Edna O'Brien
New Critical Perspectives

Edna O'Brien
New Critical Perspectives

Editors:
Kathryn Laing
Sinéad Mooney
Maureen O'Connor

Carysfort Press

A Carysfort Press Book
Edna O'Brien: New Critical Perspectives
Editors: Kathryn Laing, Sinéad Mooney, and Maureen O'Connor

First published in Ireland in 2006 as a paperback original by
Carysfort Press, 58 Woodfield, Scholarstown Road
Dublin 16, Ireland
©2006 Copyright remains with the authors

Typeset by Carysfort Press
Cover design by Alan Bennis

Printed and bound by eprint limited
Unit 35, Coolmine Industrial Estate, Dublin 16, Ireland

This book is published with the financial assistance of
The Arts Council (An Chomhairle Ealaíon), Dublin, Ireland

This publication was grant-aided by the Publications
fund of the National University of Ireland, Galway

Contents

Acknowledgements

The editors would like to thank the Department of English, National University of Ireland, Galway. We are also grateful to the Centre for Irish Studies, the Women's Studies Centre and the Faculty of Arts of the National University of Ireland, Galway, all of whom supported 'Edna O'Brien: A Reappraisal', the conference (held in April 2005) from which several of the essays in this volume are drawn. Our thanks also go to the contributors for their prompt responses to all our questions and queries.

We acknowledge the Irish Research Council for the Humanities and Social Sciences Postdoctoral Fellowship which has helped support the project, and also the financial support of the Arts Council of Ireland. We are also grateful for permission to reprint a version of 'Edna O'Brien, Irish Dandy' by Maureen O'Connor, which originally appeared in *Irish Studies Review*, Vol.13 (2005), pp. 469-477 (http://www.tandf.co.uk).

Finally, for their support in various ways, we thank Mark, Jamie and Gregory Munday, Ian Flanagan, Tadhg Foley, Louis de Paor, Faith Binckes, Patrick Lonergan, Irene O'Malley, and Charlie Byrne's Bookshop.

Introduction

Kathryn Laing
Sinéad Mooney
Maureen O'Connor

> [Edna O'Brien's] auspicious literary debut with *The Country Girls* marked the beginning of a career that now encompasses a body of work including fifteen novels, six short-story collections, plays, television and motion-picture screenplays, poems, children's books, and non-fiction ranging from essays and reviews to a biography of James Joyce (1999). She always seems to have a novel and poems in progress and continues to write short stories, many published in the *New Yorker*. In all her work O'Brien continues to shock, puzzle, delight, and scandalize her readers as she ventures into new territory.

So ends Robert Hosmer's recent entry in the *Dictionary of Literary Biography* on 'Ireland's best known female writer' (16). It would be fair to say that O'Brien is best known as a writer of fiction. She is known particularly for the autobiographical nature of her work, and for her exploration of 'the agonies of love and loss that attend women's experiences' (16); the construction of female sexuality and the consequences of this for women within a specifically Irish context, and within broader contexts too. These issues have been particularly the focus of her short fiction but, as critics have noted, her latest trilogy (*House of Splendid Isolation* [1994], *Down by the River* [1996], and

Wild Decembers [1999]) has shown a significant shift in her fiction, reworking familiar themes within a sharply-defined political framework. In her forthcoming novel, *The Light of Evening*, O'Brien draws on her mother's experiences, particularly as an Irish emigrant to the United States, and returns to a pervading theme of much of her own writing, 'the primal relationship twixt mother and daughter, their shared and their separate existences'.[1]

It has become characteristic of Edna O'Brien scholarship to begin with a lament about the relatively limited selection of criticism dedicated to a writer who has produced such a considerable body of work. That O'Brien is a prolific and often controversial writer is consistently acknowledged. That she is a 'good' writer, worthy of scholarly interest, even a place in the canon of contemporary Irish writing, is an assertion either stated with less certainty in many of the reviews and essays on her work, or with forceful defensiveness by those scholars who have chosen her as the subject of critical attention. Her status as a 'literary' figure, rather than a popular Irish woman writer with a history of controversial novels and a notoriously flamboyant persona, continues to fuel a debate within British and Irish scholarship in particular. And yet, a brief glance through Irish literature course websites, dissertation topics, and across the shelves of bookshops, in Europe and North America, testifies to an international interest, both on the part of academics and 'the common reader'. Many of O'Brien's novels are now available in translation, not only in French, German, and Dutch, but also Greek (her biography of James Joyce has recently been translated into Portuguese), suggesting the breadth of her appeal outside the sphere of British and Irish criticism.

Although the number of O'Brien critics remains remarkably small, there is a nexus of scholars who have challenged existing hostile and repetitive readings of her work. Rebecca Pelan's often-quoted article, 'Edna O'Brien's "Stage-Irish" Persona', published in 1993, set the scene for considering the actual reception of O'Brien's writing, the ways in which criticism of her work has been conflated with at once fascinated and cynical responses to her public persona. More recently, Heather Ingman, in her article, 'Edna O'Brien: Stretching the Nation's Boundaries', has shown how reductive readings of O'Brien's work as simply autobiography and romance have excluded the possibility of recognizing her as 'a political writer, concerned to challenge her nation's particular brand of gendered nationalism' (253). Amanda Greenwood's monograph, published in 2003, offers the fullest assessment of O'Brien's *oeuvre* up to that date, usefully outlining a history of O'Brien criticism as well as providing alternative readings and perspectives on her fiction. As full as this work is, Greenwood does not discuss the short stories or drama, apart from the stage play, *Virginia*, in any detail, highlighting, as she acknowledges, the gaps and possibilities for future scholarship. Maureen O'Connor's and Lisa Colletta's forthcoming collection of essays, generated by the singular attention paid to Edna O'Brien's work following a general call for papers on Irish women writers, promises a continued broadening of critical approaches to her work. Robert Ellis Hosmer, Jr's entry in the *Dictionary of Literary Biography* (*DLB* 319) provides the most up-to-date information on all of O'Brien's publications, productions, and interviews, a broad survey of her work and a useful (although not all-inclusive) bibliography of O'Brien criticism.

Our own edition, in this more vigorous spirit of critical engagement, offers further assessment of the responses to O'Brien's work in the media and in the academy, as well as building on existing revisionist approaches to offer new readings, and also suggesting further possibilities for alternative critical approaches. Many of the essays in this collection are drawn from our conference, 'Edna O'Brien: A Reappraisal', held at the National University of Ireland, Galway, in April 2005. The conference was organized both to acknowledge O'Brien's importance as a contemporary Irish woman writer whose work is ongoing, and to elicit innovative approaches to her writing. The specific rubric for this conference marked an attempt to shift criticism away from the well-trodden paths of religion, nationalism, and feminism into broader critical frameworks that might include postmodernist, postcolonial, and intertextual readings, reception theory, and other perspectives on O'Brien's extensive *oeuvre*. The international response to the call for papers, mainly from European, Scandanavian, and American scholars, confirmed the curious split in the reception of O'Brien's work that remains prevalent — an ambivalence and anxiety in the case of British and Irish critics, which is met with some astonishment by those who have studied her work outside that sphere.

Rebecca Pelan's essay, the first in the collection, is partly dedicated to a consideration of the ambivalent reception of O'Brien's work, tracing the shifting responses in reviews and in media commentary from her earliest publication, the infamous and now perhaps most widely read *The Country Girls*. Pelan shows how the increasing hostility or incomprehension that started to greet her publications paralleled an emerging iconography that began to overshadow her texts. The 'Irish Colette' or 'Irish Françoise Sagan', the Connemara Dietrich invoked in reviews suggests at once exoticism, foreignness, and a suspicion about authenticity and literariness. This short history of reception and the emergence of an iconic figure, revealed by the range of photographs of O'Brien accompanying reviews and used on book covers, touches on the as yet under explored area of the marketing of her image and texts. The 2005 exhibition of Penguin cover art at the Victoria and Albert Museum, in which some of O'Brien's books feature, highlights specifically how, in the case of O'Brien, the material text, its physical appearance, has contributed significantly to the shaping of assumptions about O'Brien's fiction. Commenting on the marketing of her work, O'Brien has stated:

> I cannot say that the different covers for my novels have always pleased me. Some have erred rather on the sensational side. It could be said that there is a big difference between an author's intentions and a marketing mogul. In fact I would love a white cover with black lettering to convey all (O'Brien to the editors, 31 January 2006).

The uncertainty as to what kind of writer O'Brien is, or how she should be appraised, already established by some of the images used to market her work, is continued in academic discourse too. For one of the distinctive features of O'Brien criticism is that much of it is scattered through diverse collections of critical essays that reveal a difficulty in categorizing her work, in placing her in relation to other Irish women writers, for example, or in relation to a broader selection of her contemporaries, and so on.

Lorna Sage, for example, in her *Women in the House of Fiction*, groups O'Brien, somewhat curiously, with Iris Murdoch and Margaret Drabble. While Sage's essay does accord her work serious attention, both her evident difficulty in 'placing' O'Brien, and a rhetoric which comes close to endorsing long-established clichés, demonstrate a certain critical uneasiness. O'Brien's idiom, for Sage, is 'splendidly untidy', and she 'veer[s] dangerously from irony to dewy sentiment, only to rise dripping from her sorrows with a fey smile' (83). Clearly dissatisfied with her initial 'placing', she suggests that O'Brien 'might perhaps more plausibly be cast as a "straight" Bohemian', going on to intimate that the heroines of her 1960s and 1970s work 'seem natural successors to Rhys's ghostly lost women, close cousins to Sagan's glamorous outsiders' (83). In fact, O'Brien is frequently cast as 'glamorous outsider' by virtue of her frequent omission from studies of twentieth-century Irish fiction, a position from which she is occasionally recuperated by her treatment of rural Irish childhood, which allows her to be tentatively grouped with more canonical male names under the rubric of a shared thematics, as in James M. Cahalan's 'Male and Female Perspectives on Growing Up Irish: Edna O'Brien, John McGahern, and Brian Moore'. She is linked with a variety of Irish women writers – Tamsin Hargreaves, for instance, puts O'Brien in a highly disparate group composed of Julia O'Faolain, Molly Keane, and Jennifer Johnston in her 'Women's Consciousness and Identity in Four Irish Women Novelists' – while an investment in the short story and self-avowed Joycean traces have allowed her to be seen, along with

Seán O'Faoláin and Mary Lavin, in terms of a shared Joycean heritage.[2] She is also grouped with her near-contemporary John McGahern as 'the most controversial writers of the 1960s in Ireland' in Julia Carlson's *Banned in Ireland* (17), but the fact that the obvious correlation between O'Brien and McGahern – signalled by an often cognate fictional territory, and the early targeting of both by Irish censorship – has never been fully made, speaks eloquently of their very different positioning in the post-1960 Irish canon.

What many of the essays in this collection do is recontextualize O'Brien's writing, and indeed that much-debated persona, refiguring what have become established and staid critical parameters. Maureen O'Connor, for example, considers O'Brien in the company of Sydney Owenson (Lady Morgan) and Oscar Wilde, suggesting she might be seen as an example of the 'Irish female dandy'. Reading O'Brien through the history of the dandy, with its European and Irish roots and celebrated conflation of aesthetics and dress, resituates the persona and texts, creating an alternative context in which her personal and literary style might be seen as subversive through dandiacal posturing. Michelle Woods introduces a very different and hitherto unexplored backdrop through her reading of Ernest Gébler's fiction in relation to O'Brien's. Gébler, a published and successful writer (at least early in his career) who, as O'Brien's husband, inspired the portrait of Eugene Gaillard in *The Country Girls*, and even less appealing male characters in later fiction. Woods makes a case for re-considering some of Gébler's now forgotten work and, through reading the fictionalization of each other in O'Brien's and Gébler's writing, suggests there is textual dialogue, hostile as it is, worthy of further exploration. Bertrand Cardin does not so much recontextualize O'Brien's fiction as redirect attention to the textuality and intertextuality of her work. Tracing her use of the epigraph reveals a writer whose self-conscious literariness, suggested in part through her use of the epigraph, provides a counterpoint to the potency of her image as a writer of popular, lightweight fiction.

O'Brien's self-conscious literariness is at its most un-disguised through her affiliations with the work of her celebrated literary forefather, James Joyce, culminating in her biography of Joyce, published in 1999. Rebecca Pelan and Ann Norton both reflect on O'Brien's 'writing back to Joyce' in their essays. Reading O'Brien's 'Irish Revel' and *Night* alongside 'The Dead' and *Ulysses*, Pelan highlights O'Brien's indebtedness and also the power of her creative reworking of these literary masterpieces. For Pelan,

> As one of O'Brien's finest, yet most critically-neglected pieces of fiction, *Night* epitomizes all that is central to her writing: the theme of women's disillusionment, the desperate, yet futile attempts at escape from Irish society only to discover other forms of entrapment, and, finally an acute awareness of her place in a literary tradition which is, at once, revered and undermined (33).

Ann Norton considers O'Brien's reworking of the Joycean epiphany, specifically in relation to the controversial *Down by the River*, 'The Love Object', and finally *The High Road*. Norton argues for a reading of O'Brien's adaptation of the epiphanic form from her modernist predecessors as feminist discourse, and as revealing the possibilities of a secular spirituality, the privileging of compassionate love over sexual passion.

Eve Stoddard and Michael Harris offer readings of O'Brien's most recent fiction, in particular *House of Splendid Isolation* and *Wild Decembers*, in the context of postmodernist and postcolonial criticism. By comparing O'Brien's writing with that of Jamaica Kincaid, Stoddard broadens the critical context for O'Brien studies by considering her as a postcolonial writer who, with Kincaid and other postcolonial writers, shares a pre-occupation with sexuality, land and national identity. Suggesting that

> while both writers draw intensely on their own experiences to craft autobiographical fiction, both also move beyond the parameters of the *Bildungsroman* in complex ways in order to comment on the politics of postcoloniality (105)

Stoddard highlights the untapped vein of critical possibilities of reading O'Brien both within and beyond purely Irish contexts. Harris continues this as he suggests *House of Splendid Isolation* might well be read in the company of J.M. Coetzee's *Waiting for the Barbarians*, Arundhati Roy's *The God of Small Things*, and Thomas Pynchon's *Mason & Dixon*. Establishing the novel's postmodernist credentials, Harris considers the ways in which O'Brien spatializes the drama and narratives of history as they are played out in the novel, showing how these narratives imprison and destroy lives, impeding political change.

Since Edna O'Brien has been considered primarily as a novelist and short fiction writer, there is very little criticism that addresses her drama and screenplays specifically, despite her having written at least ten plays that have been produced, and over ten scripts for film and television. Her most recent play, *Family Butchers*, a reworking of an earlier version, *Our Father* (1999), was staged in San Francisco in 2005 (see Hosmer's bibliography for more details about plays and screenplays). Loredana Salis, in her analysis of O'Brien's adaptation of Euripides's *Iphigenia*, in a sense introduces this play to a wider audience for the first time (it was first staged in 2003), and by doing so alerts us to this neglected genre that constitutes a significant portion of O'Brien's *oeuvre*. In addition, O'Brien's *Iphigenia* is one of several recent adaptations of the play by Irish playwrights, suggesting multiple comparative possibilities and an entirely unexplored context for her work. Salis's interpretation of the play concentrates on O'Brien's aesthetics and a shift away from the female-centredness of her earlier work. Such a perspective concurs with critics of O'Brien's most recent work (see Norton, Harris, and Pelan in this volume, for example) who discuss her more complex treatment of male characters, portrayed as victims as well as victimizers. Reading O'Brien's fiction in the context of her drama, her drama in its own right and in the context of her work as a whole, all remains to be done.

The final cluster of essays in this volume does not so much resituate O'Brien's novels into broader or entirely new contexts,

or offer analysis of neglected aspects of her work, as delve
deeper into some of the themes and images that have made her
work controversial. O'Brien's attention to the body, in
particular the female body, especially in her earlier fiction, is
examined in these essays using a variety of theoretical
approaches that overlap and establish unexpected dialogues.
Extending the much-mulled-over themes of sex and sexuality in
The Country Girls Trilogy, Shirley Peterson draws on theories that
apply 'some basic principles of sexual S/M to nonsexual
dimensions of human relationships', showing how 'sadomasochism determines the individual tragic life as well as the
larger social system' in these early novels (153). Patricia
Coughlan turns to Julia Kristeva's work on abjection in her
analysis of the recurrence of references to and images of the
body and human filth in O'Brien's writing, as well as to
references to the unmentionable, to what remains taboo in
narrative fiction. O'Brien's preoccupation with the abject and
abjection is another example of her 'writing back to Joyce', and
recurring images of abjection feature as structuring devices in
her narrative. Specifically for Coughlan, O'Brien's writing forms
a striking parallel with Kristeva's work on the abjection of the
mother. O'Brien 'does not celebrate the abjection of the
maternal and of Ireland in her work, but rather chronicles,
agonizes, and mourns over it' (182). Sinéad Mooney's detailed
psychoanalytic reading of the 'the politics of feminine
adornment' in O'Brien's fiction is revelatory about the intensity
and significance of the attention paid to dress, the female body,
and identity:

> In an *oeuvre* which takes as its main theme the compromised
> nature of female subjectivity, dress, if considered as a
> 'representative trifle', is extremely significant, in that it
> represents the body as a fundamentally liminal phenomenon,
> precariously located between the physical and abstract, symbolic
> and imaginary (201).

Finally, Mary Burke's study of the themes of food, drink,
alienation, and sex in the *Country Girls Trilogy* and *August is a
Wicked Month* provides an additional layer of critical perspective

on O'Brien's representations of the human body, female bodies, and the ways in which these are constructed through societal constraints and expectations. The ways in which the female characters experience their bodies is shaped not only by attention to dress, but by the changing attitudes to food in Irish society. Burke reveals the preponderance of images of food, eating, and anxieties about food in O'Brien's writing, showing in addition how issues of class and consumption exacerbate these anxieties, and how the association of the commodification of food in the narratives is increasingly associated with the commodification of female sexuality.

The essays collected here illustrate some of the range, complexity, and interest of Edna O'Brien as a fiction writer and dramatist. It is to be hoped that they will contribute to a broader appreciation of her work and to an evolution of new critical approaches, as well as igniting more interest in the many unexplored areas of her work. O'Brien's plays and film or television scripts, her children's fiction, and admittedly minor poetry remain largely neglected in the canon of O'Brien criticism. In addition, among the numerous uncollected short stories and essays (published in a variety of journals, papers, and magazines, notably the *New Yorker*), there lies a wealth of material awaiting rereading and critical engagement.

Works Cited

Cahalan, James M. 'Male and Female Perspectives on Growing Up Irish: Edna O'Brien, John McGahern, and Brian Moore'. *Double Visions: Women and Men in Modern and Contemporary Irish Fiction*, ed. James M. Cahalan (Syracuse, New York: Syracuse University Press, 1999), 105-34.

Carlson, Julia. *Banned in Ireland: Censorship and the Irish Writer* (Athens: University of Georgia Press, 1990).

Hosmer, Robert, Jr. *Dictionary of Literary Biography: British and Irish Short Fiction Writers, 1945-2000* (Stamford, CT: Thomson Gale, 2005), 319.

Ingman, Heather. 'Edna O'Brien: Stretching the Nation's Boundaries'. *Irish Studies Review* 10.3 (2002): 253-65.

Pearce, Sandra Manoogian. 'Snow Through the Ages: Echoes of "The Dead" in O'Brien, O'Faoláin, and Lavin'. *Joyce through the Ages: A*

Nonlinear View, ed. Michael Patrick Gillespie (Gainesville, FL: University Press of Florida, 1999), 165-78.

Pelan, Rebecca. 'Edna O'Brien's "Stage-Irish" Persona: an "Act" of Resistance'. *Canadian Journal of Irish Studies* 19 (July 1993): 67-78.

Sage, Lorna. *Women in the House of Fiction: Post-War Women Novelists* (Basingstoke: Macmillan, 1992).

---

[1] We wish to thank Edna O'Brien for sending us information about her new novel (due to be published by Weidenfeld & Nicholson, September 2006), responding to our questions about her writing, and for permission to draw on this material.

[2] See, for instance, Pearce.

1 | Reflections on a Connemara Dietrich

Rebecca Pelan

Edna O'Brien's most recent novel, *In the Forest* (2002), is based
on actual murders that took place in County Clare in 1994.[1] In a
prominent and highly critical review of the novel, *Irish Times*
journalist Fintan O'Toole stated that:

> The hepatitis C scandal, Bloody Sunday and the career of
> Charles Haughey are all major historical and political issues,
> which have been dramatized recently. But Edna O'Brien's new
> book, which tells the story of the murder of Imelda Riney, her
> son Liam and Father Joe Walsh, has broken an unspoken rule
> and crossed the boundary into private grief (50).

O'Toole's main problem with O'Brien's use of the factual
material of the murders rests on what he sees as a very clear
distinction between public and private meaning: Bloody
Sunday, the hepatitis C scandal, and the career of Charles
Haughey are all in the public realm, says O'Toole, while the
murders of Riney and the others, although occupying the same
territory in O'Brien's novel between the real and the imagined,
constitute an example of unethical intrusion into the private
realm: 'They [the murders] were a dreadful catastrophe visited
on innocent people by a disturbed, deranged man. They did not
and do not have a public meaning' (50). Even in an Irish literary
context, O'Toole can find no redeeming aspect to O'Brien's use
of this private material. He cites both John Banville's 1989

novel, *The Book of Evidence*, which was clearly inspired by the murderer Malcolm Macarthur, as well as Eoin McNamee's 1994 *Resurrection Man*, which is based on the life of Lenny Murphy and the Shankill Butchers, as examples of a key difference between what those authors did and what O'Brien undertook:

> Neither the Banville nor McNamee books presented themselves as being about the Macarthur killings or the Shankill Butchers. The blurb on the book makes no reference to Macarthur or indeed to any relationship between the novel and the real events (50).

By contrast, O'Brien's novel makes explicit the connection between her characters and the real lives of those involved in the murders.

O'Toole's emphasis in the review on the private/public realms is one that would appear to be logical and reasonable, but is actually a sleight of hand common to journalism. Throughout the lengthy review, O'Toole refers to the way individuals mentioned had become public figures by choice: as a politician, for example, Charles Haughey knowingly placed himself in the spotlight; Frank McCourt and Nuala O'Faolain, who might otherwise be criticized for writing about private material relating to their mothers and families, were able to do so, according to O'Toole, because 'there is a real sense in which their mothers belong to them, since they are woven into the fabric of their own lives' (50). In pursuing this line of thinking further, O'Toole suggests that, in her novels *House of Splendid Isolation* (1994) and *Down by the River* (1997), O'Brien meticulously researched the life of republican terrorist Dominic McGlinchey, and the events of the X-case, as the material on which to base these fictions, respectively. But, these are acceptable because McGlinchey, O'Toole says, was a notorious killer who has deliberately imposed himself on public consciousness, and the family in the X-case were, and remain, anonymous.

In all these examples, O'Toole talks about the individuals themselves who have entered the public arena, and yet when it comes to the Imelda Riney murders and O'Brien's use of the material, he shifts from a discussion of the individuals involved to the people closest only to those murdered. No mention is made of the loved ones of Charles Haughey or Malcolm Macarthur or Lenny Murphy or Dominic McGlinchey. And, equally, no mention is made of the loved ones of Brendan O'Donnell (the murderer of Riney and the others) – only of Imelda Riney's loved ones. It seems, then, that O'Toole has no difficulty in deciding who the outright victims of this atrocity are – Imelda Riney, her son, and Father Walsh – and he makes what he sees as an ethical choice in doing so. O'Brien, on the other hand, whilst displaying a great deal of sympathy for those murdered, has always been much less clear about the notion of victimhood, a point to which I will return later in the essay.

O'Brien is castigated by O'Toole for not recognizing the difference between events that are personal, private and no-go areas for authors, and all those other events, which O'Toole describes as being 'very clearly in the public realm of history and politics' and which 'ask questions about the use of power' (50). What arises for me in reading O'Toole's review is, frankly, astonishment at how it can continue to escape the notice of an otherwise astute critic, such as O'Toole, that for over forty years, Edna O'Brien has displayed an almost pathological need to enter the very no-go areas that O'Toole refers to, precisely for the purpose of asking questions about the use of power. This is a writer who has consistently cast a forensic eye on the most private aspects of (primarily, though not exclusively) Irish life in order to show that the distinction between the private and public realm is a false one, and she has done so through an engagement with the social, political, and literary worlds that contribute to who she is.

O'Toole suggests that an explanation for O'Brien's lack of discretion in *In the Forest* lies in her having had to leave Ireland, and the County Clare of Brendan O'Donnell and Imelda Riney, described as her own heartland: 'Had she been able to live and work in Ireland', O'Toole says, 'it is likely that she would not have needed to approach the social world in which the murders happened as an outsider' (50). In a real sense, he argues, *In the Forest* is a

> product of the distortions wrought on Irish writing by a history
> of censorship and exile that is now, for a generation younger
> than Edna O'Brien, a thing of the past. She was effectively
> forced into exile in the late 1950s ... and she is far too
> intelligent and honest a writer not to be aware of the difficulty
> of writing about a place you have not inhabited for so long,
> especially a place that has changed as rapidly and profoundly as
> Ireland has in the decades of her exile (50).

I would argue that O'Toole is wrong in suggesting that O'Brien has lost touch with her own heartland, and I'd like to suggest just one example of how things haven't changed in the world that O'Brien writes about.

The title story to O'Brien's collection, *A Scandalous Woman and Other Stories* (1974), investigates the communal response to the scandal created when Eily, childhood friend of the narrator, is found in the lime kiln with Jack, a Protestant bank clerk, 'in the most satanic position, with her belly showing' (25). The response is an almost knee-jerk reaction to restore respectability no matter what the cost to the individuals involved. As is so often the case with O'Brien's stories, 'A Scandalous Woman' is set in a remote Irish village where the passing of a tapeworm is a talking point for a week, and Sundays are passed longing for visitors who never come. O'Brien's focus in the story is with Eily herself who, we are told, had 'joined that small sodality of scandalous women who had conceived children without securing fathers and who were damned in body and soul' (27). O'Brien's choice of the word 'sodality' is interesting here, since, apart from its general meaning of fellowship or society, the word has a specific meaning within the Roman Catholic Church, ironically, a society with religious or charitable objects. Part of the community's task of enforcing conformity and reinstating order, involves three strong men impeding Jack's attempted escape, after which

> He was indisposed, and it is said that his black eyes were
> bulbous. It left a permanent hole in his lower cheek, as if a little
> pebble of flesh had been tweezed out of him (35).

But while Jack's loss is a mere 'pebble of flesh', Eily is reduced
to a shell, the real-life enactment of a game played in childhood
by Eily, her sister Nuala, and the narrator, in which Nuala, who
was happiest 'when someone was upset' (11), played doctor,
Eily the nurse, and the narrator the helpless patient at the hands
of Nuala especially, who

> liked to operate with a big black carving knife, and long before
> she commenced, she gloated over the method and over what
> tumours she was going to remove. *She used to say that there would
> be nothing but a shell by the time she had finished*, and that one
> wouldn't be able to have babies or women's complaints ever
> (11, emphasis added).

The degree to which the young women are perceived, by
their elders, to be undisciplined beings who threaten the status
quo, is shown by O'Brien through the use of animal imagery in
relation to both Eily and the narrator. Prior to the scandal, Eily
'worked like a horse' and 'was swift as a colt' (9) in her eager-
ness to get to the main road before dark in order to enjoy the
excitement offered by its cars, bicycles, buses, and passers-by.
After 'the scandal', however, Eily is like a wilful animal which
needs to be watched at all times, a task left largely to the
women of the village. She is locked in a room off the kitchen
which houses cats and mice and where:

> Her meals — a hunk of bread and a mug of weak tea — were
> handed into her twice a day ... she had nothing else to do, only
> cry and think and sit herself upon the oats ... and probably
> have to keep making noises to frighten off the mice (29).

Eily's only outing is attendance at Mass where she is 'hemmed
in by her mother and some other old woman' (28). During one
other rare venture outside, Eily is made to dress in a
mackintosh, Mrs Miniver hat, and sunglasses as a disguise, while
her father 'wanted to put a halter around her', but is reminded
by the narrator's mother that it isn't the Middle Ages (30). The

shotgun wedding over, 'Eily tried to dart into the back of the car, tried it more than once, just like an animal trying to get back to its lair' (37).

With the social and moral codes forcibly reinstated, attention is turned to the other young girls of the village who now need to be watched so that a similar upset is not repeated. Although praising her for being 'such a good, such a pure little girl' (37), the narrator's mother is advised to have the child's ringlets cut since 'fine feathers make fine birds' (38), and ever since the scandal the teacher 'was enjoining us to go home in pairs, to speak Irish, and not to walk with any sense of provocation' (37). Snatches of news concerning Eily reveal that she has become 'odd', talks to herself, and then, her 'lovely hair began to fall out in clumps' (39). The madness into which Eily descends is eventually witnessed by the narrator herself when, while walking in a city street with her mother, she sees

> This wild creature coming towards us, talking and debating to herself … she looked at us, and then peered, as if she was going to pounce on us; then she started to laugh at us, or rather, to sneer, and she stalked away and pounced on some other person (40).

When, years later, the narrator seeks Eily out, she finds the animal in Eily not only tamed, but broken: 'my first thought was that they must have drugged the feelings out of her, they must have given her strange brews, and along with quelling her madness, they had taken her spark away' (43). Any uncertainty as to who 'they' might be is answered in the final paragraph of the story when the narrator concludes that, 'ours indeed was a land of shame, a land of murder, and a land of strange, throttled, sacrificial women' (43).

Anyone familiar with O'Brien's work will recognize that the name given by O'Brien to the fictionalized character of the murdered Imelda Riney in *In the Forest* is also Eily, and I suggest that this is not coincidental since there are strong connections between the early story and the later novel, particularly in terms of this idea of 'sacrificial women', which brings me back to my earlier point about the distinction between Fintan O'Toole's and Edna O'Brien's respective interpretations of the notion of 'victim'. There is no doubt about where O'Brien's sympathies lie in relation to the Imelda Riney murders – absolutely none. But where O'Toole is very clear in his understanding of Riney as absolute victim, he would probably only concede O'Donnell as product of the same society. O'Brien, on the other hand, clearly constructs both as victims in quite different ways. Mich O'Kane, O'Brien's fictionalized version of the murderer Brendan O'Donnell, has, himself, been brutalized by the society in which he lives: violence and sexual abuse at the hands of a priest who was meant to be looking after him contribute to who he is. That is not to suggest here that O'Brien offers us excuses – she rarely does that – but she does attempt explanations. Eily of 'A Scandalous Woman' and Eily of *In the Forest* are clearly two of the 'throttled, sacrificial women' in O'Brien's land of shame and murder – one purely fictional and metaphoric, the other factional and literal. But, equally, Mich O'Kane (read Brendan O'Donnell) is a victim of a society that turned its back on him. I think O'Brien has been writing about women like Eily (whether purely fictional or factional) and men like Mich O'Kane for most of her literary career. She has certainly been consistent in taking as her fictional theme the disillusionment and destruction of women in society; not necessarily as actual victims in the style of *In the Forest*, but more often as victims of their own general social powerlessness.

So, how is it that critics, like Fintan O'Toole – though he is only one of many – can continue to ignore just what Edna O'Brien has so consistently been concerned about in so much of her writing? The answer, I suggest, lies in the fact that Edna O'Brien exists as a writer who remains one of the most commercially successful ever to come out of Ireland, who is known to readers in many different places, who has never been ambiguous about her Irish identity (she may have expressed ambivalence about it, but never ambiguity), yet who continues to be largely assessed by the literary critical world as someone who is, on the one hand, a personality who should not be taken too seriously as a writer — the 'Irish Colette' (Woodward 42) —

and, on the other, as a likeable, but bold, girl who keeps misbehaving, and who regularly has her work assessed on grounds other than its literary qualities.

Edna O'Brien entered the consciousness of the literary world in the early 1960s as a fresh, new writer of some talent.[2] Reviews of her first two novels, *The Country Girls* and *The Lonely Girl* (later published by Penguin as *Girl with Green Eyes*) focussed on her writing style consistently described as 'fresh', 'charming', 'honest', 'lyrical', and 'uncluttered'.

In a 1960 review for the *New Statesman,* for instance, V.S. Naipaul wrote that O'Brien

> does not appear to have to strive to establish anything: the novel [*The Country Girls*], one feels, is so completely, so truly realized in the writer's mind that everything that comes out has a quality of life which no artifice could achieve (97).

By contrast, however, when the third novel of the early trilogy, *Girls in their Married Bliss*, was published in 1964, critics detected what Sean McMahon described as a 'move away from the fresh, unselfconscious charm ... acute observation of life and fine, ribald sense of humour' (82) towards a sharper, less pleasant tone. Part of the problem associated critically with *Girls in their Married Bliss* was the fact that Caithleen, the sensitive narrator of both preceding novels, was replaced by an alternating narrative structure by both Caithleen and Baba, beginning with the latter's much more coarse and cynical assessment of their lives generally:

> Not long ago Kate Brady and I were having a few gloomy gin fizzes up London, bemoaning the fact that nothing would ever improve, that we'd die the way we were – enough to eat, married, dissatisfied (7).

Perhaps of more significance to the reception of *Girls in their Married Bliss*, however, was the withholding of its release in the United States until 1967, one full year after the publication of O'Brien's next two novels, *August is a Wicked Month* and *Casualties of Peace*, published respectively in 1965 and 1966, both of which were so far removed in tone and subject from the first

two novels, that critics were left to wonder if they were
assessing the same author they had praised just six years earlier.
Both *August is a Wicked Month* and *Casualties of Peace* deal with
emotionally scarred women who seek different solutions to
their problems, and although both contain central Irish
characters, the novels are set in England and offer as harsh a
view of life there as the earlier ones had done of Ireland.

Similarly, in Britain, although first published by Hutchinsons
in 1964, the third episode of the trilogy does not appear to have
been widely reviewed at that time, though both *The Times* and
The Times Literary Supplement reviews suggest that it was not well
received. The novel was not republished in Britain by Penguin
until 1967, the same year of its publication in America. Just how
much the reception of *August is a Wicked Month* and *Casualties of
Peace* influenced the reception of *Girls in their Married Bliss* is
uncertain, but it seems likely that the influence was substantial
since neither novel was well received in England or America:

> Miss O'Brien seemed in places [in *Girls in Their Married Bliss*] to
> be writing a kind of neo-feminist propaganda. This committed
> writing continued in *August is a Wicked Month* and in *Casualties of
> Peace* ... Miss O'Brien is still young and there is no reason to
> suppose that the present retardation is anything but temporary
> (McMahon 79).

McMahon's 'retardation' theory was, of course, proved in-
accurate once and for all with the publication of *A Pagan Place*
in 1970 and *Night* in 1972, both of which had Irish narrators,
but neither of which, once again, bore any resemblance to *The
Country Girls*. Both were also experimental in style, and did
nothing to alleviate suspicion that O'Brien was a novelist who
threatened to defy easy classification – one of the cardinal sins
in the eyes of a literary reviewing world that requires con-
sistency and homogeneity at some level in order to categorize
(and discuss) authors and their work. The two novels polarized
critical opinion. Reviews of *A Pagan Place* ranged from:

> Near the end Miss O'Brien tries for something grand, but it is
> too late for profundity, so she settles for a seduction ... she
> arranges to have the heroine seduced by a priest. But it is

> nothing, merely an emigrant Irish novelist taking a swipe at
> Holy Ireland. It should not be taken too seriously (Donaghue 6)

to those who felt that it was her 'finest book' (McManus 34).
Reviews of *Night* attracted praise of the kind that suggested
that, 'few living authors use language as richly and sensuously as
O'Brien' (Avant 4003) to condemnation of the novel as 'self-
indulgent whimsy … a mixture of narcissism and Irishry as
before, but with stylistic knobs (or balls) on … gift-wrapped
porn … one long act of public literary masturbation' (*The Times
Literary Supplement* 1184). Until the early 1970s there is little
evidence of much emphasis on the authorial persona in English
reviews. Certainly there was interest in this new and decidedly
different writer, but it was of the most general kind. By 1965 in
the United States, however, the first signs of an interest in the
persona appeared. The *New York Times,* reviewing *August is a
Wicked Month*, wrote:

> Edna O'Brien came on like a brass band with cymbals clanging.
> And she did it speaking in a soft, sweet Irish brogue and
> looking like a cousin in from the country. It was hard to believe
> that this was the young woman who slathered those four-letter
> Anglo-Saxon words all over her latest novel, about the sex-wild
> woman (Rader 57).

And, again, from the *New York Times* in 1965:

> The skin was peaches and cream, and the blue eyes were very
> clean, guileless, at once mirrors to the viewer, yet windows
> opening into a serious, intelligent mind. The hair, a red-gold
> mane, was pinned up on each side of her head. Looking like a
> schoolgirl in green little heel Mary Janes and a high-waisted,
> tight collar flowered print, the author of *August is a Wicked
> Month* … gestured with long-fingered hands to underscore her
> point (Levin 32).

Increasingly, however, throughout the 1970s and 1980s, both
European and American critics reveal a greater interest in
O'Brien and her Irishness than in her writing:

> A smashing red-haired Irish beauty, much more attractive than
> the photograph above, Miss O'Brien proved to be both

articulate and friendly on a recent first visit to New York'
(B.A.B. 21).

Edna O'Brien is a fertile woman, having birthed eight novels in
10 years, plus one play, two sons, two volumes of short stories,
and one book of non-fiction … she selects her spoken words
painstakingly and has cultivated an ethereal image of dressing in
feminine clothes and speaking softly in a sort of blank verse
with musical Irish accents (Anderson 73).

Now in her forties, O'Brien resembles one of her own heroines:
beautiful in a subtle, wistful way, with reddish-blond hair, green
eyes, and a savage sense of humour … the day I was there, the
room was warmed by a log fire burning in the fireplace and
even more so by O'Brien's rich, softly accented Irish voice
(Guppy 26).

And this one – my favourite:

Edna O'Brien read interminable prose-poems beautifully from
under a chestnut tree of red hair … while adjusting her belt like
a Connemara Dietrich (Holmes 10).

The authorial persona, certainly in England and America, has
ensured the denial of serious critical analysis of O'Brien's work
by diverting attention away from the heterogeneity of the texts
to the homogeneity of the author. It permits an acknowledgement of the writer and her talent, while at the same time
allowing an avoidance of any real engagement with the nature
of that talent. The personality cult that surrounded O'Brien at
her peak indicates that the authorial persona became the critical
focus in direct contradistinction to the perception of O'Brien as
a writer who challenged the status quo.

The projection of an externally imposed authorial persona is
by no means new or unfamiliar, particularly to women writers,
of course. Colette has long been associated with a saucy
personality and an obsession with cats; Dorothy Parker was
known as a wit, and Katherine Mansfield as something of an
enfant terrible. Perhaps the most notable example is Virginia
Woolf who was known for a good deal of her career, as the
invalid lady of Bloomsbury – an impressionist who said very
little of substance, but did it beautifully – an image that has

been shattered by a wealth of new critical readings of her work, spearheaded by a number of influential feminist analyses.

In her essay, 'On Being a Woman Writer', Margaret Atwood reveals the findings of a study on 'sexual bias in reviewing'. Under the heading 'Interviews and Media Stereotypes', Atwood discusses the reviewers' habit of slotting an author into an existing stereotype – in the case of male authors, she names such examples as Potted Poe, Bleeding Byron, Doomed Dylan, Lustful Layton, and Crucified Cohen. For women, she suggests, there are fewer to choose from – Elusive Emily, Recluse Rossetti, and, of course, Suicidal Sylvia. Atwood concludes by saying:

> The point about these stereotypes is that attention is focussed not on the actual achievements of the authors, but on their lives, which are distorted and romanticized: their work is then interpreted in the light of the distorted vision (200).

But, in addition, there are commercial interests to be served, and these interests do seem to play a greater part in the promotion of women's writing than of men's. In 1984, Doris Lessing, under the pseudonym Jane Somers, wrote *The Diaries of Jane Somers*, a book which was turned down by her British publisher, Cape, and ultimately published by Michael Joseph in Britain and Knopf in America. Without the backing usually given to Lessing's books, the *Diaries* sold 1,600 copies in Britain and 2,800 copies in the United States. Reviews of the book were pleasant, though unenthusiastic, until it was finally revealed that Doris Lessing was Jane Somers, when the *Diaries* were found by some to have merit after all. In the Preface to the reprinted *Diaries*, Lessing wrote that:

> In order to sell a book, in order to bring it to attention, you need more than the book, you need the television appearance. Many writers have at the start resisted, have thought it over, have understood that this, now, is how the machinery works, and they have decided that if – even if it is not acknowledged – they have become part of the sales department of their publishers, then they will do the job as well as they can (9).

O'Brien, too, has not been without pressure to become part of the sales department of her various publishers, and she has done so with an enthusiasm and skill that has been off-putting for many.

Similarly, the authorial persona explains the most significant part of the reluctance of feminist literary critics to engage with O'Brien's work to date. To a large extent, Anglo-American feminist literary criticism is still, predominantly, concerned with defining contemporary feminist texts as those that contain significant gender identification. O'Brien's writing, even without the intrusive persona, fails to qualify through its representation of women's social and political powerlessness with no apparent attempt to analyse those conditions. We know, of course, that feminist criticism is not homogenous, yet there is a sense in which, in its dominant characteristics, it adopted a structure parallel to that of traditional Anglo-American literary criticism in analysing women writers in particular. Despite extensive British and American academic debates on feminist issues in the 1970s and 1980s, the expression of a culturally different feminist politics largely remains on the margins when it comes to the treatment of individual women who appear to be outside any feminist parameters. A certain prescriptiveness and cultural homogeneity began to be challenged only in the latter half of the 1980s by black and lesbian critics, later tentatively augmented by postcolonial feminists. Writing in the early 1960s, at a time when the contemporary feminist movement was in its infancy, O'Brien's work was often labelled by traditional critics in a way that might surprise a now powerful feminist criticism, as evident in some of the reviews cited. That O'Brien wrote from within a relatively marginalized position about women in similar positions is often given small consideration by a feminist criticism which too often assumes female reality and experience as homogenous, thereby also denying diversity and difference. Again, as I've argued elsewhere, O'Brien has proved too 'stage-Irish' for the Irish, too Irish for the English and too flighty and romantic for feminists of the day.[3] As a result, she continues to be neglected as a writer whose work merits serious critical attention, in favour of a kind of uneasy and uncertain success based on her early novels and as a writer who knows a lot about sex. Anyone tempted to buy an O'Brien paperback based on the titillation promised by the cover, or by reviewers' regular mention of her portrayal of sex, will be seriously disappointed by the largely pedestrian nature of her characters' sexual exploits, if they exist at all.

As an Irish woman writer, O'Brien inherited a nationality, a gender and a literary tradition, all of which carry expectations of conformity over which the individual has limited control. In their focus on singular readings of her work, critics have ignored so many other aspects of O'Brien's writing, not least her acute consciousness of form as a vital means of reworking an Irish literary tradition that she is part of, and yet stands aloof from: a tradition that has not embraced women, either as real women or as writers. In keeping with aspects of her work that challenge the social mores, O'Brien has been equally icono-clastic in relation to the literary tradition that she is part of, something that has been largely neglected by the critical world. Reading these texts in the light of an Irish literary tradition offers us interpretations of her work that go far beyond the limited ones that we've become used to. O'Brien's most anthologized short story, 'Irish Revel', and her novel, *Night*, provide two good examples of texts that offer themselves for such alternative readings. In both examples, O'Brien can be seen to 'write back' to James Joyce from a specifically gendered and class-based position.[4]

Originally entitled 'Come Into the Drawing Room, Doris', O'Brien's first story to be published in *New Yorker* (1962), was later published (with minor alterations) as 'Irish Revel'. The story tells of a young farm girl, Mary, from the west of Ireland, who attends her first party at the local hotel of a nearby town. This takes place during the course of one evening and early morning in which Mary's expectations regarding the party and her hopes of meeting a certain young man she had met two years earlier, are shattered when she finds out that her invitation

to the party was based on the need for her domestic help, and
that the young man who had asked about her was not the one
of her dreams. In its similarity of plot, 'Irish Revel' can be seen
as a rewriting of what is probably the most famous Irish short
story ever written, namely James Joyce's 'The Dead'.

Joyce's portrayal of the paralysis and decay of the middle-
class Dublin society he knew so well is brilliantly captured in
the annual party of the Misses Morkan, which, like 'Irish Revel',
takes place during one evening. The celebration of Irish hos-
pitality is mocked throughout the story by Joyce's urbane and
egotistical protagonist, Gabriel Conroy, whose facade of
geniality and confidence is systematically stripped away to
reveal a man as dead in life as the deceased Michael Furey is
alive in death. However, despite the fact that each step in
Gabriel's revelation is brought about by a female character
(Lily, his aunts, Molly Ivers, and Gretta), their function within
the story is principally plot-related. Only Gretta Conroy is
glimpsed more than superficially, although she too becomes
subservient to the plot as symbolic of a particular type of Irish
woman – one of immense sensibility, loyalty, and passion, and,
not insignificantly, from the west of Ireland, a region seen by
Gabriel as best left to those without ambition or vision. In
exposing Gabriel's egotism and continental aspirations,
however, Joyce repeated what many other Irish writers have
done by implicitly mystifying both woman and the West, perpetuating the myth of both as either mysterious, wild, and
unknowable, or subservient and domestic.

In contrast to the pedantic and pompous Gabriel, whose
male perspective is confident to the point of being patronizing
towards all those around him, O'Brien reveals the uncertainty
and limitations of her protagonist's life, expressed in the
opening words of the story – 'Mary hoped' (87). Mary's hopes
on leaving her home to attend the party are not limited to the
front tire of her bicycle remaining intact, but extend to various
aspects of the life of a seventeen year old who, for as long as
she could remember, had been 'pumping bicycles, carting turf,
cleaning out-houses, doing a man's work' (87). More than

anything else, though, Mary hopes to see John Roland, an English artist who had visited her home some two years before and whom 'she had never given up hoping' to see again (87, 88). Mary is so buoyed up by her romantic hopes towards the young man who rode a motorcycle 'at ferocious speed' (90), she imagines her world as a wonderful place in which her 'father and mother were rich and cheerful; the twin had no earache, the kitchen fire did not smoke ... she forgot about the rotted tire, got up, and cycled' (90).

O'Brien uses the rotted front tire of Mary's bike as a metaphor for Mary's hopes. The air slowly leaking out of the tire, and the pump with 'no connection' (87) parallels the 'joy leaking out of her heart' (93) on discovering that the 'someone special' who awaited her was not the one she hoped for, but O'Toole, 'the lad from the slate quarry' (93), causing Mary ultimately to yearn for 'a sweetheart, something to hold on to' (113). By the end of the story, 'the front tire was dead flat' (112), just as Mary's hopes are, confirming her mother's cynical belief that 'all outings were unsettling – they gave you a taste of something you couldn't have' (88).

The party of O'Brien's story is in honour of the local Customs and Excise Officer, Brogan, whose wife's good fortune in winning two thousand pounds has permitted him to retire 'a rich man' (93). It is attended by three other female guests apart from the hotel's owner and Mary herself: Crystal O'Meara, a hairdresser, whose real name is Carmel and who either cries or talks in a foreign accent when drunk; Eithne Duggan, an 'unfortunate girl with a squint, jumbled teeth, and almost no lips' (94); and, finally, Doris O'Beirne, famous for being the only Doris in the village and 'for the fact that one of her eyes was blue and the other a dark brown' (92). While the men each pay two pounds to cover costs, the ladies 'did not have to pay anything, but were invited to lend a pleasant and decorative atmosphere to the party, and, of course, to help' (102).

In a neighbourhood where 'girls were two a penny' (91), it might be assumed that Doris O'Beirne – with her sole owner-

ship of the name, and her differently coloured eyes – would be
easily distinguished from those like Mary who have 'pink skins
and matching eyes ... with long, wavy hair and gorgeous figures'
(91), yet, on at least four occasions, O'Toole directly entreats
Mary to 'come into the drawing-room, Doris' (104, 106, 109,
109). Unlike others who might think Mary 'streelish', O'Toole

> liked long hair and simple-minded girls; maybe later on he'd get
> her to go into one of the other rooms where they could do it.
> She had funny eyes when you looked into them, brown and
> deep, like a bloody bog hole (100).

O'Toole's confusion over Mary's name seems connected, at the
most superficial level, with 'funny eyes,' the implication being
that it makes very little difference to him who she is or what her
name is. By next morning, 'very little of Mary's face' is
remembered by one of the guests, who only recalls the 'sleeves
of her black dress, which dipped into the plates' as she served
the food (113).

The hotel at which the party is held has not had a coat of
paint since the time of de Valera's campaign visit five years
before, when he signed his name in an autograph book while
sympathizing with Mrs Rodgers on the recent death of her
husband, and the fire in the parlour where de Valera signed the
book is the first to be lit since his visit. The yellow-washed walls
of the hotel, together with the cold, damp room from which
steam issues in response to the rare heat, reflect the neglect and
inertia of life generally. Quite apart from the symbol of the
drawing-room, which is the hub of the festivities in 'The Dead',
but which, in 'Irish Revel', is a room that 'no one ever sets foot
in' (104), there are a number of features in O'Brien's story that
contrast with Joyce's. The sumptuous and elegantly-presented
meal of 'The Dead', for instance, is parodied in O'Brien's story
by the coarseness and vulgarity of a greasy and undercooked
goose (101), which Mrs Rodgers tears at with her fingers:

> 'A fork supper' was how Mrs Rodgers described it. She had
> read about it in the paper; it was all the rage now in posh
> houses in Dublin, this fork supper where you stood up for your
> food and ate with a fork only (198).

The potato stuffing which spills out of the goose recalls Gabriel's reference to that which 'vulgar people call stuffing' (246), while the sausages and the giblet soup, served in cups with grease which floats 'like drops of molten gold on the surface' (103), mock the elegance of the Misses Morkan's meal, but, at the same time, cause Mary to reflect on what a 'rough-and-ready party it was', and to ponder on whether people washed themselves in 'that big basin with the jelly in it' (104): 'A party! She'd have been as well off at home, at least it was clean dirt attending to calves and pigs and the like' (104).

While the balcony scene from *Romeo & Juliet* engages Gabriel's attention in 'The Dead', the protagonists of O'Brien's story are, tellingly, watched over by Mrs Rodgers's brother the bishop, described as a 'flaccid-faced cleric' (100), whose portrait hangs over the rarely-lit fireplace. The increased suspicion of art in rural Ireland is further reflected in the fate of a drawing of Mary sent as a gift from her beloved John Roland. Her mother, expecting a gold bracelet or brooch, reveals the utilitarian values of a people with no time for anything not serving an immediate, practical purpose. Hung on a nail in the kitchen, the drawing eventually falls and someone – 'probably her mother' (97-8) – uses it to sweep up the dust.

In its original form, 'Irish Revel' contained a direct reference to 'The Dead':

> Frost was general all over Ireland, frost like a weird blossom on the branches, on the river-bank from which Long John Salmon leaped in his great, hairy nakedness, on the ploughs left out all winter; frost on the stony field, and on all the slime and ugliness of the world (55).

In its altered state, this passage reads:

> Frost was everywhere; it coated the bare branches and made them like etchings, it starched the grass and blurred the shape of a plough that stood in a field, above all it gave the world an appearance of sanctity (198).

While the later version offers a less explicit comment on the ugliness of Mary's world, O'Brien retained frost to represent the brittle, cold reality of Mary's life as opposed to the soft,

blankety snow of Gabriel's. Significantly, Gabriel Conroy's
contemplations and observations take place from within a com-
fortable room, while Mary's take place outside as she cracks the
frost with the heel of her shoe, the implication being that, for
women like Mary, the world of self-centred contemplation is
denied by the cold, hard reality of their lives. This is further
reinforced in O'Brien's story in her description of Mary's means
of arrival and departure. While Gabriel's arrival is eagerly
anticipated by all, his actual appearance in 'The Dead' is sudden
and immediately immerses the reader in the events of the party,
to which Gabriel is central:

> 'O, Mr Conroy', said Lily to Gabriel when she opened the door
> for him, 'Miss Kate and Miss Julia thought you were never
> coming' … A light fringe of snow lay like a cape on the
> shoulders of his overcoat and like toecaps on the shoes of his
> galoshes; and, as the buttons of his overcoat slipped with a
> squeaking noise through the snow-stiffened frieze, a cold,
> fragrant air from out-of-doors escaped from crevices and folds
> (229).

Mary, on the other hand, arrives at her party after considerable
physical and mental effort to be admitted, ungraciously,
through the back door by Doris O'Beirne:

> 'God, I thought it was someone important', she said when she
> saw Mary standing there, blushing, beholden, and with a bottle
> of cream in her hand … 'Come in or stay out', said Eithne
> Duggan (91).

And in contrast to Gabriel's continental aspirations and
moments of revelation (or epiphany), which are aspects of his
privileged, albeit misguided, self-indulgence, Mary's backward-
looking perspective – to her house (88), to her experiences with
John Roland (89-90, 96-97), to her life at home (88-9, 99), and
to her bicycle tracks in the snow (112) – reflects a distinct lack
of future or aspirations.

Its direct relationship to 'The Dead' is just one aspect of the
intertextuality of 'Irish Revel'. O'Toole's repetition of 'come
into the drawing room, Doris' throughout the story recalls both
Tennyson's 'Come Into the Garden, Maud', and the nursery

rhyme, 'Come into my parlour, said the spider to the fly', each of which suggests entrapment of one form or another. But in making clear O'Toole's aim of getting Mary 'to do it' (100), O'Brien responds directly to Lily's comments in 'The Dead' that 'the men that is now is only all palaver and what they can get out of you' (230), which leaves Gabriel mortified and only able, hastily, to offer the girl money. Perhaps of more significance is that, by inverting Gabriel's perspective, O'Brien also inverts the myth of the West and woman as Other. 'Irish Revel' explicitly 'writes back' to Joyce and a profoundly male, urban, and classed perspective, but it is just one of a number of O'Brien's stories to deal with the almost inevitable oppression of women within a society whose moral and political values demand the denial of certain individual and social liberties, a society which O'Brien portrays as less a return to a proud and glorious past, than a retreat into medieval repression.

Conversely, however, in their largely unsuccessful search for positive role models in O'Brien's fiction, critics – and especially feminist critics – have consistently failed to recognize the importance of figures such as the narrators of 'A Rose in the Heart of New York' and *A Pagan Place*, Baba of *The Country Girls* and, perhaps the most powerful of all, Mary Hooligan of *Night*, in whom the pathetically fearful and ill-equipped narrator of much of O'Brien's fiction, best represented by Caithleen Brady of *The Country Girls*, is fused with the outrageous and fearless Baba figure.

Consistently compared to the 'Penelope' section, Episode 18, of *Ulysses*, in which Molly Bloom's unstructured and impressionistic thoughts emerge as she lies in bed, *Night* is much less an imitation of that section than a response to it and Joyce, through an altered and structured stream-of-consciousness technique, in which Mary Hooligan, alone in a fourposter bed and unable to sleep, recalls her life with a degree of cynicism, disillusion and ambivalence which is absent in Joyce:

> I lie with my God, I lie without my God. Into the folds of sleep. Oh Connemara, oh sweet mauve hills, where will I go, where will I not go, now? Fucking nowhere (8).

Having left her home in Coose, 'that old Alma Mater. Low lying. A glorified bog' (34), after her first sexual encounter in an attempt to escape an 'amplification of the event, cudgels, the ecclesiastical intervention and opprobrium from within the family' (38), Mary Hooligan's position 'among the foe. The Brits, the painted people. A land where the king has piles' (39), brings about the realization that escape is impossible. Memories of Coose, her mother Lil, her father Boss, her son, affection-ately known as 'the lad', as well as the numerous friends and lovers she has known, are interwoven in a narrative which constantly moves between past and present. Once again, the familiar themes are there: the beauty of Ireland, the narrow-mindedness, the violence, the suffering, and the longing, but, in Mary, the head-on confrontation with memory is, apparently, cathartic:

> I am up now, limbering … I am in command of an unusual feeling, a liking for everything … I have that nice feeling that one has after a convalescence, the joints are weak and the head inclines to reel but the worst is over, the lurid fever has been passed (12).

An Irish reader could hardly fail to note the significance of the narrator's surname, Hooligan, as one which not only plays on Cathleen Ní Houlihan, the literary personification of Irish womanhood and nationhood during a period of nascent nation-alism, but its meaning of hoodlum or ruffian. As caretaker in someone else's house (46), Mary is hardly the ideal: the kitchen is left in a state of disarray likely to appal the owners (33); a table, broken by Mary, is locked away and the key dropped into a pond (48); and, engrossed in playing Patience, Mary allows 'long grey tenders of cigarette-ash' to burn into the furniture (49). As part of her ruminations, Mary seems to relish the fact that:

> Little does my mistress know. I have wrought innumerable stains and I am champion at spilling. Also, I scratched the hinges of the escritoire with my thumb nail (53).

She has also managed to 'pick the lock of the wardrobe' and is 'on the lookout for a crowbar to invade the cellar' (68). Rejecting the possibility of further contact with the house's owners lest it become an 'umbilicus' from their 'shrivelled store', Mary leaves the breakages, the dining-room table, the sugar bowl, the ignoble graffiti, and the 'brandy snifters that so joyously got severed from their stems' (121) as evidence of her presence. Seen in conjunction with the epigraph to the novel –

> The original Hooligans were a spirited Irish family whose proceedings enlivened the drab monotony of life in Southwark towards the end of the nineteenth century

– *Night* can also be seen as an address to the Big House tradition (a tradition most often associated with Irish women writers), since Mary's reminiscences and, more importantly, her destructiveness, takes place in a house which is not hers and which she, literally, rejects by leaving: 'Already I have such a dislike for the place, such a loathing, an aversion, vengeance for the roof under which all the auspices were tawdry ...' (121). Viewed in this light, Mary Hooligan's reminiscences are a form of exorcism. By virtue of her role as destroyer, Mary becomes symbolic of Irish women in both the literary and social contexts, since she not only rejects the house, but her inheritance as an Irish woman:

> Au revoir Tig, au revoir Jonathan, au revoir Boss and Lil and all soulmates, go fuck yourselves. I have been saddled long enough. It is time for memory to expire (121).

As one of O'Brien's finest, yet most critically neglected pieces of fiction, *Night* epitomizes all that is central to her writing: the theme of women's disillusionment, the desperate, yet futile attempts at escape from Irish society, only to discover other forms of entrapment, and, finally, an acute awareness of her place in a literary tradition which is, at once, revered and undermined. Like Joyce, O'Brien often ironizes her protagonists through the choice of name – Mary in these examples – parodying, on the social level, the custom familiar to colonial discourse of allocating women a generic name. The enforced enslavement of O'Brien's generic 'Marys' to Patrick Pearse's idea of women's service and suffering as 'the highest thing' reveals them as not only generic colonized, but as generic Catholic.

For me, O'Brien remains one of the most important Irish writers of the modern period precisely because she has so consistently interrogated the values entrenched, particularly, in Irish rural society, and she has done so via a consistently gendered perspective. Despite the critical outrage, O'Brien has, from the very beginning of her literary career, spoken out about aspects of Irish life that had remained hidden for too long, and she spoke about them when few other writers – male or female – were doing so: inventive forms of contraception appear in stories such as 'A Fanatic Heart' and in the novel *A Pagan Place*; self-abortion is undertaken by the doctor's maid in *A Pagan Place*, while in stories of illegitimate pregnancies, such as 'Savages', abortionists are hinted at, usually in the form of unknown visitors to the house; lesbianism is the subject of 'The Mouth of the Cave', and takes a different form again in 'Sister Imelda,' while the sterilization of Caithleen in *The Country Girls*, as well as numerous illegitimate pregnancies and illicit love affairs, all contributed to make O'Brien's work 'obscene' in the eyes of the Irish censors and others, but amazingly brave for many of the rest of us. Her short stories, in particular, are often sociological documents that record aspects of Irish rural life as experienced by women during a particularly harsh time in Ireland's history. Most of the stories, far from being either sexual or sentimental, are quite simply brutal.

O'Brien has been extraordinarily consistent throughout her work in representing the brutality of societies that must, for their very survival, suppress the individual at the private level, and maintain order at the public. Her stories vary, of course, in that we find people who attempt to escape from these situations – sometimes physically (as in the case of the early novels) and sometimes psychologically, often through madness (as in so many of the short stories). And there are those who rebel against their oppression through behaviour that is considered outrageous by their society's standards, and those who conform and still pay a high price. It is also the case that in the vast majority of her novels and stories, the repressed individual at the heart of the narrative is female. With the exception of only two examples – 'Tough Men' and 'Clara' – O'Brien's short stories are exclusively concerned with a female perspective. In her novels, too, there has been a consistent use of a central female narrator or protagonist. Even if we look at the more recent 'political' trilogy – *House of Splendid Isolation* (1994), *Down By the River* (1995), and *Wild Decembers* (2000) – we can see O'Brien's interest in what she calls 'the unwelcome tale' as it relates to women, or, at the very least, the relationship between women and men in societies that expect and, if necessary, enforce, certain restrictive kinds of behaviours. I suggest that if there is any crossing of lines in relation to the telling of these stories, it is in some kind of emotional or irrational confusion between the real and the imaginary on the part of critics, rather than on the part of O'Brien herself.

Works Cited

Anderson, Susan Heller. 'For Edna O'Brien, Writing is a Kind of Illness'. *New York Times* 11 Oct. 1977. 73.

Atwood, Margaret. 'On Being a Woman Writer'. *Second Words: Selected Critical Prose* (Toronto: Anansi Press, 1982).

Avant, J.A. Review of Edna O'Brien's *Night*. *Library Journal* 15 Dec. 1972: 4003.

B.A.B. 'Authors and Editors'. *Publishers Weekly* 25 May 1970: 21-2.

Banville, John. *The Book of Evidence* (London: Minerva, 1989).

Donoghue, Denis. 'The Idiom of Stephen Dedalus in Rural Terms'. *New York Times Book Review* 3 May 1970: 5-6.

Guppy, Shusha. 'The Art of Fiction LXXXII: Edna O'Brien'. *The Paris Review* 92 (1984): 22-50.

Habich, John. 'Ireland on the Dark Side'. *Star Tribune* 20 April 2002: 1E.

Holmes, Richard. 'Poetry International', *The Times* 22 June 1972:10.

Joyce, James. *Ulysses* (Harmondsworth, Middlesex: Penguin, 1983).

--- 'The Dead'. *The Oxford Book of Irish Short Stories*, ed. William Trevor (Oxford: Oxford University Press, 1989), 228-66.

Lessing, Doris. Preface. *The Diaries of Jane Somers* (Harmondsworth, Middlesex: Penguin, 1985).

Levin, Martin. Rev. of Edna O'Brien's *August is a Wicked Month*. *New York Times Book Review* 13 June 1965: 32.

McMahon, Sean. 'A Sex by Themselves: An Interim Report on the Novels of Edna O'Brien'. *Éire-Ireland* 2.1 (1967): 79-87.

McManus, Patricia. Rev. of Edna O'Brien's *A Pagan Place*. *Saturday Review* 25 April 1970: 34.

McNamee, Eoin. *Resurrection Man* (London: Picador, 1994).

Naipaul, V.S. Rev. of Edna O'Brien's *The Country Girls*. *New Statesman* 16 July 1960: 97.

O'Brien, Edna. *August is a Wicked Month* (Harmondsworth, Middlesex: Penguin, 1964).

--- *Casualties of Peace* (Harmondsworth, Middlesex: Penguin, 1965).

--- 'Come Into the Drawing Room, Doris'. *New Yorker* 6 Oct. 1962: 47-55.

--- *The Country Girls* (Harmondsworth, Middlesex: Penguin, 1960).

--- 'Dear Mr Joyce'. *Audience* (July/Aug. 1971): 75-77.

--- *Girl with Green Eyes* (Harmondsworth, Middlesex: Penguin, 1962).

--- *Girls in Their Married Bliss* (Harmondsworth, Middlesex: Penguin, 1964).

--- 'Irish Revel'. *The Love Object* (Harmondsworth, Middlesex: Penguin, 1968), 87-114.

--- *James Joyce* (London: Phoenix, 1999).

--- 'Joyce and Nora'. *Harpers* (September 1980): 60-4.

--- *Night* (Harmondsworth, Middlesex: Penguin, 1974).

--- *A Pagan Place* (Harmondsworth, Middlesex: Penguin, 1971).

--- 'A Scandalous Woman'. *A Scandalous Woman and Other Stories* (Harmondsworth, Middlesex: Penguin, 1976), 9-43.

--- 'She Was the Other Ireland'. *New York Times Book Review* 19 June 1988: 3.

O'Toole, Fintan. 'A Fiction Too Far'. *Irish Times* 2 March 2002: 50.

Paterno, Domenica. Rev. of Edna O'Brien's *A Pagan Place*. *Library Journal* 15 May 1970: 1861.

Pelan, Rebecca. 'Edna O'Brien's "Stage-Irish" Persona: An "Act" of Resistance'. *Canadian Journal of Irish Studies* 19.1 (1993): 67-78.

--- 'Edna O'Brien's "World of Nora Barnacle"'. *Canadian Journal of Irish Studies* 23.2 (December 1997): 49-61.

Rader, Barbara. 'Those Clear Eyes Hide a People-Watcher'. *New York Times* 2 June 1965: 57.

Roth, Philip. 'A Conversation with Edna O'Brien: "The Body Contains the Life Story"'. *New York Times Book Review* 18 Nov. 1984: 38-40.

Senn, Fritz. 'Reverberations'. *James Joyce Quarterly* 3 (1966): 222.

The Times Literary Supplement. Rev. of Edna O'Brien's *Night*. 6 October 1972: 1184.

Woodward, Richard. 'Edna O'Brien: Reveling in Heartbreak'. *New York Times* 12 March 1989: 42.

---

[1] This essay represents a composite of three pieces of my work on O'Brien: a plenary paper, presented at the 'Edna O'Brien: A Reappraisal' conference, as well as excerpts from two published essays, see Pelan 1993 and 1997.

[2] My discussion here is drawn from my article 'Edna O'Brien's "Stage-Irish" Persona: an "Act" of Resistance'.

[3] Pelan, 'Edna O'Brien's "Stage-Irish" Persona: an "Act" of Resistance'.

[4] Echoes of Joyce permeate O'Brien's writing and could easily form the basis of a separate study. O'Brien stated to Philip Roth that in the 'constellation of geniuses, [Joyce] is a blinding light and father of us all', p.39. Her interest in Joyce is reflected in 'Dear Mr Joyce'; in her review of Brenda Maddox's biography of Nora Barnacle, 'She Was the Other Ireland'; and in her book, *James Joyce*. Joyce's influence on her own style of writing is revealed in Senn, p.222, who compares a passage from O'Brien's *The Country Girls* with the closing paragraph of 'The Dead'.

2 | Edna O'Brien, Irish Dandy

Maureen O'Connor

In explaining 'Why Irish Heroines Don't Have to be Good Anymore', in a 1986 *New York Times* article of that title, Edna O'Brien recalls this scene:

> One day in the early 1950s I saw a very tall woman in St Stephen's Green in Dublin, bending over to talk to someone; she was dressed completely in black, almost like a nun, and indeed had what Yeats's sister Lily described as a sort of royal smile. It was Maud Gonne, the 'burning cloud' as Yeats described her. Seeing her sent a shiver through me. I had touched or rather glimpsed both politics and poetry. Unwittingly it spurred me to write (13).

This Irish heroine is one of two 'living legends' distinguished 'both for their beauty and their patriotism', according to O'Brien; the other being Constance Markiewicz, whom O'Brien quotes as saying, 'I'll have a pistol here and a pistol here and my best hat'. Terry Eagleton similarly links the two women in his claim that they

> resisted the left-utilitarianism of some of [their] male comrades with a concern for style, elegance and ornament, an attention to the small beauties and stray pleasures of life which could be easily dismissed as female vanity (295).

The avant-gardists uniting style and politics in both Eagleton's and O'Brien's accounts are instances of the Irish female dandy, a contemporary example of which, this essay will argue, Edna O'Brien herself belongs.[1]

In the above-quoted description, Maud Gonne figures as inspiration for O'Brien's writing, but the qualities detailed are not obviously literary. They are, however, what Max Beerbohm, in his disquisition on the artist-dandy, called the 'subtle symbols of ... personality'; that is, style. In his consideration of the special problems of audience for the Irish writer, Gerry Smyth has observed that 'style is the most political consideration of all' (54), and W.J. McCormack similarly asserts that for the Irish writer 'style is a miniature politics' (846), suggesting the continuities between the affecting appearance of Gonne — muse, artist, political activist, and revolutionary — and her importance for O'Brien's subsequent literary production. Just before this passage, O'Brien calls Gonne the 'undoubted queen' — echoing 'the walk of a queen' Yeats attributes to Gonne at the end of his play *Cathleen Ní Houlihan* — who 'dazzled' people with 'her passion and her appearance'. In the paragraph we have, Gonne's smile is 'royal', reiterating her queenliness, her 'natural' nobility, an instance of a central tenet of dandyism, that is, an aristocracy based on merit, not birth or blood. One of 'nature's gentlemen', she is not simply tall, but 'very tall', not only unusually lofty and imposing, but also deviating from conventions of female beauty that prize smallness and delicacy, an approach to the hermaphroditic or androgynous dandiacal ideal. Of herself O'Brien has said,

> I want to write and hope to write with vigor, with muscle. I don't care whether I'm a man or a woman, I want to write as an androgynous person for whom language is sacred (*The Book Show*)

and Angela Carter names O'Brien specifically as one of the 'women writers ... [who] pretend to be female impersonators' (499). But to return to Gonne and her height: though very tall, she is not too tall to bend herself to speak to less heroically-proportioned mortals, and the twentieth-century dandy is an eminently democratic, even demotic, creature, as we will see. Gonne is dressed simply, yet strikingly, in the Brummellian

mode of exquisite, even excessive understatement, and in black,
a colour — or perhaps more significantly for the meiotic
extreme exacted by the Brummellian standard, an absence of
colour — approved by the nineteenth-century dandy. Charles
Baudelaire's ruminations on the colour, in the course of a
discussion of the dandy, refuses to read surfaces as frivolous:

> The black suit and the frock coat not only have their political
> beauty as an expression of general equality, but also their poetic
> beauty as an expression of the public mentality — an immense
> cortège of undertakers ... We all observe some kind of funeral
> (qtd in Benjamin 77).

Note that in both Baudelaire and O'Brien the figure attired in
mourning absorbs and unites politics and poetry.

Of dandyism Baudelaire also says that it 'borders upon the
spiritual and the stoical' (28), and O'Brien's Gonne appears
nun-like, suggestive of the dandiacal virtues of self-discipline
and detachment — another example of excess moving in an
unexpected direction — as well as an asexuality that challenges
bourgeois heterosexist imperatives. Most important, Gonne is
an electrifying personality on public display in an urban space in
whose synaesthetic body appearance does passion's work and
who so dazzles the senses that to glimpse is to touch. O'Brien
describes the visceral effects produced by her own spectacular
appearance, her initiation into celebrity, when recalling that on
her first trip to Ireland following the publication of her first
novel *The Country Girls*, 'people were said to have fainted at the
sight of me' (qtd in Woodward 42). Like Gonne, O'Brien
provokes intense emotional reactions while evincing no
emotion herself. She claims not to even have been a witness to
others' responses to her — 'people were *said* to have fainted',
she reports — an example of dandy cool; as Baudelaire puts it:
'the joy of astonishing others, and the proud satisfaction of
never oneself being astonished' (27). In a 1970 *Times* book
review, Nuala O'Faolain speaks of just such an effect in
O'Brien's novel *A Pagan Place* which demonstrates, in the
reviewer's words, the novelist's 'devious cool' (4).

Maud Gonne as signal inspiration escapes O'Brien critics. James Joyce is the figure more frequently cited as O'Brien's most significant literary influence, but he is another dandy, considered by Michael Gillespie, specifically in relation to O'Brien, to be 'perhaps the most imaginatively androgynous writer of prose fiction' (110). As recently as June 2004 Ulick O'Connor, in the *Sunday Independent*, referred to Joyce as a 'flâneur', and Richard Ellmann's biography traces Joyce's 'first stirrings of dandyism' to his time in Pula in 1904 and 1905 (194). In the 1920s, according to Ellmann, whose source for this information is Samuel Beckett, 'Joyce formed a large collection of ties in Paris and came to pay almost dandiacal attention to his clothes' (532). In her own biography of Joyce, O'Brien recurs frequently to the dandiacal details of her subject, including his velvet smoking jacket and silk cravat, a snakeskin stick, a silk handkerchief worn with a sombrero, the arrogant piquancy of completing an ensemble comprising 'frayed clothes' with a yachting cap, his Rimbaud-like pose of a 'bohemian rake savoring the decadence of Paris', his unshakable insouciance, that is, in dandy-speak, his 'cool' (10, 19, 29, 127, 135). I have yet to come across an interview with O'Brien that does not exhibit a similar interest, though often half-sneering, half-swooning, in remarking on every detail of the writer's clothes, hair, face, voice. One journalist described her as reading 'interminable prose-poems beautifully from under a chestnut-tree of red hair ... adjusting her belt like a Connemara Dietrich' (Holmes 10), an image that recalls Angela Carter's musings on 'the type of Baudelarian dandy Dietrich impersonated so well' (112). O'Brien has complained that 'If you happen to have your hair done, well then you can't be a serious writer' (qtd in Carlson 73), an observation which she follows by asserting that any woman writing is 'scandalous', 'a rebellion' (76), a recognition of the anxiety an inconveniently 'feminine' writer arouses. As Susan Fillin-Yeh explains:

> negative assessments of the modern woman illuminate the crucial importance of 'womanly' markers in her sartorial style

and the reassurance those markers provided men threatened by
the social changes she represented (174).

Walter Benjamin, drawing on Baudelaire, connects the dandy
to the Parisian flâneur, the wanderer, the eternal observer.
Jessica Feldman identifies this as 'one particular aspect of the
dandy, his sense of exile' (123), the restless motion of the
outsider. The flâneur is, after all, by definition an ambler, an
aimless wanderer. O'Brien manifests just such mobility when
she declares, 'I hate stagnancy, being stuck. I detest rigidity' (qtd
in Woodward 42), and it is this 'one particular aspect' that
contributes to the pertinence of the dandy figure for Irish
writers. Declan Kiberd focuses on such nomadism when he
locates the 'dandy's tragedy' in Ireland, seeing it as

> the story of the bards who woke up to find themselves
> wandering spailpíní and of gentry who were reborn as tramps.
> All such nomads know the truth of Wilde's aphorism: that the
> first duty in life is to adopt a pose, a style, a way of being in the
> world … such a description applies as much to Gaelic as to
> Anglo-Irish writers and leaders (148).

The modern history of the dandy features at least one
wandering Irish bard, an appropriately anomalistic example of
the female dandy. Without going back as far as Alcibiades or
Ceasar, as does Baudelaire, we can say fairly safely that the
historical figures who register most vividly for us as dandies
began to emerge in the late eighteenth and early nineteenth
centuries and were the first celebrities in the modern sense,
inaugurating the cult of personality — individuals like Byron,
the Prince Regent, Beau Brummell, and I would add Madame
de Staël, and an Irish writer of the period who patterned herself
on 'la Corinnne', Sydney Owenson, or Lady Morgan. According
to Mary Campbell, one of Morgan's biographers, French
writers, including Stendhal, Balzac, and Dumas, 'recognized in
her the tradition they prized in themselves — the wit and irony
of the dandy' (208). Morgan, like Edna O'Brien, and like that
most immediately identifiable Irish dandy, Oscar Wilde, was
pilloried for being frivolous, licentious, indecent, profligate,
immoral, vulgar, vitiating of morals — and these epithets have

been applied to all three writers — and for writing fiction appealing to women, a charge, in Wilde's case, levelled specifically against his novel, *The Picture of Dorian Gray* (Gagnier 58-9).

Unlike Wilde, however, the two women share the additional imputations of being ungrammatical, sloppy, silly, and sentimental, as well as being guilty of excessive production, of publishing far too frequently, an unwomanly kind of fertility. Little has changed in nearly two hundred years, except that whereas critic John Wilson Croker had to restrict himself to violently denouncing Morgan's morals and intelligence, nowadays Kevin Myers is free to suggest physical violence, declaring he 'could willingly stick a hatchet in [O'Brien's] head only to be applauded by the nation' (qtd in Perrick 9). Ina Ferris's conclusion regarding 'the figure of Morgan's authorship — aggravating, indecorous, sprawling', that it 'tended to double as that of the Irish nation itself' (70), seems equally if not uncannily applicable to O'Brien, about whose prose one reviewer observed the words were 'plausibly Irish in their rhetorical disarray' (Nye 10). And Peggy O'Brien notes with alarm what it might mean for Irish women, that O'Brien

> is an outrageous concoction of what foreigners expect an Irish person to be — mellifluous, volatile, wanton, irrational. It is worrying to the Irish, especially Irish women, that O'Brien is viewed as their representative and their voice (185).

It is interesting to note that Markiewicz, one of O'Brien's avowed heroes, has been subjected to strikingly similar criticisms, not only by her own contemporaries, but by contemporaries of O'Brien's like Elizabeth Coxhead, biographer of Republican women, who in 1965 said of Markiewicz that

> she is remembered for the wrong reasons, in the wrong way ... regarded with a curious ambivalence, accused of undue fanaticism, and bitterness, blamed for much that was not her fault ... hers is not the image of Irish womanhood we want to present to the outside world (qtd in Steele 424).

Similarly to Markiewicz, Wilde, Morgan, and O'Brien have all been seen in their time as compounding their sins against 'Literature' by actively and openly courting publicity, and not

only achieving celebrity and success, but, worse, also relishing
these achievements.[2] For all of these figures, their interest in
style and clothing, their studied and striking self-presentations
are deprecated even in the same breath as such details are
obsessively and minutely reported, recalling Benjamin's dis-
quieting spectacle of the flâneur, whose stroll through the
marketplace makes of agency a performance, revealing its
illusoriness, and thereby linking himself to the commodity.
Each of these writers engages in a theatrical, aggressively
fictional self-fashioning, which problematizes foundational
ideas about identity, gender, social role and position, even 'race'.
They playfully encourage and abet critical and popular
confusion between their gleefully marketed, self-consciously
manipulated personae and their fictional productions. A
recurrent complaint distinguishing critical assessments of both
Morgan and O'Brien is the appearance of characters in their
fiction considered to be too transparently autobiographical.
Such objections may indicate a discomfort with boundaries
between author and text too emphatically made porous, as well
as with the constructed nature of national and sexual identities
— and the unacknowledged interdependence of those constructs — such stylization of character discloses. Each writer
'refashioned an Irishness which is both overperformed and
overdetermined', as Neil Sammells characterizes Wilde's
political deployment of style (12), but all three writers' theatri-
cality functions as social critique. Subject to frequent parody,
Morgan's 'Glorvina' character, the 'Wild Irish Girl' she
produced on the page and performed in person, stands in the
same metonymic relationship to her creator as does Wilde's
dandy persona. Just as 'Glorvina' became an object of misogynist and racist ridicule — most famously in the pages of
William Thackeray's *Vanity Fair*, in both the novelist's text and
illustrations — the Wildean aesthete also featured prominently
in satirical cartoons and articles, as well as in the Gilbert and
Sullivan operetta *Patience*, all anxious attempts to neutralize
these figures' dangerous parodic charge while attempting to
exploit their saleability.

The 'ineffectual' dandy mocked with such ferocity in Wilde's time, is first theorized in the mid-nineteenth century, after the age of Morgan and Byron (who defended Morgan against Croker's attacks). The most thorough dissertations on the subject are by Jules Barbey D'Aurevilly and Charles Baudelaire in France and in England by Thomas Carlyle, most significantly in his text *Sartor Resartus*, first serialized in *Fraser's Magazine* in 1833. Barbey's treatise, 'Du Dandysme', or 'On Dandyism', first published in 1844, claims for the phenomenon British origins and focuses on George 'Beau' Brummell as its greatest avatar. Baudelaire, who refers to himself as an 'écrivain-dandy', or writer-dandy, also emphasizes, in a series of essays written in the 1840s, dandyism's 'Englishness', a foreignness that not only lends glamour to Baudelaire's formulation, but which is also crucial to the cultural and political urgency with which he invests the figure. For both Baudelaire and Barbey, the dandy is modernity, freedom, limitless possibility, and multiplicity, a hero of opposition and controversy who throws off all conventional constraints and duties, a romantic revolutionary.[3] It is the Irish dandy, Wilde, according to Sammells, who effects progressive interventions in the development of the dandy in the twentieth century, especially its 'pop cultural versions'. Earlier dandies inverted 'social and political relations. Wilde takes the process a step further:

> those structures are not just inverted, they are collapsed ... Style comes to function not as a means by which the centre defines itself, but as a means by which that same centre is transformed and democratized — by people with style (Sammells 121).

One of the results of this process is the creation of space for theorizing the female dandy excluded from earlier formulations. It is not insignificant that it is an Irish dandy who brings such changes about, as a look at an influential British discussion of dandyism will demonstrate.

Thomas Carlyle, a less adulatory theorist of dandyism than his French contemporaries, vigorously and anxiously parodies the phenomenon in *Sartor Resartus*, portraying it as an effeminate Frenchified affectation, indeed, a kind of spreading contagion, threatening to undermine British manliness. Carlyle positions the dandy in counterpoint to the 'hero-prophet', that is, a man like himself. James Eli Adams discusses 'Carlyle's symbolic opposition of prophet and dandy' as 'introducing the tensions between autonomous and ascribed identity that haunt Victorian constructions of masculinity'.

The Carlylean hero-prophet, Adams maintains, 'also exemplifies a widespread Victorian representation of mas-culinity as a virtuoso asceticism, a rigorous discipline staged before an imagined audience' (16). In other words, the hero-prophet is, finally, as troublingly dependent on display and audience as the loathed, because self-conscious and 'theatrical', dandy. There is not enough distance between the two figures for comfort, which is why they require such obsessive delineation. Significantly, Carlyle, one of the most vicious of anti-Irish racists, draws a connection between the unmanning decadence the hero might contract from the dandy with the infectious dangers posed by the subhuman, rebellious Celt, an alignment that potentially undermines the claim made by L. Perry Curtis in his seminal text, *Apes and Angels*, that the simianized French flâneur represented in the Victorian British press is unrelated to the ape-like Celt which often appears alongside him, that the dandy-monkey poses nothing like the same threat to the social order or the state as does the gorilla-Irishman (Curtis 119).

Many of Carlyle's racially inflected anxieties around the dandy are on display in the following passage from *Sartor Resartus*:

> In strange contrast with this Dandiacal Body stands another British Sect, originally, as I understand, of Ireland, where its chief seat still is; but known also in the main Island, and indeed everywhere rapidly spreading. As this Sect has hitherto emitted no Canonical Books, it remains to me in the same state of obscurity as the Dandiacal, which has published Books that the unassisted human faculties are inadequate to read. ... [I]n England they are generally called the Drudge Sect; also, unphilosophically enough, the White-Negroes; ... While in Ireland, which, as mentioned, is their grand parent hive, they go

by a perplexing multiplicity of designations, such as Bogtrotters, Redshanks, Ribbonmen, Cottiers, Peep-of-Day Boys, Babes of the Wood, Rockites, Poor-Slaves: which last, however, seems to be the primary and generic name; ... Furthermore, they appear to imitate the Dandiacal Sect in their grand principle of wearing a peculiar Costume. Of which Irish Poor-Slave Costume no description will indeed be found in the present Volume; for this reason, that by the imperfect organ of Language it did not seem describable. Their raiment consists of innumerable skirts, lappets and irregular wings, of all cloths and of all colours; through the labyrinthic intricacies of which their bodies are introduced by some unknown process (212-3).

At first the 'White-Negroes' of Ireland are set in opposition to the 'Dandiacal Body', but this places them in too discomfiting a proximity to the hero-prophet, the security of whose quarantine requires that differentiation from the dandy be absolute. The hero-prophet cannot be seen as occurring somewhere between the two extremes of refinement and savagery; he must be unequivocally ascendant. The 'Poor Slave', then, is shifted into a closer relationship to the dandy, with whom he shares obscurity of language and a mystifying pre-occupation with costume, qualities that usefully associate them both with the abject feminine. Both the dandy and the Irish White-Negro are placed beyond the reach of human com-prehension; they elude description, remain irreducible to language, inhabiting, together, a position comfortably inferior to the hero-prophet's lofty reason and rectitude.

Fillin-Yeh, a contemporary theorist of the dandy, believes that it is the

dandy's consciousness of self and position that made this persona so useful as an appropriation for all sorts of modernist dandies and cross-dressers, and especially for women artists (143).

I would add that the appropriation is especially useful in an Irish context, where identity can only be speculative and im-provisational, where, as Carlyle testifies, designations are easily donned and discarded, intricately lapped and mysteriously, only contingently, assembled in an ever-shifting, shingled costume:

48

48 New Critical Perspectives

all dressing becomes cross-dressing. The above quoted passage from Kiberd suggests something like this in its discussion of another Irish woman writer, Elizabeth Bowen; however, a product of Bowen's Court cannot easily assume the rags of the poor-slave or incorporate the persona of outlaw or savage, figures used as frequently by admirers as by those who deplore the dandy, whether it is Baudelaire, Carlyle, Camus, Carter, or Benjamin (who uses the word 'apache' interchangeably with 'dandy'). As Anne Enright has pointed out, O'Brien does not belong to the same tradition of Irish women writing that Bowen does. Enright contends that O'Brien

> is the exception to all of those rules. The class of women who wrote were rich; they had that confidence built in already. But Edna O'Brien is the great, the wonderful mistake in all of that scheme of things (qtd in Moloney and Thompson 55).

Ina Ferris posits a similar contrast between Anglo-Irish ascendancy author Maria Edgeworth and her contemporary, the daughter of an Irish strolling player, Lady Morgan, who

> exploited and experimented with her dubious status in the literary field in ways not open to the more respectable Edgeworth, writing female authorship itself in a more aggressive, performative register than Edgeworth was willing to do (12).

Very few commentators on O'Brien discuss class, except in coded references to her rural, Catholic, west-of-Ireland origins, but class is crucial not only in approaching O'Brien's subject matter and treatment of it but also in appreciating her audience, which has remained constant through her many experimentations with form and her use of controversial material, like lesbianism, incest, abortion, and terrorism.

George Walden posits class as central to theorizing the modern dandy:

> The lines of continuity between the classical and modern dandy seem clear, and the portrait of the democratic dandy comes into focus. She or he would be a stylish creature, ultra-conscious of clothes, elegantly rather than outrageously dressed. They would be sex symbols of some kind ... They would be 'smart' rather

than intellectual ... And their vanity and detachment would entail a relentlessly sardonic view of the world ... And most important of all, in a populist age, the dandy would not ape upper class manners or dress; on the contrary, in clothes, manner and opinions they would be ultra-democratic (46-7).

Susan Sontag makes similar claims for the twentieth-century dandy when she says that

Camp is the modern dandyism. Camp is the answer to the problem: how to be a dandy in the age of mass culture ... Camp has found more ingenious pleasures. Not in Latin poetry and rare wines and velvet jackets, but in the coarsest and commonest pleasures, in the arts of the masses (116).

And it is O'Brien's appeal to the masses, 'the relegation of [her] writing to the realm of popular fiction, a less prestigious category', in the words of Rebecca Pelan, that so exercises her critics (75). But the dandy admits of no distinction between high and low art, in fact revels in transvaluing and confounding such determinate structural antinomies. Carter Ratcliff declares that 'What is most disturbing about dandyism is its knack for inconsequence' (104). The academy's discomfort with O'Brien's dandiacal, frivolous populism reveals a Carlylean privileging of the highly serious (a valuation he shares with his contemporary, Celticist Matthew Arnold, who figured the Celt as feminine, 'audacious', a creature of excesses).[4] Such lingering Victorian distrust of the popular reflects a corresponding disparagement of its non-elite audience. O'Brien, like Wilde and Morgan, is not only a dandy of personal style, but a dandy of literary style as well. The prose of all three writers can be flamboyant and lush, a linguistic excess that pushes their texts into unconventional shapes; all three have been described as intertextual in their rhetorical strategies,[5] each partaking of an aesthetics of citation, a parabola of referentiality that gathers the authors' own texts in its sweep and puts its heterogeneous sources to original uses, like the imbricated costume of Carlyle's White-Negro. These effects are all achieved without compromising popular accessibility. O'Brien, like her predecessors, does not directly oppose the official, but overlaps with it, relates to it with wittily abrasive scepticism, pulling it slightly askew, unsettling its imagined symmetry, in a twentieth-century version of the 'wayward colonial femininity' Ferris ascribes to Morgan (86). This seductive, dandiacal performance is rooted in O'Brien's Irishness, even as it exceeds it. If critics appear to emphasize her Irishness as a way of marginalizing her, as has been suggested by Pelan, they are only following her stage-directions. O'Brien cannily manipulates her Irishness to place herself at both periphery and centre, to play the roles of insider and outsider with seemingly effortless style.

Works Cited

Adams, James Eli. *Dandies and Desert Saints: Styles of Victorian Manhood* (Ithaca and London: Cornell University Press, 1995).

Arnold, Matthew. *On the Study of Celtic Literature and On Translating Homer* (New York: Macmillan Company, 1899).

Baudelaire, Charles. *The Painter of Modern Life and Other Essays* (London: Phaidon Press, 2001).

Benjamin, Walter. *Charles Baudelaire: Lyric Poet in the Era of High Capitalism* (New York: Verso, 1997).

Beerbohm, Max. 'Dandies and Dandies', first published in *Vanity* 7 Feb 1895.
    http://www.albany.edu/faculty/rlp96/beerbohm.html

Byron, Kristine. '"In the Name of the Mother…": The Epilogue of Edna O'Brien's *Country Girls Trilogy*'. *Women's Studies: An Interdisciplinary Journal* 31.4 (2002): 447-65.

Cahalan, James M. *The Irish Novel: A Critical History* (New York: Twayne Publishers, 1988).

Campbell, Mary. *Lady Morgan: The Life and Times of Sydney Owenson* (London: Pandora Press, 1988).

Carlson, Julie. *Banned in Ireland: Censorship and the Irish Writer* (Athens: University of Georgia Press, 1990).

Carlyle, Thomas. *Sartor Resartus* (Oxford: Oxford University Press, 1999).

Carter, Angela. *Shaking a Leg: Journalism and Writings* (London: Chatto and Windus, 1997).

Coxhead, Elizabeth. *Daughters of Erin: Five Women of the Irish Renascence* (London: Secker and Warburg, 1965).

Curtis, L. Perry, Jr. *Apes and Angels: The Irishman in Victorian Caricature* (Washington and London: Smithsonian Institute Press, 1997).

Danson, Lawrence. *Wilde's Intentions: The Artist in his Criticism* (Oxford: Clarendon Press, 1997).

Eagleton, Terry. *Heathcliff and the Great Hunger: Studies in Irish Culture* (London: Verso, 1996).

Ellmann, Richard. *James Joyce* (Oxford: Oxford University Press, 1982).

Feldman, Jessica. *Gender on the Divide: The Dandy in Modernist Literature* (Ithaca and London: Cornell University Press, 1993).

Fillin-Yeh, Susan. 'Dandies, Marginality, and Modernism: Georgia O'Keeffe, Marcel Duchamp, and Other Cross-Dressers'. *Dandies: Fashion and Finesse in Art and Culture*, ed. Susan Fillin-Yeh (New York and London: New York University Press, 2001), 127-52.

Ferris, Ina. *The Romantic National Tale and the Question of Ireland* (Cambridge: Cambridge University Press, 2002).

Gagnier, Regenia. *Idylls of the Marketplace: Oscar Wilde and the Victorian Public* (Stanford: Stanford University Press, 1986).

Gillespie, Michael. '(S)he was Too Scrupulous Always: Edna O'Brien and the Comic Tradition'. *The Comic Tradition in Irish Women Writers*, ed. Theresa O'Connor (Gainesville: University Press of Florida, 1996), 108-23.

Holmes, Richard. 'Poetry International'. *The Times* 22 June 1972: 10.

Kiberd, Declan. 'Elizabeth Bowen: The Dandy in Revolt', *Sex, Nation and Dissent in Irish Writing*, ed. Éibhear Walshe (New York: St Martin's Press, 1997), 135-49.

Leerssen, Joep. *Hidden Ireland, Public Sphere* (Galway: Arlen House, 2002).

McCormack, W.J. 'Irish Gothic and After'. *The Field Day Anthology of Irish Writing*. Vol. 2, ed. Seamus Deane (Field Day Publications, 1991), 831-54.

Moloney, Caitriona and Helen Thompson. *Irish Women Writers Speak Out: Voices from the Field* (Syracuse: Syracuse University Press, 2003).

Morgan, Eileen 'Mapping Out a Landscape of Female Suffering: Edna O'Brien's Demythologizing Novels'. *Women's Studies: An Interdisciplinary Journal* 29.4 (2000): 449-76.

Moskal, Jeanne. 'Gender, Nationality, and Textual Authority in Lady Morgan's Travel Books'. *Romantic Women Writers: Voices and Countervoices*, eds. Paula R. Feldman and Theresa M. Kelley (Hanover and London: University Press of New England, 1995).

Nye, Robert. 'Good words for the most part in the right order'. *The Times* 5 October 1972: 10.

O'Brien, Edna. *Speaking on The Book Show*. New York State Writers Institute – Writers Online, vol. 2, no. 3; (1998). http//www.albany.edu/writers-inst/olv2n3.html.

--- *James Joyce* (New York: Penguin, 1999).

--- 'Why Irish Heroines Don't Have to be Good Anymore'. *New York Times* 11 May 1986: 13.

O'Brien, Peggy. 'The Silly and the Serious: An Assessment of Edna O'Brien'. *Masschusetts Review* 28.3 (1987): 474-88.

O'Faoláin, Nuala. 'Devious Cool'. *The Times* 18 April 1970: 4.

Pelan, Rebecca. 'Edna O'Brien's "Stage-Irish" Persona: An "Act" of Resistance'. *Canadian Journal of Irish Studies* 19.1 (1993): 67-78.

Perrick, Penny. 'And another thing — let's have lunch'. *The Times* 3 June 1985: 9.

Raby, Peter. *Oscar Wilde* (Cambridge: Cambridge University Press, 1988).

Ratcliff, Carter. 'Dandyism and Abstraction in a Universe Defined by Newton'. *Dandies: Fashion and Finesse in Art and Culture*. 101-26.

Sammells, Neil. *Wilde Style: The Plays and Prose of Oscar Wilde* (Harlow: Longman, 2000).

Saint-Amour, Paul K. 'Oscar Wilde: Orality, Literary Property, and Crimes of Writing'. *Nineteenth-Century Literature* 55.1 (June 2000): 59-91.

Smyth, Gerry. 'Being Difficult: The Irish Writer in Britain'. *Éire-Ireland* 31.3 (1996): 41-57.

Sontag, Susan. 'Notes on "Camp"'. *A Susan Sontag Reader* (New York: Farrar/Straus/Giroux, 1982), 105-19.

Steele, Karen. 'Constance Markievicz's Allegorical Garden: Femininity, Militancy, and the Press, 1909-1915'. *Women's Studies: An Interdisciplinary Journal* 29.4 (August 2000): 423-47.

Thompson, Helen. 'Hysterical Hooliganism: O'Brien, Freud, Joyce'. *Wild Colonial Girl: Essays on Edna O'Brien*, eds Lisa Colletta and Maureen O'Connor (Madison: University of Wisconsin Press, 2006), 31-57.

Tracy, Robert. 'Maria Edgeworth and Lady Morgan: Legality versus Legitimacy'. *Nineteenth-Century Fiction* 40.1 (June 1985): 1-22.

Walden, George. *Who is a Dandy?: Dandyism and the Regency Dandy, George Brummell* (London: Gibson Square Books, 2002).

Woodward, Richard. 'Edna O'Brien: Reveling in Heartbreak'. *New York Times* 12 March 1989: 42.

---

[1] I would like to thank Tadhg Foley for his careful reading of and thoughtful suggestions for this essay.

[2] According to Cahalan, O'Brien is 'rivaled in the scope of her international fame perhaps only by Brian Moore, among Irish novelists', p.286.

[3] As Albert Camus will acknowledge in the next century, seeing, however, as did Walter Benjamin, the potential for fascism in the dandy's hyper-individualism; and, as Sammells puts it, the 'aestheticization of politics', p.119.

[4] See, especially, Arnold pp.76-77, and 82, where he famously avers that 'no doubt the sensibility of the Celtic nature, its nervous exaltation, have something feminine in them, and the Celt is thus peculiarly disposed to feel the spell of the feminine idiosyncrasy; he has an affinity to it; he is not far from its secret'.

[5] Using Morgan as an example, Joep Leerssen has recently claimed of Irish writers that 'tradition or identity is indeed actively *appropriated* rather than passively *inherited* by heirs', p.21, emphasis in the original. While subject to outraged accusations of plagiarism and lazy recycling in his day, Wilde's intertextuality and self-referentiality constitute the focus of much recent critical interest. For some examples, see Danson, Raby, St Amour, and Sammells. Similar reconsiderations of Morgan's literary praxis can be found in Campbell, Ferris, Moskal, and Tracy, among others. In addition to the work in this current volume, see especially Byron, Morgan, and Thompson on O'Brien's intertextuality.

3 | Red, Un-Read, and Edna: Ernest Gébler and Edna O'Brien

Michelle Woods

'As usual I went to the bookshop at the bottom of Dawson Street where I had a free read every week', declares Kate, protagonist of Edna O'Brien's *The Lonely Girls* (1962), 'I read twenty-eight pages of *The Charwoman's Daughter* without being disturbed ... Coming down the stone steps of the bookshop, I met him, point-blank' (195). Kate has met the man who will become her controlling husband, Eugene Gaillard, 'a dark-faced god turning his back on me' (197). That Kate has been reading James Stephens's *The Charwoman's Daughter* (1912) is significant: Stephens's novel of women's life in impoverished turn-of-the-century Dublin and their attempts to escape the bonds of patriarchy is a forerunner to Kate and Baba's story, which ends in the only escape that seems possible at the time, marriage. There is, however, a second allusion in this reading choice associated with the first meeting with Gaillard, a fictionalized version of O'Brien's husband Ernest Gébler. Gébler was also a novelist and his first novel, *He Had My Heart Scalded* (1946), follows a similar trajectory in its account of the emancipation of Maggie McLoughlin, a girl born into poverty in Dublin who is trapped into marriage, but finally escapes her family, her dying husband, and Dublin, by emigrating to England.

O'Brien described Gébler as a 'Mr Rochester' figure (qtd in Woodward 42), telling an interviewer that she had a 'Jane Eyre-type marriage … I took the Brontës a little too seriously. It was never a marriage of equals, it was always master and pupil' (qtd in Wroe 6). Controversy would reign following their divorce in 1968 as to how much influence Gébler had on O'Brien's formation as a writer, with Gébler later in life finally claiming 'that it was he who had written Edna's first two books and not her' (C. Gébler 346). When the two met in the early 1950s, Gébler was 'a much older and already internationally acknowledged author' with a huge commercial success behind him in his 1950 novel *The Plymouth Adventure* (Donleavy 372), which had sold over four million copies in the United States and had been filmed in Hollywood (Pine 16). O'Brien was nineteen and later dismissed Gébler's claims to have written her novels, suggesting his influence went only as far as his encouraging 'her to write seriously for the first time, not just the jottings she had been putting down since she was eight' (qtd in Carty 3), and in giving her 'access to a wonderful library' (qtd in Kenny 16). Her own success with her first novel, *The Country Girls*, led to the end of their marriage, according to O'Brien's and Gébler's son, Carlo, and her increasing notoriety as a writer in the 1960s generated increasing bitterness in Gébler as his own writing career declined. While O'Brien is finally now beginning to be considered a novelist of literary worth, all of Gébler's work is out of print and largely forgotten.

In this essay, I wish to revisit both Gébler's and O'Brien's work to analyze their respective fictionalizations of their relationship, and to suggest that the responses to their work and their uneasy place in the Irish canon are linked. There are obvious similarities worth pointing out: both authors were banned in Ireland because of the explicit sexual content of their novels, both (together) left Ireland to write in England, both achieved considerable success early on in their careers but were not recognized as authors of literary fiction, and both remain to some extent somewhat removed from Irish canonical writing, though O'Brien's work has recently begun to be accepted as integral to the Irish canon.

Gébler's presence as the template for male figures in O'Brien's fiction has also of late tended to go unnoticed. Though one interviewer writes that O'Brien 'does not protest unduly when I say that I seem to recognize her ex-husband in [*Time and Tide*]' (Honan 7), Gébler's obituaries only placed him as 'the inspiration for Mr Gentlemen, the cad in the early novels by his former wife ... who lured young Irish girls from the security of their families' (Donnelly 9). Yet Gébler is more clearly a model for Kate's lover and husband, Eugene Gaillard, a connection I wish to explore here in the context of his own fictionalization of O'Brien in his novel, *Shall I Eat You Now?* (1968), published as *Hoffman* in the United States.

O'Brien's entrée into the Irish literary landscape has tended to define some critical perceptions of her writing to this day, and this is bound up with her relationship with Gébler: 'With every new novel, Edna O'Brien is beset by questions about her looks, her accent, her Irishness', an *Irish Times* profile opens, 'but she has had trouble winning critical acclaim in her native land, where she remains the glamorous runaway who fled the country with an older man at 19' (Battersby, 'Life' 15). In his memoirs, J.P. Donleavy writes that O'Brien was regarded unfairly as a literary climber who

> just daintily stepped out from behind the respectability of the aspidistra in order to foster her ambitions with Gébler, a much older and already internationally acknowledged author (372).

Much of this criticism, Donleavy suggests, arose from the 'bitter, begrudging climate of Ireland' in the 1950s rather than any genuine consideration of the relationship (370), and these attacks on O'Brien's integrity were born out of 'somewhat resentful jealousies' of Gébler's commercial success as a writer (372).

O'Brien's own commercial success from the very start of her career is still often linked to her personal charm and the sexual content of the novels rather than to genuine talent, leading to a 'long battle against critics who view her work as lightweight and

her prose as overblown' (McDowell 15). Her novelistic engagement with her own past has also been criticized as a sign of
artistic inadequacy or a parasitic dependence on her autobiography for the materials of her art: 'she has plundered
somewhat recklessly from her life', one interviewer writes,
'stirring in just enough fantasy to hit the fiction shelves' (Honan
7). Gébler's nephew, Stan Gebler Davies, synthesized these
kinds of criticism to attack stringently O'Brien's fictional
portrayal of his uncle in *Time and Tide*, writing that 'it was the
sort of self-indulgent drivel written by housewives seeking to
escape Wimbledon ... [Ernest Gébler] first instructed her by
running her diaries through the typewriter, as he put it. It is a
literary technique well-known to all scribblers and, while it may
not often produce high literature, it is frequently lucrative' (11).
Gebler Davies resuscitates his uncle's claims to have written
O'Brien's first two novels – 'the two successful books', Ernest
Gébler tells his daughter-in-law (qtd in C. Gébler 308) – thus
keeping alive the image of O'Brien as, at the very least, the
'Irish Colette' (Battersby, 'Life' 15). And jealous he was, according to their son Carlo Gébler, to an extent that his
competitiveness with O'Brien may have stultified his own
writing career:

> My father talked endlessly about his novels and my mother's
> much greater success despite her mediocre talent ... In literary
> terms my father was fairly successful during the late 1960s
> (although it infuriated him that he was not as successful as my
> mother) (182, 236).

Throughout his memoir, *Father and I* (2000), Carlo Gébler
underlines his mother's talent in opposition to the artistic
inadequacies of his father, claiming that Ernest Gébler stole the
idea for his bestselling *The Plymouth Adventure*. He also cites
excerpts from his father's diaries in which he claims to have
published someone else's novel as his own and in which he
ruminates on re-submitting his first novel as a 'girl author' in
order for it to be re-published (395, 398). Carlo Gébler writes:

> he made it appear that he found writing easy, yet even as a child
> I understood he struggled to write, as opposed to my mother

who did not; his words came slowly, while her words flowed
fluently ... He's a phony (373).

Yet, within the memoir, the son comes to realize that his father
always felt a 'phony' despite – or rather because of – his
commercial success as a writer, and that this need related to the
insecurity of his upbringing (C. Gébler 385). Gébler was born in
England to a Czech Jewish father and Irish mother, who moved
to Ireland when he was a child and who moved back to
England when he was a teenager. A poor family, they left
Gébler in England at the age of fourteen to work when they
moved again back to Ireland. He was never quite Irish, and his
son contends that, following his divorce from O'Brien, he
blamed what he perceived as the children's inadequacies on
their being Irish: 'The Irish were great people,' he told them,
'but thick' (C. Gébler 19). Carlo Gébler, in turn, directly equates
his father's coldness with his foreignness: 'He was an austere
man, quite Czech, quite middle European' (qtd in Donnelly 16).
    Foreignness is the kernel of O'Brien's portrait of Kate's
relationship with Eugene Gaillard in *The Lonely Girls* and *Girls in
Their Married Bliss*; it is this, and not Gaillard's stature as an
older and established artist, that attracts Kate, who sees in his
foreignness an escape from the future her father wants to
impose on her, in desiring her to marry 'one of your own kind'
(*CGT* 291). 'I did not tell him this,' Kate thinks to herself, 'but I
now knew that I would never marry one of my own kind' (252).
Kate's immediate impression of Gaillard is that of a 'strange
man with a sallow face' (184); she is not quite sure where exactly
Gaillard is from – 'Bavaria or Rumania or some place' – and
this ambiguity leads her landlady to jump immediately to one
conclusion: 'Is he a Jew, eh?' (205). The same identification is
made by her cousin Andy when he comes with her father to
'rescue' her from Gaillard and sees Gaillard's portrait: 'Look at
the nose of him – you know what he is? They'll be running this
bloody country soon' (299). Upon Andy's direct assertion,
'You're a foreigner', Eugene answers, 'Not at all,' adding that
perhaps the Irish are not as homogeneous as they assume and
can perhaps themselves be equated with a negative foreignness:

'Not at all as foreign as your tiny, blue, Germanic eyes, my friend' (298).

An actual attempted 'rescue' of O'Brien from Gébler's clutches occurred, according to J.P. Donleavy's memoirs, and developed into a fist-fight involving himself and Gébler against O'Brien's father and his party who called the two 'foreigners' a 'hateful libertine infidel and the heinous pagan' (376). In reading Donleavy's memoir, *The History of the Ginger Man* (1994) and Carlo Gébler's *Father and I* (2000), it is evident that O'Brien bases elements of her fiction on her marriage and its break-up, most notably in the second two novels of *The Country Girls Trilogy* (1960-3) and in *Time and Tide* (1992). Even though O'Brien wrote the *Trilogy* during the break-up of her marriage to Gébler, the figure of Eugene Gaillard is a more forgiving fictional portrait than the portrayal of the husband figure, Walter, in *Time and Tide*, thirty years later, who may also be based on Gébler. In the novel, Walter, a far more nakedly unpleasant character, is not overtly a foreigner, as if the attraction of foreignness no longer provides a smokescreen for a clear-sighted mature writer. O'Brien uses the same Jane Eyre allusion to her marriage in *Time and Tide* as she had to her real one in interviews. In the novel, Nell thinks to herself that 'Jane Eyre and Mr Rochester were very near, far nearer than her neighbours' (20) , and she also revisits some of the atmosphere of Gaillard's and Kate's marriage in *The Country Girls Trilogy*: both Nell and Kate leave stifling houses in London after their husbands discover their affairs, and both leave their children behind to Irish housekeepers and custody battles. In *Girls in Their Married Bliss*, Kate finds a scribbled note underneath 'the daily sentence in block capitals for Cash to write out': 'Now and then he thought all women could not possibly be bitches, but not for long, reality was always at hand' (*CGT* 401). In *Time and Tide*, Walter communicates with Nell in notes: 'Once he wrote on a large sheet of paper – "Now and then he did not think that all women could possibly be bitches", but reality was always at hand to reassure him' (27). Ernest Gébler is presented as fiercely misogynistic in his son's memoir, using women to

further his own career and trying to control O'Brien's success
by demanding her royalty cheques. O'Brien seems to subvert
this act by appropriating it, and fictionalizing it in *Time and Tide*,
with Nell walking out on Walter.

The difference between Gaillard and Walter is that O'Brien
probes Gaillard's being and the refrains of his life – foreignness,
ambiguity, failure – in a way she does not with Walter. Walter is
all senseless, nasty reaction; Gaillard's eventual unpleasantness
and controlling domination is to some extent offset by the
reader's awareness of his outsiderness, his sense of failure, and
his impotent idealism. Gaillard is a filmmaker who made his
reputation with a documentary about 'shatteringly realistic
poverty' (*CGT* 184), and who made one film, 'a romance', in
Hollywood, but who does not want to make 'a famous picture'
(220, 333). He wants to 'compile a long chronicle about the
injustice and outrage done by one man to another throughout
the ages, and of our perilous struggle for survival and self-
protection – but,' he adds, 'who'd want to look at it?' (333) His
name is in 'such small print' on the screen that 'no-one reads it'.
He tells Kate that 'the problem of life is not solved by success
but by failure' (220). Gaillard's filmography echoes Gébler's
writing history: a first book, *He Had My Heart Scalded*, set in the
poverty of the Dublin slums, his second, a historical romance
made into a Hollywood film – and Gaillard's frustrated idealism
seems to echo Gébler's lifelong communist beliefs and his
tangential treatment of these in his increasingly ignored fiction.
For Carlo Gébler (named after Karl Marx, as was his half-
brother from Ernest Gébler's first marriage), his father's
idealism is risible and inauthentic; he brings a real East
European (as opposed to Ernest, a fake Czech and a fake
Irishman), who has lived through communism, back home to
meet his father who still blindly believes that '[i]nstead of Jesus
Christ ... it ought to be Joseph Stalin on the wall of every
house in Ireland with a perpetual light burning underneath' (C.
Gébler 289). O'Brien, however, underlines and embraces the
poignancy this idealism elicits, at least in her fiction, with Kate
reacting with a striking understanding of the tragedy of such

idealism: 'What he said reminded me of a film I had seen, of a turtle laying her eggs on the sands and then laboring her way back to the sea, crying with exhaustion as she went' (*CGT* 220). O'Brien could just as well be referring to the establishment of her own literary efforts, and it seems that the fictionalized portrayal of Gébler, written as their marriage fell apart, articulates a nostalgic and melancholic probing of the kind of man he was.

A year after their divorce, Gébler published his sixth and last novel, *Shall I Eat You Now?* It had been filmed as an award-winning TV drama, *Call Me Daddy*, and was produced as a Hollywood film, *Hoffman* (1970), starring Peter Sellers and Sinéad Cusack (bearing some resemblance to a young O'Brien in the film). The novel, described by its first United States paperback edition, as 'Lolita, with a kinky twist', is something of a revenger's farce, set in Wimbledon, with the middle-aged protagonist, Benjamin Hoffman, blackmailing and imprisoning his young secretary as a reaction to his wife's desertion. The young secretary, with her quintessentially English name, Janet Smith, is about to be married, but Hoffman, who has lusted after her at work, discovers that her fiancé is involved in criminal activity and threatens to report him if she does not agree to spend a week in bed with Hoffman. Over the week, however, Hoffman refuses to sleep with her, instead wooing her in an unnerving and controlling manner, so that finally she decides to remain with him, if only out of self-interest. Hoffman chooses Miss Smith as a docile creature he thinks he can manipulate and control, in contrast to his ex-wife, Maureen Dingle Murphy, with her quintessentially Irish name, who had been driven mad by her desire for an independent career.

If Nell and Kate, in O'Brien's fiction, leave their Mr Rochester figures because of love affairs, here, in Gébler's fiction, Maureen leaves because of her career and becomes his Bertha. During the week she spends at Hoffman's flat, Janet discovers a locked room and one night steals his keys to unlock it, finding Maureen's room as she left it, full of empty gin bottles and life-size photographs, and a still discernible moniker

on the door, 'The Museum' (*Shall I Eat You* 130). Janet, who
has become domestic in her week at Hoffman's, keeping
everything 'spick and span' is disgusted by the 'slutty state' of
the room (72, 127), learning from the life-size photos, divorce
papers, and Maureen's letter to Hoffman lying there, that
Maureen was clearly too obsessed by herself and her career to
care about domestic matters. A psychiatrist's letter, also lying
around, warns Hoffman that Maureen has left his care too early
and Janet finds a photograph of Maureen that 'looked to be
that of an escaping mad woman' (130). While the other photos
are beauty shots, some published in newspapers, this one, also
published, has the caption: 'Miss Maureen Dingle Murphy
arriving on the Isle of Man for the World Conference on
Women's Rights' (130). In her letter to Hoffman, Maureen asks
to be taken back and reminisces on their marriage:

> It was all right at the beginning because I was a nobody, I did
> not know my potential, you were my little tin god. And we
> would have had your cosy family life if I had been content to
> remain nobody ... I should have warned you that I was just not
> the absolutely marriageable type. So what about it if you are
> only thirteen years older than me? ... I married you to get a
> home in London from where I could make my career. You
> asked for that! Now you've got it. Marriage was invented by
> men to keep women subject to their will ... I'm going to be
> famous in my career and have lots and lots of handsome men
> making love to me (129).

Gébler had used some autobiographical material for previous fiction, certainly his background growing up in Dublin
slums for the setting of *He Had My Heart Scalded* (1946) and
fictionalized references to the relationship between himself and
his first wife in *A Week in the Country* (1957), in which there are
biographical parallels between the ex-communist Hollywood
screenwriter Mark and Gébler, and between Mark's American
wife, Beth, and Gébler's American wife, Leatrice Gilbert. (In
The Lonely Girls, Gaillard also has an American ex-wife living
with a daughter in the United States.) His portrait of Maureen
Dingle Murphy in *Shall I Eat You Now?* seems to have some
resemblance to O'Brien, the younger Irish woman who became

famous during their marriage, and who left him because he was attempting to limit her career, rather than for another man. O'Brien also sought psychiatric help with R.D. Laing following the divorce. It is interesting that Gébler has Maureen equating success in her career with a resulting ability to cheat on Hoffman, as if Gébler's own insecurity as a writer and husband was caused by suspicion that O'Brien, in her writerly success (achieved by the time this book was published), was cheating on him.

Shall I Eat You Now? is, on the face of it, a deeply misogynistic book, riven with cannibalistic metaphors, such as Hoffman's description of women as 'fallopian tubes with teeth', and of assertions such as '[i]t is not only homosexuals who don't like women – hardly anyone likes them ... women were animals and should be treated as animals' (62, 39). Yet there is attempted irony here: Hoffman is portrayed as being deeply flawed and hovering on the verge of an awareness of his self-delusion and the depths of his inability to control both his fantasies and women. When Janet Smith emerges from Maureen's room, she calls herself Janette Dinkie Smith and Hoffman half-realizes that his notion of controlling a docile, young, and inexperienced woman will be soon overturned and his revenge refracted on to his own self. Though Maureen, and through her perhaps O'Brien (seen in the 1960s as a liberatory chronicler of women's sexual lives, though not an avowed feminist), is satirized for her championing of women's rights, Gébler had promoted the cause in his early fiction. His portrayal of Maggie McLoughlin's life in 1940s Dublin in *He Had My Heart Scalded*, a 'Gorkyesque' novel, according to its author (qtd in Battersby, 'Entertainer' 15), has her constantly battling symbolic patriarchal figures, whether her father or the policemen who discover her losing her virginity (both of whom repair to the pub to decide her future). The novel ends with McLoughlin's bid for a new, independent life in England.

Gébler's second novel, *The Plymouth Adventure*, was also a socially and politically engaged novel with feminist elements, even though it was only received as a historical romance.

Although it narrates the voyage of the Pilgrims to America, it contains surprisingly subversive material, which is often over-looked. It can be read as an allegory of the spread of the communist movement (no mean feat given its popular acclaim in the United States during the McCarthy era) and it also contains a critique of the notion of freedom, not only because of the novel's derision of capitalists but also because of its critique of patriarchy. One of the travellers, Dorothy Bradford, eschews the notion that the Pilgrims are going to find freedom in the New World:

> We women are kindly allowed to have a soul to save, but beyond that we are reckoned with the horses. We keep a proper silence, we do not move the great and important affairs of men. Perhaps you can tell me what escape there is for a woman at this journey's end, Mr Winslow, that is not the final and great escape? Or are you shocked, to hear such things from a mere woman? (110-1)

Gébler's strong female characters in his early fiction owe more to his political beliefs in universal equality for all classes rather than to a particular sympathy for the women's movement. He returns to the issues of class and gender in his later play, *Siege* (produced at the Abbey in 1973), in which Hugh Wicker takes hostage the local lord's daughter, Antonia, who disabuses him of his bitter attitude towards women (44). In between, however, Hoffman elucidates his bitterness at being left behind and ignored, and at 'surviving a vain, malignant Catholic bitch … at surviving myself' (*Shall I Eat You* 48). It seems possible that this anger, partly ironic and partly in earnest, may be a fictionalized account of Gébler's bitterness surrounding his divorce and the anger at himself, the depression at the heart of his personality as suggested by his son (C. Gébler 401). Hoffman's 'Museum' is Gébler's own.

O'Brien and Gébler each occupies a room in the meta-phorical homes of the other's fiction, even when they literally cannot live under the same roof. Having left Ireland together, O'Brien would write about Ireland abroad and never per-manently return, while Gébler returned but never wrote about

Ireland after his first novel, set there and banned there. Most of Gébler's fiction involves some escape or exile: Maggie leaves Ireland and its constrictive social bounds in *He Had My Heart Scalded*; the Pilgrims leave Europe and religious oppression in *The Plymouth Adventure*; Mark and his brother Karl leave America in *A Week in the Country*, in part because of the McCarthy hearings, and Hoffman is never quite at home. Though never stated openly, Benjamin Hoffman's name suggests the only Jewish character in Gébler's fiction, as does Janet's accusation that he is demanding a 'pound of flesh' and a 'rotten pound of flesh' (30, 130). His blackmail of Janet is part of Hoffman's central desire to become 'an intellectual Englishman' (114). He is renovating a new home for them to settle, to compound this new identity, but realizes in his closing words that this may finalize nothing: 'And here, Hoffman thought, is where the real trouble begins' (144). The mobility in and between Gébler's novels, in style, tone, and setting, makes him difficult to pin down as a writer – the only near-constant thread in his work is the figure of the amanuensis, transcriber, or writer (Gilbert Winslow in *The Plymouth Adventure*; Mark in *A Week in the Country*; Aunt Milly in *The Love Investigator*, and Hoffman, with his scribblings, in *Shall I Eat You Now?*), but this, too, seems an uncomfortable home for a writer whose work was successful in its own time but never accepted as literary.

O'Brien gets to the heart of Gébler in a way that he does not himself (at least in his own fictional self-portraiture), through Eugene Gaillard's embrace and acceptance of failure as an artist but also the self-hatred arising from it, and his projection of this onto the Kate figure. It is a focused exploration of Gaillard's being rather than a generalized depiction of the 'lurking bastards' O'Brien once described herself as being attracted to (Simpson 6), and one which corroborates Carlo Gébler's construction of his father in his memoir. Gébler's portrait of Maureen, through Hoffman's bitter lens, on the other hand, deals only with the outward symptoms of Hoffman's self-hatred rather than penetrating its core, and points to Gébler's narrative limitations. O'Brien finds a 'home' in her voice, but

Gébler's voice seems adrift after his first two novels. O'Brien's location of her novelistic voice may have something to do with Gébler, if only in terms of inspiring certain aspects of her patriarchal characters. Gébler's voice, it seems, loses its mooring through gnawing envy of O'Brien, and her growing fame that was predicated on a re-imagining of their life together.

Gébler, banned in Ireland himself, was banned again as a fictional character in O'Brien's first novels. As O'Brien's fiction has outlived her censors, Gébler's location in them has been forgotten. 'Who remembers Ernest Gebler?' one reviewer asks (Whitebrook 7), and the question might better be posed as, why remember him? Perhaps he should be remembered solely because of the fictional dialogue between himself and O'Brien, and because of his role as a kind of malevolent muse for her fiction. Yet, perhaps, he should also be remembered for his own novels, which have slipped under the critical radar. Certainly the first two novels are worthy to be considered as important literary works as well as revealing in a cultural context; Gébler's engagement with the social failures of post-independence Ireland in *He Had My Heart Scalded*, his *trompe l'oeil* engagement with communism at the beginning of the McCarthy era and the Cold War in *The Plymouth Adventure*.

The neglect of Gébler's work may be due to the previous marginalization of O'Brien's work as non-literary writing, and in part may be connected to one of the same roots of her marginalization, the early commercial success of their novels. This success was a handicap for both, delaying acknowledgement of the literary merits of O'Brien's work and proving a stumbling-block for Gébler's literary reputation. In becoming a best-selling novelist, Gébler seemed unable to re-establish himself as a literary author. O'Brien's career followed the same trajectory initially, until her writing became valued through a re-assessment of the Irish canon and women's voices in Irish literature. O'Brien may well be the better writer, but Gébler's exclusion from mainstream Irish literature should not be considered as an accurate assessment of his literary worth, considering the similar treatment of O'Brien in the past. It seems worth re-assessing, at least, whether Gébler's exclusion is based on other factors, such as his contested national identity (Irish, but not quite), especially at a time when Irish literature reveals and promises increasing heterogeneity, or whether it is due to apparently outmoded and redundant communist beliefs, but which may still contain some relevant reminders in the days of economic boom.

Works Cited

Battersby, Eileen. 'Life of O'Brien'. *The Irish Times* 14 October 1999: 15.

--- 'The Entertainer: Carlo Gébler talks to Eileen Battersby'. *The Irish Times* 2 April 1998: 15.

Carty, Ciaran. 'Still Against the Tide'. *The Scotsman* 25 August 1996: 3

Davies, Stan Gebler. 'The Trouble with Edna'. *The Evening Standard* 19 October 1992: 11.

Donleavy, J.P. *The History of the Ginger Man* (Boston and New York: Houghton Mifflin, 1994).

Donnelly, Rachel. 'Ernest Gébler: An Emotional Dubliner'. *The Irish Times* 3 February 1998: 9.

Gébler, Carlo. *Father and I* (London: Little, Brown, 2000).

Gébler, Ernest. *Siege or a Cry for Help*. Unpublished script, National Library Dublin, 1973.

--- *Hoffman* (London: Pan, 1969).

--- *The Plymouth Adventure* (New York: Doubleday, 1950).

Honan, Corinna. 'How I Learned to Stop Loving the Wrong Men'. *The Daily Mail* 7 September 1992: 7.

Kenny, Mary. 'Women in Love'. *The Spectator* 4 May 2002: 14-16.

McDowell, Lesley. 'Happy Anniversary: Edna O'Brien'. *The Sunday Herald* 4 August 2002: 15.

O'Brien, Edna. *The Country Girls Trilogy* (New York: Plume, 1987).

--- *Time and Tide* (Harmondsworth: Penguin, 1992).

Pine, Richard. 'Ernest Gébler: No Saint in Ireland'. *The Guardian* 24 February 1998: 16.

Simpson, Ann. 'The Long Way Home, Alone'. *The Glasgow Herald* 16 April 1994: 6.

Whitebrook, Peter. 'A Despot in the Family'. *The Scotsman* 23 September 2000: 7.

Woodward, Richard B. 'Edna O'Brien: Reveling in Heartbreak'. *New York Times* 12 March 1989: 42.

Wroe, Nicholas. 'Country Matters'. *The Guardian* 2 October 1999: 6.

4 | Words Apart: Epigraphs in Edna O'Brien's Novels

Bertrand Cardin

The Oxford English Dictionary defines an epigraph as 'a short quotation or pithy sentence placed at the commencement of a work, a chapter etc. to indicate the leading idea or sentiment'. The epigraph began its career in English Gothic and historical novels from the eighteenth century onwards and became very popular throughout Europe between 1815 and 1830, as many novels by Scott, Stendhal, Maturin, or Balzac illustrate. The use of the epigraph stems from a concern to enrich the cultural tradition of the novel and establishes both collective and individual semantic interactions in writing.

Structuralist and poststructuralist theories provide a good basis to analyse these interactions. According to Mikhail Bakhtin, the unity of language and discourse is dialogue, a point on which Emile Benveniste agrees. Dialogue is collective enunciation, rather than an exchange between two sub-jectivities, for it is not only carried out through the medium of *parole*, the use which individuals make of the resources of language, but also through *langue*, the system of language shared by the collective consciousness. These remarks prove to be particularly relevant in the case of the epigraph. Indeed, in spite of its isolated location at the threshold of the narration, a quotation which serves as an epigraph can be seen, even materially, as a link between the quoted writer, the quoting writer, their respective readers, and all readers in between: hence a system of both subjective and codified relationships which, in their interweavings, alter one another. This link establishes what Gérard Genette calls a transtextual relation between the quoted 'hypotext' and the quoting 'hypertext' (*Palimpsestes* 397). As a result, the epigraph is transtextual insofar as it is connected with other texts. The epigraph, as Genette argues in *Palimpsestes*, also takes part in paratextuality because, as a form of 'framing', it highlights the relation between the periphery and the main body of the text (86). As a quotation of a text in another text, it is obviously intertextual, its presence inter-relating two texts to each other. Finally it also takes part in hypertextuality, like parody, insofar as it transforms, modifies a preceding hypotext, de-locates, and re-locates it. These sub-categories may be found all the more useful in the study of Edna O'Brien's work as, with the exception of *The Country Girls Trilogy*, which is not preceded by a quotation, all of O'Brien's novels begin with one or even two epigraphs. The presence of these quotations perfectly illustrates Bakhtin's opinion that the dialogic form tends to be typical of the novel. This paper focuses on these para-, inter-, and hypertextual characteristics of the short quotations which introduce Edna O'Brien's novels.

Paratextual epigraphs

The epigraph is outside the text, but its ordinary place is as close as possible to the text, usually on the page after the title, or the dedication if there is one, and before the beginning of the first chapter of the novel. Being situated at the threshold of the text makes it a part of the paratext along with the title, but also the possible preface, the acknowledgements, the author's notes, and so on. As a foretaste of the novel, like the title, it indirectly brings the reader to the text, but through the medium of an original quotation taken from another text.

In O'Brien's novels, the paratextual links are reinforced by the fact that both the epigraphs and the titles of the novels often echo each other. Indeed, titles such as *Night*, *Wild*

Decembers, Down by the River, or *In the Forest* are clearly evocative of dark, wild nature, which is, in its turn, reminiscent of the epigraph of *August is a Wicked Month* with its phrase, 'mortal nature', taken from Keats's poem, 'The Human Seasons' (1818):

> He has his winter too of pale misfeature,
> Or else he would forgo his mortal nature.

The title *House of Splendid Isolation* draws attention to the word 'house', which is recurrent as well in the epigraphs of *In the Forest*, taken from a folk song:

> Turn back, turn back, thou Bonnie Bride,
> Nor in this house of death abide;

and *A Pagan Place*, which is from Bertolt Brecht: 'I carry a brick on my shoulder in order that the world may know what my house was like'. Together with 'house' and 'home', the word 'mother' deserves attention, in its echo of O'Brien's memoir, *Mother Ireland. Johnny I Hardly Knew You* contains an epigraph about 'a mother'.[1] Similarly, in *The High Road*, the epigraph reads: 'Mother, mother I am coming/home to Jesus/ and to Thee'. This epigraph, which is defined as a 'hymn', invokes religion, which is parodically mirrored by a title such as *A Pagan Place*.

All of these words which keep recurring, along with the motifs they evoke, are keywords in O'Brien's fiction. As a result, the epigraphic texts can be seen as a microcosm of the greater texts to come. They suggest the chief concerns of the narratives themselves. To a certain extent, on a smaller scale, they reflect the diegeses and the plots of the novels. There is undoubtedly semantic interaction between the epigraph and the novel, the former offering a gloss on the text to follow.

Likewise, the novel *Time and Tide*, the title of which refers to the proverb, 'Time and tide wait for no man', is mirrored by an epigraph which is also identified as a proverb: 'The spider spins her web on dark days'. Do these quotations, right from the beginning of the novel, aim at showing how true and trustworthy these proverbs are? Or do they intend to lay emphasis on their unchanging, fossilized, stereotypical aspects which mirror the mentalities of their users who perceive proverbs and sayings as irrefutable truths, and consider that there is no point in digging any further? The novel itself tends to illustrate the literal sense of the words 'time' and 'tide', since it focuses on a mother's inextinguishable suffering after the drowning of one of her children, but such superficial reflections on the title only incite deeper considerations.

By the same token, a folk song is used as an epigraph in *In the Forest* and the title of another novel, *Johnny I Hardly Knew You*, is also taken from an Irish ballad.[2] Besides highlighting the particular lyrical qualities of the narratives, these two borrowings from songs are in keeping with the poetical sadness of the diegeses they precede.

In the paratextual relationships linking epigraph and title, one of the many functions of the former is to justify the latter. For instance, *Wild Decembers* is preceded by a line by Emily Brontë from which the novel also borrows its title:

> ... fifteen wild Decembers
> From those brown hills
> Have melted into spring –
> Faithful indeed is the spirit that remembers ....[3]

This line echoes and reflects O'Brien's narrative and grants the title a more precise meaning. The epigraph can also explain how the work is to be understood. It can be read as a comment on the text or a way to underline its significance. It could thus become metatextual, though it is too short to be a real critical commentary on the text. Because of the brevity of the epigraph, this comment is often laconic, mysterious, and appeals to an implicit knowledge. The reader may be able to make sense of the work, to solve the riddle only once the text is read. This paratext can shed a strange light or a particular shade on the text. It can be seen as a means to provide readers with food for thought and, thus, to increase their literary competence. The epigraph urges readers to play an active part, to be writerly readers, *des lecteurs scriptibles* as Barthes puts it, the real object of poetics being the intelligibility of the work (*S/Z* 10). Whether before or after reading the novel, the message of the epigraph needs to be recognized and understood anyway. The epigraph introduces a sign system in which the semiotic and semantic aspects coexist, according to the distinction made by Benveniste: the semiotic aspect comes under a univocal sign system where the sign works as discrete unity and must simply be recognized, whereas the semantic aspect, which is part of discourse, of sentence, must be understood (91). From then on, the dialogue with the epigraph is no longer implicit, but becomes explicit in connection with the text of the novel. This dialogic characteristic of the epigraph is an essential one.

The epigraph denotes the interdependence of any one literary text with a preceding text. It bridges a gap between two texts, establishes a dialogue between them and incites the reader to put forward hypotheses and interpretations or to wonder about the writer's motivations, the validity of the epigraph, and how far its presence enriches the novel.

Intertextual epigraphs

By starting her novels with these quotations, O'Brien suggests how the use of other texts may influence and, in a sense, disrupt the authority of a single voice. Her novels are all the more polyphonic as these epigraphs establish a dialogue with the text which follows and are representative of the general spirit of her novels. In Bakhtin's words, they speak a plurality of voices and consciousnesses, independent and un-merged, a genuine polyphony of fully valid voices which are nevertheless subject to the control of the author herself, insofar as O'Brien chooses the epigraphs of her novels.

In this heteroglossia, this diversity of languages, O'Brien simultaneously refers to and identifies with the voices from outside. Through the epigraph, she allows the world into her discourse, thus transcending the binary relationship of the narrator and the reader. By identifying with this voice as a subject of enunciation, the narrator is, together with the narratee, placed in a value system established by the epigraph. If the epigraph and its author are familiar to the reader, the implicit relationship is amplified, together with the ideology informing

the text. Moreover, the identity of the quoted writer arouses the
reader's curiosity and allows the reader to perceive the heritage
of which O'Brien is a part. In placing a quotation before her
text, O'Brien appropriates the qualities, the fame of other texts
and writers as if they had been transmitted by filiation. Indeed,
the fact that an epigraph is placed before the actual text is
suggestive of genealogy. This is the case for *Down by the River*
which is preceded by a quotation from *Ulysses*:

> Darkness is our souls do you not think?
> Flutier. Our souls, shame-wounded by our sins.

The quotation is interesting for its poetic musicality which rests
on repetition, and the symmetry of the mirror-image which is
reminiscent of the intertextual echo. It is also noticeable that it
is the sole epigraph to appear in O'Brien's novels which is
borrowed from an Irish literary work.

As Joyce belongs to the generation before O'Brien's, he can
indeed be considered as a symbolic father – a model acknowledged by O'Brien herself, as her biography, *James Joyce*, testifies.
In a review of this book, Ann Skea writes that O'Brien's
enthusiasm for Joyce's work is 'contagious' and that she
'delights in borrowing his words', a Joycean praxis de-
monstrated through her epigraphs (47, 59).

In *Down by the River*, the epigraph is composed of a quotation
followed by a reference to the text from which it is extracted,
and also names its author, which is exceptional, because the
epigraphs in O'Brien's novels do not tend to acknowledge both
writer and title. This detail tends to prove that what is important does not lie so much in the contents of the epigraph, as
in the identity of its author, whose presence is latent behind
O'Brien's text. In *Down by the River*, the epigraph reads like a
dedication to Joyce and shows O'Brien's respect and un-
willingness to de- or re-contextualize her famous predecessor.
Besides, with a quotation borrowed from Joyce, O'Brien
honours herself with a prestigious filiation with her native
culture, but also affiliation with it through scholarly work,
according to the distinction established by Edward Said: 'The
filiative scheme belongs to the realms of nature and of "life"

whereas affiliation belongs exclusively to culture and society'
(20). A strong relationship of filial piety between O'Brien and
Joyce can be denoted in these notions of filiation and affiliation.
According to Gérard Genette, the epigraph is deeply connected
with this concept of affiliation, being in itself a signal, an index
of culture, a password of intellectual affiliation.[4]

In addition to the admiration she feels for Joyce, it may also
be in order to give more credit, more value to her own works
that O'Brien systematically uses epigraphs and establishes a
form of dialogism with some of the famous texts that precede
her own. Possibly the epigraphs help her to place herself within
a 'serious' literary lineage. For, as has often been noted, O'Brien
is not usually recognized as part of the Irish canon. This
borrowing could be interpreted as contributing to the consecration of the writer who chooses her peers. This self-
consecration is also illustrated by Joyce who affiliates himself to
Homer, although he did not introduce *Ulysses* with any
epigraphs, despite the parodic nature of his novel. However, if
Michele Hannoosh is correct to argue in her essay that there is
something parodic in the epigraph, then epigraphs also take
part in hypertextuality.

Hypertextual epigraphs

In their numbers or in their symmetrical structures, epigraphs
are often based on a binary pattern. Such is the case with the
two epigraphs in *The High Road*, in which a 'hymn' responds to
a 'curse' as a tit for tat:

> God that berreth the crone of thornes
> Distru the prud of womens hornes ...
> Curse

> Mother, Mother, I am coming
> Home to Jesus
> And to Thee ...
> Hymn

These two extracts introduce the reader to an emotional,
religious, Manichean approach to the text, confirmed by the

clear dichotomy that separates the characters of the novel. This divided structure parodically and subversively mirrors the un-bridgeable gap that keeps the characters apart in the novel.[5]

The same duality is at work in the paratext of *August is a Wicked Month*. The epigraph, quoted above, which is composed of the last two lines of Keats's poem 'The Human Seasons', refers to winter,[6] in sharp contrast to the reference to summer in the novel's title. This opposition anticipates the happiness of the protagonist turning quickly into bleak misery. Such epi-graphs can be compared to mock songs or satirical mimicry, insofar as they are ironically based on antinomy. They announce the forthcoming parodic devices that are at work in the texts.

Both epigraph and parody share a certain number of similarities. Indeed, both quote a text in a different context and endow the quotation with a new meaning and a new 'story'. As with parody, the particular meaning of the quotation depends on its connection with its new context. The epigraph simul-taneously implies a gap between the quoted literary work and the following text, but nevertheless establishes a connection between them. By doing so, it really works like parody, which relies on resemblance and distortion between the hypotext and the hypertext. Even if it connects two different texts, the epigraph can also distort the initial meaning of the quoted sentence, as it is out of context, by relocating and using it as a reflecting model of the text it precedes. The epigraph establishes a new articulation, an intricate dialogue between the texts. It denotes a transformation of another text, a trans-position of one or several sign systems into another or others.

For example, *Night* starts with a quotation from Ernest Weekley which defines the original Hooligans:

> The original Hooligans were a spirited Irish family whose proceedings enlivened the drab monotony of life in Southwark towards the end of the nineteenth century.[7]

Firstly, it is significant that, by giving one etymology of the word 'hooligan', O'Brien endows the epigraph with a didactic value which is all the more serious as it refers to a historical context.[8] Here again, the epigraph, with its scholarly explanation, may urge the reader to consider the book in earnest. Besides, the connection between the epigraph and the novel is obvious, insofar as 'Hooligan' also proves to be the protagonist's surname in the novel. Furthermore, this name seems to determine the behaviour of Mary Hooligan, who causes havoc in the house she has to look after, borrows clothes from the absent owners, and lets a couple of wanderers sleep in the fourposter bed. Interestingly, this behaviour is in complete contrast with the genteel behaviour of Anglo-Irish families usually depicted in the traditional 'Big House' novel. As a result, the values of aristocrats, together with literary tradition on its whole, are parodied and subverted in this novel.

History and the traditional visions of nationalism are also parodied in the aforementioned recurrence of the words 'house' or 'mother' in the paratexts of O'Brien's novels. Indeed, these words implicitly convey a traditional, nationalistic approach to Ireland which is parodic in the universe of O'Brien's fiction, because both mother and home are neither soothing nor comforting there. Parody is at work in O'Brien's fiction according to Linda Hutcheon's definition of the word: 'Parody is the repetition with critical distance that allows ironic signalling of difference at the very heart of similarity' (26).

Ireland, for example, is clearly central to the epigraph of *House of Splendid Isolation* with an extract from a speech by the Attorney General in Ireland, Sir John Davies, in 1606:

> For Saint Patrick did only banish the poisonous worms, but suffered the men full of poison to inhabit the land still; but his Majesty's blessed genius will banish all those generations of vipers out of it, and make it, ere it be long, a right fortunate island ...

The identity of 'the epigraphed', the historical context, and the reference to 'his Majesty', prepare the reader for the background of British colonization and its aftermath in Ireland, which is one of the major motifs in the novel that follows. But, for today's readers, isn't such a declaration somewhat parodic and subversive in its tone? Centuries later, the power of hindsight renders ironic such as 'the poisonous worms' or 'those generations of vipers'. The speech shows such anglo-centric prejudice and exaggeration that there is something of a cartoon caricature in such metaphoric usage. The epigraph incites today's reader to revise these traditional clichés, to become aware of the biased, excessive viewpoints that were officially expressed in the past. Being placed on the paratextual periphery of the body of the text, the epigraph confirms French poststructuralist theory which argues that the margin is the ultimate place of subversion and transgression. Besides, the allusions to male authority – Saint Patrick on the one hand and 'his Majesty' on the other – may also be read as questioning masculine subjectivity and criticizing the sexist version of Irish nationalism that developed in response to colonial oppression. The core of the novel that follows this quotation implies that masculinist imperatives keep alive new versions of historical conflicts, with women often the victims.

Similarly, in the same novel, the second epigraph is an excerpt from a speech delivered by Lloyd George after dis-patching the Black and Tans to Ireland in 1920: 'We have murder by the throat'. Such violent English statements account for the tragic events that are narrated in the plot of the novel and can be read as foils to some of its characters' nationalistic ideologies. Here again, the selection of such terms emphasizes the deadlock that both sides had reached during the Troubles, a situation which was prolonged by such violent rhetoric. The choice of such an excerpt as an epigraph appeals to a revised reading of past events and implies that history is a human construct, which is necessarily biased, and which cannot be written without ideological interpretation. O'Brien's epigraphs re-evaluate such rhetoric, challenging and questioning the traditional notion of 'official' history.

In the epigraphs that allude to the history of Ireland, the semantic field of violence and bloodshed can be picked up with words such as 'wounded' (*DBR*), 'wild' (*WD*), 'death' (*IF*), 'blood' (*TT*),[9] 'murder', 'poison(ous)', 'vipers' (*HSI*), 'crone of thornes' (*HR*). In the most obviously political of these epigraphs, images are deliberately exaggerated to lay stress on the responsibilities of the authorities and to highlight the fact that by using such words, politicians kept the conflict going and fuelled the feelings of animosity between the two communities. Nowadays, these epigraphs incite the reader to look coolly at these past events. Their messages are hypotexts to be read with a renewed, revised, hypertextual eye. This detached, ironic approach to the past, encouraged by such quotations, is quite in keeping with the parodic, postmodern revisiting of history.

Postmodern epigraphs

Postmodernism suggests a re-evaluation of the past in the light of the present and makes possible a vast dialogue between history and fiction, implying that history may be no more than just another fiction, and thus highlighting the fluidity of borders. This postmodern interrogating of limits is at work in O'Brien's novels, which are not fossilized in the novel genre. Indeed, the epigraphs chosen by the author are not necessarily taken from novels. On the contrary, they are often extracted from texts belonging to different genres: for instance, in *August is a Wicked Month,* the epigraph is a quotation from Keats's poetry; in *Wild Decembers,* it is from a poem by Brontë; in *A Pagan Place,* it comes from a play by Brecht. In *Time and Tide,* the epigraph is a line from the Russian poet Ossip Mandelstam. Any literary text, and especially a novel by Edna O'Brien, is not an isolated phenomenon but is explicitly made up of a constellation, a mosaic of quotations. These quotations from texts which are not novels, written by authors who are not Irish, are in keeping with the hybrid, cosmopolitan spirit of O'Brien's novels. When they are borrowed from literary works, they are either taken from texts that belong to poetry and drama, or are extracted from non-Irish works, the quotation from *Ulysses* opening *Down by the River* being the only exception.

Furthermore, many epigraphs are not taken from literary works of any kind, but from political speeches or psycho-analytic essays: in *Johnny I Hardly Knew You*, the quotation from Freud's *Interpretation of Dreams* incites the reader to adopt a psychoanalytic interpretation of the novel in which a mother has a symbolically incestuous relationship with her son's best friend. Religious hymns or folk songs, whose authors remain anonymous, are also quoted. With such references, O'Brien, whose work testifies to a specific Irish heritage, nevertheless also belongs to the community of contemporary Irish writers whose models are, according to Ferdia MacAnna, those of international writing and music (qtd in Corcoran 123). Her work successfully brings together tradition, modernity, and postmodernity. Indeed, it refers to tradition and, at the same time, disrupts it. It returns to the past, but to revise it. O'Brien's work is postmodern insofar as it both prolongs and is opposed to modernity. It also proves to be hybrid and transcultural because it provides links not only between various texts, but also between the arts, between different disciplines. O'Brien's epigraphs downplay boundaries by juxtaposing several voices, several genres, and several contexts: they range from Keats to Freud via Mandelstam, from the Song of Solomon to Brecht via a seventeenth-century speech given by the Attorney General of Ireland. Linked to liminality, these quotations are 'contact zones', cross-overs of ideas, points of view, exchanges of words, times, and places. O'Brien's systematic use of epigraphs, which borrows from other works on so large a scale, parodies parochialism and restricted, narrow-minded nationalism, and the obscurantist religious bigotry from which the author personally suffered so much. O'Brien's fiction is an atemporal, displaced, dislocated network, endowed with intercultural hybridity. It confirms that Ireland today is not an isolated entity, that its culture and aesthetics are intertwined with other nations. The potential that her books offer – that is, the creation of multiple links across genres and epochs – might then indicate a new kind of metanarrative for Irish studies: one that insists on the local and parochial as having relevance, on the paradigmatic axis, to the universal and international, but one that is neither predetermined nor monological, being instead multi-textured, heterogeneous, and performatively polyphonic. The hybrid, synchretic characteristics of these translations between cultures are reinforced by translations between languages, since some of the epigraphs (Brecht's, Freud's, and Mandelstam's) have been translated into English. Translation plays a major part in this dialogue between epigraphs and novels. A homogeneous language unifies the quotation with the text and favours interactions. In this dialogue, disparate cultures meet, crisscross, and are brought into contact with one another by disseminating borrowings and lendings which surpass all binary oppositions between Ireland and its 'others', thus creating a dissemination which proves to be very promising in its transculturality.

Works Cited

Bakhtin, Mikhail M. *The Dialogic Imagination: Four Essays*, ed. Michael Holquist. Trans. Caryl Emerson and Michael Holquist (Austin, TX: University of Texas Press, 1986).

Barthes, Roland. *S/Z* (Paris: Seuil, 1970).

Behan, Kathleen and Brendan. *Mother of all the Behans* (London: Arena, 1985).

Benveniste, Emile. *Problèmes de linguistique générale* (Paris: Seuil, 1966).

Brontë, Emily. *Collected Poems and Prose* (Manchester: Carcanet, 1981).

Corcoran, Neil. *After Yeats and Joyce. Reading Modern Irish Literature* (Oxford and New York: Opus, Oxford University Press, 1997).

'Epigraph'. *The Oxford English Dictionary*. 2nd ed. (Oxford: Clarendon Press, 1989).

Genette, Gérard. *Seuils* (Paris: Seuil, 1987).

--- *Palimpsestes. La littérature au second degré* (Paris: Seuil, 1982).

Hannoosh, Michele. *Parody and Decadence* (Columbus: Ohio University Press, 1989).

Hutcheon, Linda. *A Poetics of Postmodernism. History, Theory, Fiction* (New York and London: Routledge, 1988).

Joyce, James. *Ulysses* [1922] (London: Penguin, 1973).

Keats, John. *The Complete Poems* [1821], ed. John Barnard (Harmondsworth: Penguin Books, 1973).

O'Brien, Edna. *August is a Wicked Month* (London: Jonathan Cape, 1965).

--- *Casualties of Peace* (London: Penguin, 1968).

--- *The Country Girls Trilogy* (London: Jonathan Cape, 1987).

--- *Down by the River* (London: Weidenfeld & Nicolson, 1996).

--- *The High Road* (London: Weidenfled & Nicolson, 1988).

--- *House of Splendid Isolation* (London : Weidenfeld & Nicolson, 1994).

--- *In the Forest* (London: Weidenfeld & Nicolson, 2002).

--- *James Joyce* (London: Penguin, 1999).

--- *Johnny I Hardly Knew You* (London: Weidenfeld & Nicolson, 1977).

--- *Night* (London: Weidenfeld & Nicolson, 1972).

--- *A Pagan Place* (London: Weidenfeld & Nicolson, 1970).

--- *Time and Tide* (London: Viking, 1992).

--- *Wild Decembers* (London: Weidenfeld & Nicolson, 1999).

Said, Edward. *The World, the Text and the Critic* (Cambridge, Mass.: Harvard University Press, 1983).

Skea, Ann. 'James Joyce'. *Eclectica Magazine* 3 (1999): 47-59.

Song of Solomon, *The New English Bible* (Oxford: Oxford University Press, 1982).

Weekley, Ernest. *The Romance of Words* (London: John Murray, 1912).

---

[1] The quotation from Freud reads: 'A mother is only brought unlimited satisfaction by her relation to a son; that is altogether the most perfect, the most free from ambivalence of all human relationships.'

[2]   It was on the road to sweet Athy, hurroo, hurroo
     It was on the road to sweet Athy, hurroo
     It was on the road to sweet Athy
     With a stick in your hand and a tear in your eye
     A doleful damsel I heard cry
     Johnny, I hardly knew you.

       . . .

     Where are the legs with which you run, hurroo, hurroo?
     Where are the legs with which you run, hurroo?
     Where are the legs with which you run,
     When first the Jerry pointed a gun?
     I'm thinking your dancing days are done
     Johnny, I hardly knew you.

In *Mother of all the Behans*, Brendan Behan writes that this song was written by his uncle, Peadar Kearney, Kathleen Behan's brother, p.95.

[3] As usual, the initial title of the quotation is not given. This extract proves to be taken from 'Remembrance', a poem Emily Brontë wrote in 1845. Yet, here again, the original stanza is not completely respected. Indeed, the third stanza in the poem reads:
     Cold in the earth, and fifteen wild Decembers
     From these brown hills have melted into Spring.
     Faithful indeed is the spirit that remembers
     After such years of change and suffering!
Notice that 'From these brown hills have melted into Spring' constitutes one line in Emily Brontë's poem whereas O'Brien makes two lines with it since she cuts it between 'hills' and 'have'. Likewise,

'these' is changed into 'those' and 'Spring' loses its capital letter. Is the source of the original quotation not given to hide the slight distortions in the epigraphs?

[4] The French text reads: 'Les jeunes écrivains des années soixante et soixante-dix se donnaient ... le sacre et l'onction d'une (autre) filiation prestigieuse. L'épigraphe est à elle seule un signal (qui se veut *indice*) de culture, un mot de passe d'intellectualité', *Seuils*, p.163.

[5] As is often the case in O'Brien's vocabulary, a 'hymn' and a 'curse' also refer to religiosity or religion which are echoed in other epigraphs by references to 'our souls' and 'our sins' or by a line from the Song of Solomon, 'And thy belly be like a heap of wheat set about with lilies' (first and second epigraphs to *DBR*); to the word 'spirit' (*WD*) or 'spirited' (*N*); or to the patron saint of Ireland, 'Saint Patrick' (*HSI*).

[6] The reference to this season is also present in Emily Brontë's quotation which opens *Wild Decembers* (see note 4).

[7] Although the epigraph does not mention it, this quotation is taken from *Romance of Words* by Ernest Weekley (1912). It originally reads 'the drab monotony of life in Southwark about fourteen years ago', a phrase Edna O'Brien changed into 'towards the end of the nineteenth century'. Perhaps she does not give the exact reference to the quotation because her epigraphs are not always quite faithful to the original quotations. A slight difference can be noticed as well concerning the epigraph taken from Emily Brontë's poem.

[8] Together with history, the past is explicitly mentioned in other epigraphs with phrases like 'turn back, turn back' (*ITF*) or 'the spirit that remembers' (*WD*).

[9] The epigraph, a quotation from Ossip Mandelstam, reads:
Pour your eternal dreams, samples of blood,
From one glass to another.

5 | From *Eros* to *Agape*: Edna O'Brien's Epiphanies

Ann Norton

Edna O'Brien based her 1997 novel, *Down by the River*, on the actual case of a fourteen-year-old Irish girl – referred to in the press and in court as 'Miss X' (named 'Magdalene' in the novel) – who was purportedly raped by her uncle by marriage and impregnated, and who sought an abortion in England in 1995. When she was discovered and initially prevented from terminating her pregnancy by forcible return to Ireland, she became a media emblem for the abortion wars in Ireland and the world. *Down by the River* emphasizes the fact that this happened to a human being and not to a symbol; it is an empathetic imagining of the trauma she must have experienced. O'Brien ups the ante of the original case by making her fictional rapist the alcoholic father of fourteen-year-old Mary and by graphically depicting the rapes themselves, which Mary does not fully understand and which her father denies to himself and others. The story of Mary's manipulation by priests, politicians, and anti-abortion activists, who use her for their own purposes and never consider the girl's health, her future life, or her own desires, clearly indicates O'Brien's belief that it is the girl's choice alone to continue or terminate her pregnancy. It is a fierce defense of legal abortion and an excoriation of what

O'Brien presents as the personal hypocrisy or fanaticism of its opponents.

Yet O'Brien's plea for mercy toward all the characters – even, especially, those who use and hurt Mary – ultimately becomes more prominent, and this harsh novel, unlike many of O'Brien's earlier works, ends hopefully. After miscarrying, Mary resumes her interrupted adolescence and, in a karaoke disco, she dares to sing. As she walks toward the stage, the narrator makes a heavy-handed allusion to the last paragraph of James Joyce's 'The Dead', one significantly paraphrased in many previous O'Brien novels and stories:

> Across the land the snow is falling, the silver-thorn flakes meshing and settling into thick, mesmerizing piles, sheeting the country roads, looping the winter hedges to a white and cladded stillness, and down at home their house is empty, the vacant rooms waiting for life to come back into them, for windows to be lit up again and the sloshing crowd waiting too ... Her voice was low and tremulous at first, then it rose and caught, it soared and dipped and soared ... and they were silent then, plunged into a sudden and melting silence because what they were hearing was in answer to their own souls' innermost cries (264-5).

This evident reference to literature's most famous epiphany has many layers of meaning. Gabriel Conroy suddenly sees his wife Gretta as a real, vulnerable human being rather than as an appendage to his ego, or merely a vehicle for sexual pleasure. Likewise in O'Brien, the Irish audience's 'innermost' selves, uncensored by social, political, or cultural rules and memories, recognize that Mary is more than an ill-educated country girl impregnated out of wedlock. As a scapegoat, and as a human being who has suffered and survived, she merits reconciliation, respect, and love, as do the people who hear her sing. This recognition of Mary's humanity will bring 'life' back to the 'vacant rooms' of these people, whose former callous treatment of Mary – and by extension others like her – has caused their metaphorical deaths, represented in 'The Dead' as snow. The 'melting' silence implies that the snow that in the Joyce story was 'general all over Ireland' at last will disappear.

Like Joyce's male protagonists, O'Brien's female protagonists grapple with Ireland's paternalistic Catholic culture for
freedom of expression and experience, showing, as Stephen
Dedalus says in *A Portrait of the Artist as a Young Man*, that 'this
race and this country and this life produced' them (203). And,
like Joyce's, O'Brien's characters experience 'epiphanies',
'sudden spiritual manifestation[s]' within the mundane world
(*Stephen Hero* 211), the word coined from Christian thinkers
who used it to signify the manifestation of God's presence in
the world. Joyce famously adapted it to demonstrate secular
revelations that, as Morris Beja describes, may come from
'some object, scene, event, or memorable phase of the mind'
whose 'manifestation' may be 'out of proportion to the significance or strictly logical relevance of whatever produces it'
(18). O'Brien's characters' epiphanies, and their allusions to
Joyce's more famous epiphanies, work both subtly and obviously almost as thematic shorthand.[1] Three texts from
different points in O'Brien's career – 'The Love Object' (1968),
The High Road (1988), and *Down by the River* (1996) – will serve
here to illustrate this point.

In some contradiction to O'Brien's reputation as a rebellious
Catholic, her female characters' epiphanies are more traditionally spiritual than Joyce's. They suddenly recognize the
value of love as Christ preached it and not as patriarchal
religious regimes interpret it; specifically, they see that the
puritanical obsession with sex as sin (and, by extension, the
masculinist world focus on women as primarily sexual beings)
ironically privileges sexual desire over empathy and compassion, or *eros* over *agape* – exactly the opposite of its apparent
doctrinal intention.

Father William T. Noon describes Gabriel Conroy's epiphany in 'The Dead' as a turn 'from *Eros* to *Agape*' (84), and I
suggest that O'Brien focuses primarily on this interpretation in
her characters' epiphanies. Anders Nygren defines and dif-
ferentiates them as two 'fundamental motifs' of Platonic and
Christian thinking:

[Eros] is a human love for the Divine, a love of man for God.
But ... not everything which can be called man's love for God
is to be identified with Eros. Eros is an appetite, a yearning
desire, which is aroused by the attractive qualities of its object;
and in Eros-love man seeks God in order to satisfy his spiritual
hunger by the possession and enjoyment of the divine
perfections. But the love of man for God of which the New
Testament speaks is of quite a different stamp ...God's love,
Agape in the fullest sense of the term, has neither the appetitive
nature of Eros nor the responsive character of Faith ... [it]
consists, not in getting, but in doing good ... [and] it is
'indifferent to value' ... neither kindled by the attractiveness
nor quenched by the unattractiveness of its object. ... Eros, on
the other hand ... is far from 'indifferent to value' ... Eros
[seeks] to gain possession of [the loved object] (viii-ix).

This dichotomy appears relentlessly throughout O'Brien's
fiction. In early novels and stories her characters struggle to
possess elusive, deified love objects, men they idealize as heroes
from Christian and romantic literature, and they seek in sex a
mystical experience that is missing from their unhappy lives,
hoping for love from an 'other' – an 'object' who will give them
identity and meaning. Yet in many works the protagonists
eventually turn to a selfless love, recognizing the other – the
object – as subject, as someone not unlike themselves, and
embrace the moral law of many religions: to love and to give to
others selflessly and mercifully. O'Brien in fact gives this point
more weight than depictions of sexual desire and activity,
though her erotica has garnered far more attention than her
embrace of agape.

O'Brien uses epiphany for feminist purposes as well. She
contrasts female defeats after epiphany with the comparative
male triumphs after epiphany Joyce so memorably depicts, in
order to show that for women, such artistic, moral, and social
victories are usually thwarted by cultural and religious insistence
on their sexual and reproductive identities.[2] Yet, ultimately,
O'Brien's female protagonists are not confined to the private
worlds of home, marriage, or adultery; they are reformers working, without desire for glory, toward a more compassionate

world. In fact, O'Brien's epiphanies unabashedly imply that women's sufferings make them superior to men, granting them a Blakean ability to see beyond their initial visions to a re-visioning, a fresh perception of those they had seen very differently.

Interestingly, when O'Brien turns in the 1990s from dissections of sexual relationships to politics and history, this embrace of the other includes presenting men much more empathetically than in her earlier work. She combines these new explorations of masculinity with an implicit agenda: to inspire similar revelations in her readers and in the hypocritical society she criticizes (and which Joyce criticized). Amanda Greenwood describes O'Brien's 1990s trilogy as acknowledging 'the need for direct engagement with the dominant discourse as a means towards the realization of social and symbolic reform' (75). *Down by the River* demonstrates clearly O'Brien's movement toward a broader context, as she stages publicly a real-life story that engages issues she has explored as private in earlier texts – incest, sexuality, abortion, constructions of the feminine – and urges readers to see all the characters as unique human beings rather than religious, political, or gendered stereotypes.

Down by the River also marks a major difference between Joyce's and O'Brien's purposes for epiphany. Joyce delineates, especially in 'The Dead', *Portrait*, and *Ulysses*, the phases of a writer's development toward dramatic form and away from the more subjective lyrical and epic. He mocks Stephen and Gabriel not only for deficient artistic abilities before their epiphanies, but also for the self-absorption and lack of empathy that cause such limitations, and which they recognize as they progress toward greater artistry. Mary, in comparison, is pathetic rather than ludicrous, struggling to find any voice rather than refine one already forming, and she needs to translate her epiphanies into lessons that will allow her to live with some happiness and safety. Mary's singing in a karaoke bar may seem trivial, but for her any self-expression or assertion can be risky, since even in contemporary Ireland her rejection of home, country, and church leaves her vulnerable as Stephen Dedalus or Gabriel

Conroy would never be. Rebecca Pelan cogently argues in her comparison of 'The Dead' with O'Brien's short story 'Irish Revel' that '[t]he world of self-centered and self-indulgent contemplation is denied by the cold, hard reality of their lives' (56), and this certainly describes Mary. Yet Mary's epiphanies are in a sense purer than Gabriel's or Stephen's since they focus on loving others for their own sakes rather than as a corrective to past ethical or aesthetic mistakes. This focus on agape – as well as her thoughts and actions, which are free of selfishness – makes her at some level superior to Stephen or Gabriel.

Down by the River in fact begins with an ironic reference to Stephen's 'bird girl' epiphany, when the sight of a young beauty seems the material manifestation of his vow to reject a religious vocation and embrace 'the snares of the world' as part of his artistic path. Stephen joyfully muses on a 'day of dappled seaborne clouds' as he questions why words about colour have such beauty and power (*Portrait* 180). The omniscient narrator of *Down by the River* – imbued with Mary's voice as the omniscient narrator of *Portrait* contains Stephen's – contrasts Mary's squalid experience with Stephen's ecstasy by imitating his language:

> O sun. O brazen egg-yolk albatross; elsewhere dappled and filtered through different muslins of leaf, an after-smell where that poor donkey collapsed, died and decayed; the frame of a car, turquoise once; rimed in rust, dock and nettle draping the torn seats, a shrine where a drunk and driven man put an end to himself, then at intervals rubbish dumps, the bottles, canisters, reading matter and rank gizzards of the town riff-raff stowed in dead of night (1).

When Mary's father James rapes her for the first time directly after this, the narration seems again to mimic Stephen's rapturous speech, but in a frantic attempt to make sense of this violation: 'O quenched and empty world' (4). Mary, the novel ruthlessly reminds us, as a lovely young girl – rather like the bird girl – cannot choose to encounter or not the snares of the world. Indeed, she cannot escape the sexual roles her father and her society foist upon her, becoming both mother and

Magdalene in one fell swoop. James immediately blames her as
a sexual temptress: 'What would your mother say … Dirty little
thing' (5). Mary's name emphasizes her entrapment in cultural
stereotypes, and here, as elsewhere, O'Brien fictionalizes in the
baldest terms Marina Warner's discussion of 'Mariolatry':

> Mary establishes the child as the destiny of woman, but escapes
> the sexual intercourse necessary for all other women to fulfill
> this destiny. Thus the very purpose of women established by
> the myth with one hand is slighted with the other (336).

Yet Mary's thought-language shows that she, like Stephen,
takes joy in the variety and colour of the world. It also echoes
the voices of Molly Bloom in *Ulysses* and Anna Livia Plurabelle
in *Finnegans Wake*, both of whose last-chapter monologues represent a kind of ultimate epiphany in their respective texts.
They repeat 'O' in their more lyrical moments and speak — or
think — in fluid, ungrammatical sentences and fragments,
creating words from synonyms or freely altering their syn-
tactical usage. These famous Joycean women represent life-
giving, sexually-celebrant femininity rather than victimized girl,
and they are curious people, avid for experience and to know
themselves and others. Mary's association with them implies
that she will survive and thrive, despite her degradation, and
eventually experience the compassion and joy they evoke. For
instance, when Mary's father forces her to perform fellatio, she
thinks almost objectively about the experience as a physical
union, describing it to herself both to minimize its terror and
degradation and to understand it, recognizing her father's essential humanity even as he commits violence.

> Not sight, not words, only touch. Touch telling her what to do.
> Almosting it. Touch decreeing the momentum, of fast or slow
> … the girth that of her mother's deodorant knob but of a
> different taste. Rapidity. Then volitionlessness. Sea foam, sea
> horses, a lavering in her mouth … (28).

Molly, in very different circumstances but with similar vivid-
ness, remembers Blazes Boylan's sexual prowess with
humorous interest:

yes when I lit the lamp because he must have come 3 or 4 times
with that tremendous big red brute of a thing he has I thought
the vein or whatever the dickens they call it was going to burst
through his nose is not so big after I took off all my things with
the blinds down after my hours dressing and perfuming and
combing it like iron or some kind of a thick crowbar standing
all the time he must have eaten oysters (611).

Anna Livia's references are harder to pinpoint, but she
thinks with like curiosity and relish about sexuality, encom-
passing subject and object in her ruminations:

Why? One's apurr apuss a story about bird and breakfedes and
parricombating and coushcouch but others is of tholes and
oubworn buyings, dolings and chafferings in heat, contest and
enmity. Why? ... It is a sort of swigswag, systomy dystomy,
which everabody you ever anywhere at all doze. Why? Such me
(597).

O'Brien writes in *James and Nora* 'that [no] man' but Joyce
'has ever wanted so to be a woman' or 'composed and
descanted words that so utterly depict the true and desperate
heart' of women (35). She also claims in her biography of Joyce
that he depicts women who, 'despite being victims, attain a
moral superiority' (91), and that Joyce trusted women more
than men partly because 'relationships between men were
founded on competitiveness, jealousy, rivalry', emotions that
masquerade as friendship. Mary's echoes of Molly and Anna
Livia stress her affinity with their feminine strength and wisdom
– free from the 'male collusion' that forces women to 'maintain
a mystique and conceal their deepest sexual impulses' (*James
Joyce* 74) – and imply her moral superiority to those who would
prefer she represent virgin or whore. Indeed, Mary will survive
incest, reject suicide, and embrace love despite her desperate
situation and the social 'collusion' that creates it.

Tellingly O'Brien skewers the women in *Down by the River*
who mete out self-righteous punishment for Mary's (apparent)
dual sins of premarital sex and attempted abortion. Significantly, they are contrasted with men whose first impulses are
kindness and concern. A conversation between Mary's head-

master and Mary's friend Tara's mother illustrates the lack of reflection or mercy typical of those women who promote the 'impossible bind' Warner articulates (336). The headmaster recognizes the father as the rapist, as Tara's mother will not; and while she fumes that Mary's 'soiled undergarments' were proof of a sexual indulgence, the headmaster suggests that she will need 'all the friends she can find' (150). The novel extends sympathy even to Mary's apparently despicable father. Soon after his initial sexual abuse of his daughter, James heroically saves a mare and her foal by manually effecting a difficult breech delivery '[w]ith a taut and terrible delicacy, as if it is a child that he is assisting into the world' (62). Mary recognizes from this miraculous feat his 'absolute and instantaneous rapport with the animal, so tender and true such as he had never shown her or her mother or possibly anyone' (63), and sees, in a crucial epiphany, that her father is good as well as evil, that he has the capacity for love even as he manifests its opposite.

The most evident angel of mercy in *Down by the River* is a man, Luke, the street musician who, in spite of his own poverty, houses and feeds Mary when she runs away from her poor rural home to Galway. He offers her friendship and shelter, not from sexual desire, but from sheer spontaneous sympathy. Still, the inhabitants of Mary's village will automatically assume that Luke is the father of her unborn child, and Luke and Mary are punished for sharing a love the people around them cannot envisage, in spite of their apparently religious motivations for censure. Consequently, Luke rejects his own innate compassion, thinking that '[o]nly a moron would trust' (174). Mary finally loses her baby in a sudden bloody miscarriage that seems to symbolize just this bitter loss of love, as if the child has seen the fight its existence caused and has chosen not to live in such a world, or as if it was murdered by the very people who sought ostensibly to protect its life.

But Mary's sense of agape survives all the brutality she suffers, and she recognizes the necessity of compassion throughout the novel, unlike Stephen in *Portrait*, whom Cranly asks whether he has 'ever felt love towards anyone or anything'. Stephen answers by stressing an abstract notion of loving God: 'I tried to unite my will with the will of God instant by instant. In that I did not always fail. I could perhaps do that still ...' Cranly cuts short this hubristic exercise with a concrete question: 'Has your mother had a happy life?' (261-2). O'Brien returns constantly to Cranly's question, implying both the potentially selfish nature of Stephen's quest for ideal intellectual comprehension and aesthetic expression – a point Joyce also makes throughout *Portrait* – and Stephen's lack of empathy for, or even recognition of, women in any but sexual roles.

O'Brien particularly utilizes the authorial irony of Joyce's epiphanies in her pre-1990 fiction, her characters experiencing, like Stephen, only an initial stage of revelation. These female protagonists look to satisfy a 'spiritual hunger' through possession of what they perceive as the 'divine perfections' of their lovers, though they recognize their own urgent quest for romantic sexual love partly as a sublimated search for religious faith. Such recognition manifests itself in the Christ-like or priest-like imagery that describes these early heroines' perceptions of the beloved men, who are usually older, more educated, more accomplished, and more powerful. But these women eventually drop the need for their lovers to be God-like when they are able to see people – especially desirable men – truthfully, and to forgive them and love them unselfishly and spontaneously, accepting the good and the evil within them, giving without obligation to receive in return: in short, when they can experience agape even toward those for whom they have felt intense erotic love.

This progression away from immersion in eros and toward this vision of agape is reflected both by individuals within texts and in her work chronologically as a whole, culminating in the 1990s trilogy. O'Brien refers to mistaken 'erotic' obsession in an early interview with Nell Dunn when she deplores sexual attraction dominated by religious, literary, and mythic meanings. Saying that such love has done her 'a lot of harm', O'Brien describes it as 'destructive ... one should like the man or woman one loves whereas I probably, deep-down, fear them, and therefore hate them' (78). In fact, O'Brien claims in the same early interview that 'the meaning of love' can be found in Yeats's 'pity beyond all telling' that is 'hid in the heart of love' ('The Pity of Love'), where the lover is not concerned with romantic or sexual longings or his need for requited love, but only in protecting the beloved from harm.

'The Love Object', one of O'Brien's most frequently discussed (and disparaged) stories, contains in miniature the progression many of her protagonists make from romantic self-absorption toward empathetic awareness of, and pity for, others who suffer, such as Kate in *The Country Girls* trilogy, Willa in *Casualties of Peace*, and Ellen in *August is a Wicked Month*. Each of these texts portrays a wounded, self-destructive woman whose problems are partly attributable to a sexist world that rewards male selfishness, and partly to what Kiera O'Hara calls an 'obsession with love [that] seems to stand in the way of its attainment' (317). The cagey first-person point of view employed in 'The Love Object' leaves ambiguous whether Martha tells the truth when she claims finally to see 'the real' man and not an object. But the *means* for this epiphany are all in place, and they are subtly linked to the progression of Gabriel Conroy's famous epiphany, paraphrased in this story as it is in 'Irish Revel', 'Lantern Slides', and other O'Brien texts. To dismiss, as O'Hara does, Martha's ultimate revelations as 'no real letting go' minimizes the importance of Martha's hard-won, if incomplete, empathy and what it bodes for her future. It also undercuts what Maureen L. Grogan identifies as Martha's ability in the midst of her pain to use 'the combined faculties of memory and imagination to re-create and revise' her actual experience with her lover and her ability to fashion 'a new reality' (10).

Martha realizes – incompletely – that her sin consists not of adulterous sex, but selfishness, as she clumsily follows the clues that point the way out. Martha manages both to see her lover as a fellow human being and to lose her sense of him as a 'stranger' whose attention she craves and for whom she will act selfishly. This echoes the 'strange friendly pity' Gabriel feels when looking at Gretta sleeping (2267); for him it is a step toward separating her identity as wife and lover from her reality as a human being. Similarly, O'Brien's title refers not only to Martha's sense of her lover as an 'object', but also to the fact that she remains the love 'object' for the unnamed lawyer.

The reader can see from the start – as Martha does not yet – that his indulgence in an affair with Martha is purely selfish and in fact 'cruel', the word that will blaze in her head as her one remaining image of the affair. He is deliberately associated with patriarchal power and privilege, even spiritual authority. An 'elderly' wealthy lawyer with 'praying hands', a 'very religious smile' (147), a 'row of war medals' (155), and a third 'trophy' wife about half his age (the same as Martha, thirty), she revels in the fact that he is both 'stranger and lover', which she *used to think* was the ideal bed partner' (148, emphasis added). Just as Gabriel's vision of his wife as a stranger on the stairs makes her a symbol of 'distant music', which inspires his 'lust' for her 'body, musical and perfumed and strange' (2260, 2263), Martha romanticizes her lover as the other whom she longs to possess. And just as Gabriel initially hates Michael Furey as a rival, Martha at first feels 'no pity' for her lover's wife. She appreciates the fact that he 'took great care to speak like a single man, and he allowed time after [their] lovemaking to stay for an hour or so and depart at his leisure' (150); he 'saw and admired parts of [her] that no other man had ever bothered with' (151). It is obvious to the reader, if not to Martha, that such 'kindness' constitutes calculated moves meant to keep Martha in what is in fact the 'mean and squalid little affair' neither will name (150).

Still, from the start Martha recognizes and appreciates kindness and knows that in fact her lover manifests its opposite, as her long, complex dream of their lovemaking reveals. First envisioned as a devil, he attends to her orgasm but then becomes rough, saying, 'I'm not considering you now, I think we've considered you' (154), as if their sexual pleasure must always be separate, one person giving only for the sake of receiving in return. Moreover, his remonstrance that they should never apologize to each other or express anger confirms his power to control the dialogue about their relationship. And Martha's love becomes its opposite as he begins his physical and emotional withdrawal. She feels a 'lump of hatred' for him as he dresses after their tryst for a formal dinner to which he'll take his wife, seeing his body as ugly and herself and her lover as 'enemies' (155-6) who will always be 'outside one another' (157). Yet exactly when she should most hate him – he condescendingly says, while she performs fellatio, 'It just occurred to me that possibly you love me' (160) – her ironic epiphany begins, with strong echoes of 'The Dead'.

The language in this crucial scene suggests that Martha should be seeing the truth about her lover's selfishness, as Gabriel sees the truth of Gretta's humanity and his own egotism, but the male and female roles are reversed. Ironically, this occurs on the morning of the day she is to get a 'prize' for the (never described) television announcing that Martha does for a living. Unlike Gabriel, who craves recognition for his literary reviews, she disregards this professional recognition. Even more ironically, the lover claims that Martha should become his 'friend', though she recognizes that he speaks 'without conviction' (160). When he finishes, Martha stares through the blinds at 'the beam of raw light coming through' and says, 'I think there's frost outside', to which he replies that 'winter was upon' them – like the falling snowflakes in 'The Dead' – and takes the bulb out of the bedside lamp to plug in his razor. She does not see that he robs her of light and creates the 'frost' by his selfish actions. After he leaves, all that remains of him are the 'thick turds of his dark-gray cigar ash', which she compares to 'the ashes of the dead': clearly a reference to the death in life Joyce portrays in Gabriel's Dublin society (161).

The 'suggestion of frost outside' remains the next morning as a reminder of the selfishness they both still show. As Martha schemes to coax him back, she pictures a 'miracle' (162) she knows is 'inhuman': the death of his wife and children. Martha imagines replacing her lover's 'black tulip' with a 'white narcissus'. Red tulips traditionally signify declarations of love and yellow tulips hopeless love, so the black tulip – besides its obvious connection with death – could symbolize both his 'official' love for his wife and Martha's hopeless love for him. But the narcissus represents her self-interest in brutally hoping for his family's demise, matched by his brutality in coldly sending back a card indicating merely that he had received her passionate love letter.

Slowly, Martha begins to recognize the part that her own selfishness has played in their affair, and she wants to warn the plumber she has tried to enlist to aid in her suicide 'about so-called love hardening the heart' (165). And the answer lies in her pity for Michael, the plumber, as Gabriel's pity is inspired by the story of Michael Furey. For the first time Martha really looks at him and notices his 'scaled eyelids' – as Gabriel sees Gretta's face 'that was no longer beautiful ... no longer the face for which Michael Furey had braved death' (2267) – and Martha sees with compassion that if Michael 'abets' her suicide he will then be 'committed to the memory of it' (166). She still lacks Michael's unforced empathy, however. He thinks immediately of Martha's sons, about whom she had rationalized that her 'being alive or dead made little difference in the course of their lives' (164). And though he 'wistfully' describes 'a lovely young girl' who commits suicide when her husband left her, she has to 'muster ... up pity' (166), just as Gabriel realizes that he has never felt 'love like that for any woman but he knew that such a feeling must be love' (2035). Two things prevent Martha's suicide: Michael's empathy, which 'shames' her out of her plans to kill herself; and the fact that she suddenly must care for her sons because one is sick, and her ex-husband 'could not take care of a sick child' (167). This links the ex-husband and the lover; they are equally indicted as lacking the empathy Michael has and that Martha at least envisions. And the two men are further connected when Martha hears their father with his sons 'delivering information with the self-importance of a man delivering dogmas'. Shuddering at the 'poison that lay between us when we'd once professed to love', she transfers the feeling to her lover, only to see that this makes her a 'stranger' to herself (169).

Eventually, Martha begins to think 'less harshly' of her lover and hopes he is experiencing pleasures, though she has to fight to keep hate away, the truth once again represented by light: 'It was like carrying a taper along a corridor where the drafts are fierce and the chances of it staying alight are pretty meager' (170). When he calls again 'out of the blue', he asks patronizingly if her 'nerves were steady enough'; yet he is disappointed to see that she has 'recovered' (170). Recognizing that he cannot share in her new awareness, Martha imagines his alienated human condition in a final epiphany that shows her his 'imprisonment', where he too 'face[s] the self without distraction', and she decides that she 'cannot weigh him down' with the burden of her inappropriate erotic love (171). It is possible that the 'something' Martha clings to at the story's baffling conclusion is just this vision of agape that she still struggles to maintain. She no longer believes that a 'stranger' makes the best lover, and her sense of him as a stranger has completely changed – he is no longer the consummate masculine god/lover she longed to connect with, no longer an object, but a human being like herself. But she remains an object to him; and O'Brien implies that neither her lover nor her ex-husband will reach this crucial awareness of their shared human condition.

The High Road (1988) contains several epiphanies that stress the protagonist Anna's ability to love and notice those around her as fallible, forgivable human beings who share her own fragile dreams and fears: in short, as subjects rather than objects. Yet the violent resistance to these ideas Anna meets – even in the warm, sensual, Mediterranean world of Spain, so different from the cold London and Ireland of her memories – shows a hypocritical world still obsessed with eros, finding its fulfillment in possession.

The novel contains the clearest example of an O'Brien protagonist conquering her need for a lover to be God, and, unusually, one who cleaves to a female lover she does not

objectify. Significantly, it also portrays harsh masculine retaliation for this new freedom. Like many O'Brien characters,
Anna has run away from the intense pain of losing her married
lover. It opens on Easter morning in Spain, emphasizing both
Anna's real need to be resurrected in a new life, and her desire
to be soothed in the old way in a new place and with a new
lover she conflates sex and faith, reverently remembering her
recent lover as maybe 'the last to partake with me at that fount
of sensuality, and vertigo, and earthly love' (12-13). She will
forget him, but this loss will 'kill that part of [her] that for all its
pain is the most sacred' (13), as she still believes that
heterosexual erotic love is the highest joy. But her adventures
lead her away from the obsession with this married and distant
man whom she can never possess, and toward a fascination
with the women who share her Spanish enclave. She finds
solace in thinking of others more than herself, and, significantly, noticing the women as well as the men and reveling in
the feminine, earth-based spirituality she encounters in Spanish
culture. She meets a man to whom she is attracted, but they talk
instead of making love, sitting and watching over one another
'like sages' (33). He tells her that sex is 'overrated', sensing her
lingering belief that it is 'the most important thing in the world',
and she realizes as they 'touch without touching' that 'this
would be enough forever, this moment of pure life, this stream
of abstract love' (34).

As the story progresses, this realization strengthens, and she
remembers as a past phase her young self who believed in each
new lover as a Christ figure, when 'every new love affair
brought [her] ... to the brink of a sustained happiness' (49),
regretting as the worst of her life 'the eternity of years that I had
solemnly waited for him, believed in his coming' (66). Later she
has a 'dreadful little revelation':

> I had run away not because I loved him too much but because I
> feared I had not loved him enough, that I had not loved him in
> the selfless way in which as a child I had loved the saints and
> the martyrs, and that maybe now I did not know how to love at
> all. I was not capable of the sacrifice (148).

The bond Anna shares with Catalina reverses the usual power relations for O'Brien's women. As a young Spanish maid whose age and experience do not match Anna's, who is very much a 'stranger' at some level, Catalina could play the supplicant to Anna's power and privilege. But their friendship gives them 'invisible sustenance' and is deliberately 'not what [they] sought from men, something other-womanly, primordial' (185). From the start they have an attraction based as much on sympathy as sexual desire. Anna senses that Catalina 'pities' her for 'being among such dull folk' as the money- and sex-obsessed tourists (60). Anna also visits her home and sees Catalina, unwashed and living in squalor, under the thumb of her cruel macho father: in short, losing illusions about the lover before their sexual consummation but still desiring her. Yet Catalina, like Anna, suffers from obsession with a classic O'Brien love object: an older, married university professor with 'El Greco eyes and [a] long, beautiful El Greco face' (162) whom she believed would 'save' her from unhappiness, but who has now rejected her. On a revelatory outing together, Anna helps Catalina see that this obsession will only hurt her, and they make love expressed in language that deliberately enacts feminist theories of female *jouissance*. As Helen Thompson describes it, Anna and Catalina's desire is 'characterized by each woman's being both subject and object … the boundaries between self and other blur as each sees her own body and her own desire mirrored in the other' (26):

> I stretched out and cleaved to her, through her opening to life; arms, limbs, torsos joined as if in an androgynous sculpture, the bloods going up and down merrily … back, back in time to that wandering milky watery bliss, infinitely safe … boundaries burst, bursting, the mind as much as the body borne along, to this other landscape that was familiar yet unfamiliar … slipping through a wall of flesh, eclipsed inside the womb of the world (*HR* 186).

As they pour bottles of water over themselves as baptism in this new life and understanding, Anna connects this epiphany with her reaction to a bullfight – a glorification of masculinity as

power – after which she 'bled' for a week imagining Christ's
body as feminine,

> in sympathy ... its gore brought to my mind too vividly Christ's
> bleeding wounds and the women I knew, including myself, as if
> Christ was a woman and woman was Christ in the bloodied
> ventricles of herself. Man in woman and woman in man. The
> impossible (187).

Anna also admits that a fortune teller said she 'hasn't done it
right, she's not doing it right ... what she was telling me was
that I drank and ate and perceived life the wrong way', for
which she once believed 'death would be [the] only redemption'
(188). Now she has turned a corner: as they leave their camp
she no longer sees death as the only escape from this way of
life, and believes that this new understanding, like religious
faith, will be 'a constant ... that one does not see, simply knows
to be there' (188).

But following the women's symbolic baptism into a new life
of equal, empathetic sexual love, Catalina's estranged husband
murders her for the double transgressions of adultery and
homosexuality, both deemed religious sins, but which actually
stress the loss of his wife as his sole possession. In fact, in an
ironically Christian act, Catalina dies *for* Anna, since her
husband actually intends Anna as his victim. Heather Ingman
explains that their brief vision has proved 'impossible' since
'Anna and Catalina have trespassed against the family and
against the Catholic religion, twin imperatives as powerful in
Spain as in Ireland' (259). Nonetheless, in spite of this violent,
pessimistic conclusion, *The High Road* presents a potential
remedy for women's mistaken erotic obsessions, suggesting the
specific embrace of lesbian love as a healthy replacement for
men's cruelty and domination, what Ingman calls 'the most
positive note so far in the context of her challenge' to
'masculinist nationalism' (259). While *The High Road* contains
complexities that this brief discussion cannot plumb, its story
and imagery point to ideal love's embrace not of an 'other' who
will dominate, but a partner who will pity and join with the
beloved.

Thus Edna O'Brien not only rewrites Joyce's epiphanies to stress her own feminist points; she rewrites her characters' experience of the most basic message in Christian doctrine. Of course, it is far-fetched to call O'Brien a deliberately, or conventionally, Christian writer. Still, as she explains in relation to Joyce, whose work is 'permeated' with 'religious motifs', 'leaving the Church is not the same as leaving God' (*James Joyce* 13). She might have been speaking of herself. Her women in particular are capable of internalizing Christ's essential point, best expressed in Matthew 25:31:

> I was hungry and you gave me food, I was thirsty and you gave me something to drink, I was a stranger and you welcomed me, I was naked and you gave me clothing, I was sick and you took care of me … just as you did it to one of the least of these who are members of my family, you did it to me.

This is part of what Sandra Manoogian Pearce explains as a major progression in 'O'Brien's once isolated, lonely women', who find 'self-redemption through reconciliation – either with themselves or through others – emerging as strong, independent women' (63). While O'Brien has explored as fully as any writer the destructive erotic archetypes within Christian and romantic narratives, she also portrays women, and men, who embrace a golden rule that abrogates and transcends gender stereotypes. O'Brien's epiphanies conflate feminism with humanitarianism: only when people embrace and enact the realizations of O'Brien's female protagonists can societies actually promote the moral code they proclaim.

Works Cited

Beja, Morris. *Epiphany in the Modern Novel* (Seattle: University of Washington Press, 1971).

Dunn, Nell. Interview with Edna O'Brien. *Talking to Women* (Bristol: MacGibbon and Kee, 1965).

Greenwood, Amanda. *Edna O'Brien* (Horndon, UK: Northcote House Publishers, 2003).

Grogan, Maureen L. 'Using Memory and Adding Emotion: The (Re)Creation of Experience in the Short Fiction of Edna O'Brien'. *Canadian Journal of Irish Studies* 22.2 (1996): 9-19.

Ingman, Heather. 'Edna O'Brien: Stretching the Nation's Boundaries'. *Irish Studies Review* 10.3 (2002): 253-65.

Joyce, James. 'The Dead' [1914]. *The Norton Anthology of English Literature Volume II*. 7th edition, eds M.H. Abrams and Stephen Greenblatt (New York: Norton, 2000), 2240-68.

--- *Finnegans Wake* [1939] (New York: Penguin, 1967).

--- *A Portrait of the Artist as a Young Man* [1916] (New York: Penguin, 1992).

--- *Stephen Hero* [1944] (New York: New Directions Books, 1963).

--- *Ulysses* [1922] (New York: Vintage Books, 1986).

Noon, William T. *Joyce and Aquinas* (New Haven, CT: Yale University Press, 1957).

Nygren, Anders. *Agape and Eros*. Trans. Philip S. Watson (London: SPCK, 1953).

O'Brien, Edna. *Down by the River* (New York: Plume Books, 1997).

--- *The High Road* (New York: Farrar Straus Giroux, 1988).

--- *James Joyce* (New York: Viking Penguin, 1999).

--- 'The Love Object'. *A Fanatic Heart: Selected Stories of Edna O'Brien* (New York: Plume, 1985), 147-72.

--- *James and Nora: Portrait of Joyce's Marriage* (Northridge, CA: Lord John Press, 1981).

O'Hara, Kiera. 'Love Objects: Love and Obsession in the Novels of Edna O'Brien'. *Studies in Short Fiction* 30 (1993): 317-25.

Pearce, Sandra Manoogian. 'Edna O'Brien's "Lantern Slides" and Joyce's "The Dead": Shadows of a Bygone Era'. *Studies in Short Fiction* 32 (1995): 437-46.

--- 'Redemption through Reconciliation: Edna O'Brien's Isolated Women'. *Canadian Journal of Irish Studies* 22.2 (1996): 63-71.

--- 'Snow Through the Ages: Echoes of "The Dead" in O'Brien, Lavin, and O'Faoláin'. *Joyce through the Ages: A Nonlinear View*, ed. Michael Patrick Gillespie (Gainesville: University Press of Florida, 1999), 165-78.

Pelan, Rebecca. 'Edna O'Brien's "World of Nora Barnacle"'. *Canadian Journal of Irish Studies* 22.2 (1996): 49-61.

Thompson, Helen. 'Uncanny and Undomesticated: Lesbian Desire in Edna O'Brien's "Sister Imelda" and *The High Road*'. *Women's Studies: An Interdisciplinary Journal* 32.1 (2003): 21-44.

Warner, Marina. *Alone of All Her Sex: The Myth and the Cult of the Virgin Mary* (New York: Knopf, 1976).

Yeats, William Butler. *Selected Poems and Three Plays*. 3rd edition, ed. M.L. Rosenthal (New York: Macmillan, 1986).

---

[1] See in particular Pearce, 'Snow through the Ages' and 'Edna O'Brien's "Lantern Slides"'.

[2] I believe that O'Brien also draws on epiphanies in Virginia Woolf's novels, but there is not enough space in this brief essay to develop or support this claim.

6 | Sexuality, Nation, and Land in the Postcolonial Novels of Edna O'Brien and Jamaica Kincaid

Eve Stoddard

> That Antigua no longer exists. That Antigua no longer exists partly for the usual reason, the passing of time, and partly because the bad-minded people who used to rule over it, the English, no longer do so ... And so all this fuss over empire — what went wrong here, what went wrong there — always makes me quite crazy, for I can say to them what went wrong: they should never have left their home, their precious England, a place they loved so much, a place they had to leave but could never forget.
>
> Jamaica Kincaid, *A Small Place*

> Fields that mean more than fields, fields that translate into nuptials into blood; fields lost, regained, and lost again in that fickle and fractured sequence of things; the sons of Oisin, the sons of Conn and Connor, the sons of Abraham, the sons of Seth, the sons of Ruth, the sons of Delilah, the warring sons of warring sons cursed with that same irresistible thrall of madness which is the designate of living man, as though he had to walk back through time and place, back to the voiding emptiness to repossess ground gone for ever.
>
> Edna O'Brien, *Wild Decembers*

Both Edna O'Brien and Jamaica Kincaid are feminist writers who live in a metropolitan nation and write about the oppressive conditions of life, especially for women, in their countries of origin, Ireland and Antigua, respectively, both former British colonies. Juxtaposing their novels brings to light certain shared features of their parallel positionalities, but also the differences of race, geopolitical location, and narrative style and voice in their works. As the more prolific writer, O'Brien is also much more varied in style and form in her novels, especially her later novels, while Kincaid continues to develop and refine her very distinctive voice — at once flat, bitter, angry, and yet inflected with self-undermining irony and contradiction. They share a focus on the experiences of women exploring their sexuality in social contexts where this is deeply painful and problematic. This essay will focus on questions of indigeneity, women's bodies, and the land, and how their representation is shaped by the ruptures of colonialism, and the often equally negative consequences of nationalism, for women in newly independent states. I will use O'Brien's *Wild Decembers* and Kincaid's *Autobiography of My Mother* to suggest that, while both writers draw intensely on their own experiences to craft auto-biographical fiction, both also move beyond the parameters of the *Bildungsroman* in complex ways in order to comment on the politics of postcoloniality.

After two decades of 'postcolonial' analysis and theory, most discussions of the field begin with critiques of its tendency to create a monolithic object of study, to imply that the world is somehow 'post' colonialism, and to exploit the approach for the gain of the critic who remains politically detached from the issues of inequality and oppression that mark the colonial condition (Slemon 101-3). An assumption of my approach is that there are some intersections among the histories and conditions of disparate nations caused by the fact that the British Empire was part of a world system that ruled subjugated peoples militarily, economically, and culturally, transporting its people, its education, and its law around the earth, and then gradually withdrawing over the course of the twentieth century. This imperial history has created some commonalities among widely disparate experiences, for instance in educational and parliamentary structures, but there are also many differences, not least of which are racial and economic inequalities today resulting from that system.

Kincaid herself somewhat playfully poses the question of the relationship between Irish and West Indian experience in her novel *Lucy*, which fictionalizes an account of Kincaid's having been taken out of school and sent to New York City as an *au pair*. In *Lucy*, Kincaid deliberately juxtaposes the Irish and Caribbean experience through a conversation between Lucy and her friend Peggy, who plays a 'bad girl' alter ego for Lucy, like Baba to Kate in O'Brien's *Country Girls* trilogy. When they first meet, Peggy says, 'You're not from Ireland, are you? You talk funny' (62). This exchange draws attention to the crux of the comparison between Irish and Caribbean postcolonial experiences. Lucy appreciates it so deeply because she has moved from a world of black and brown people, where no one would stick out for being black. In the United States she is suddenly marked by her colour on the outside, by her history on the inside. Peggy is simultaneously enacting her family's preference for their own ethnic group and an un-American disregard for the black-white opposition as the primary determinant of status and identity.

The texts of O'Brien and Kincaid make manifest the acute losses resulting not only from colonialism, but also from the regime that follows. In her autobiographical *A Small Place*, Kincaid meditates unforgettably and paradoxically on her perceptions of her nation of origin when she revisits it after independence, and discovers how the political and cultural economies of tourism have recreated plantation relations. The repressiveness and corruption within Caribbean society are seen as direct products of the ways colonialism constructed self-hatred and an alienated and false epistemology (*A Small Place* 34-6). In Ireland, the yoking of nationalism and agrarian reform in the late-nineteenth century supported the Anglo-Irish intelligentsia's cultural nationalist agenda (Hirsch 1125). In the early decades of independence there was an affirmation of the rural way of life and an increasing sense that the real Ireland was the non-modern rural one. As tourism became the primary economic hope of the Republic, it was this romantic, backward, peasant Ireland of the small cottage and the tweed-dressed man on a bicycle that was sold, especially to all those descendants of Irish exiles who lived with the desire to return to the land of origin, to see the place they had heard of in song and story.

Because nationalism implies unity and tends to suppress internal dissent, in newly independent countries minority groups and women may find themselves no better off, perhaps worse off, than they were under colonialism. Focusing on the particular history of India's achievement of independent nationhood, both Partha Chatterjee and R. Radhakrishnan critique the erasure of women's issues after independence. Ireland's history shares with India's the presence of women's activism in the move toward decolonization, followed by the erasure and suppression of women as historical actors after independence. Instead, they become the carriers of what is now held to be 'traditional' culture in their roles as wives and mothers (Ingman 254). In the British West Indies, the figures identified with decolonization and early independence are exclusively male. However, the power and leadership of women has tended to be in the domain of oral praxis, in the semi-secret traditions retained from Africa, such as religion and healing. This knowledge and energy has emerged powerfully in Caribbean literature and society since the 1980s. Thus the narrative of national and nationalist history, especially in the era of independence, is one that cannot accommodate the representation of women as protagonists, until the insurgence of a specifically feminist intervention. That intervention has also been interconnected with forms of mental decolonization that have rejected the superiority of European paradigms of knowledge, with some success.

The relationship of the modern nation and the land to a precolonial past is entirely different in Ireland and the Caribbean, since the Irish people have an imagined continuity on the land. In the Caribbean, the indigenous people were all but extinguished, though fragments of their cultural practices

survive in words, foods, and agriculture. The people who constitute the nation were brought from elsewhere, mostly Africa;
thus the sense of rupture is immense. A number of postcolonial
projects, such as that of the Indian Subaltern group, address the
problem of writing or recovering lost histories from the point
of view of the colonized.[1] Among the African diaspora,
autobiography in a continuum from non-fiction to fiction has
been especially important for representing metonymic individual experiences and subjectivities of those always inscribed
only as objects to be feared, controlled, manipulated, defined,
and studied by the colonial writer. For indigenous peoples,
another approach to recovering absent narratives of history is
expressed in Eduardo Galeano's *Memory of Fire: Genesis* for its
answer to the problem of absent voices:

> And he will teach them to smell history in the wind, to touch it
> in stones polished by the river, and to recognize its taste by
> chewing certain herbs, without hurry, as one chews on sadness
> (qtd in Slemon 109).

The land of Ireland remains marked with the monuments of
many layers of history, from passage tombs to holy wells to
ruined monasteries and big houses to abandoned famine fields.
Hence, in the opening of *House of Splendid Isolation*, O'Brien
writes: 'History is everywhere. It seeps into the soil, the subsoil.
Like rain, or hail, or snow, or blood. A house remembers. An
outhouse remembers. A people ruminate. The tale differs with
the teller' (3). The prologue to *Wild Decembers* describes the bog
thus:

> Fathoms deep the frail and rusted shards, the relics of battles of
> the long ago, and in the basins of limestone, quiet in death, the
> bone babes and the bone mothers, the fathers too. The sires.
> The buttee men and the long-legged men who hacked and
> hacked and into the torn breathing soil planted a first potato
> crop, the diced tubers that would be the breath of life until the
> fungus came (1).

In O'Brien's later novels, the land shifts from facticity to a
synecdoche for the Irish history of battle, conquest, rebellion,
and re-conquest, to a sense of presence in the land's traces, to

its imagined witnessing of past struggles, to seeming almost alive — a breathing, victimized, yet threatening beauty and power, gendered female and often mirroring the central female character of the novel, as in *A Pagan Place, House of Splendid Isolation*, and *Wild Decembers*.

By contrast, while Afro-Caribbeans embrace the archipelago as their native land, they know that their ancestral ties are to Africa and that archeological traces in the land derive from peoples who were nearly obliterated by European conquerors. Thus Kincaid writes about England:

> But what I see is the millions of people, of whom I am just one, made orphans: no motherland, no fatherland, no gods, no mounds of earth for holy ground, no excess of love which might lead to the things that an excess of love sometimes brings, and worst and most painful of all, no tongue. (For isn't it odd that the only language I have in which to speak of this crime is the language of the criminal who committed this crime?) (*A Small Place* 31)

In *Autobiography of My Mother*, Kincaid has created a brilliant and tragic consciousness of foundational loss. Xuela, the first-person narrator, opens the novel by saying, 'My mother died at the moment I was born' (3). Her father turns her over to his laundry woman to be raised. Addressing the facts of loss and poverty, Xuela says that '[i]n a place like this, brutality is the only real inheritance' (6). The novel quickly establishes the role of empire in creating such a world. Xuela accidentally breaks a treasured plate belonging to her foster mother, a plate inscribed with the word 'Heaven', and on the plate is a picture of the English countryside. She identifies herself as

> of the African people, but not exclusively. My mother was a Carib woman, and when they looked at me this is what they saw: The Carib people had been defeated and then exterminated, thrown away like the weeds in a garden; the African people had been defeated but had survived (15-16).

Thus the impossible task of autobiography by a dead person becomes an allegory of the project of subaltern history. The novel is told as an individual story, but each element of it represents metonymically the history of the entire region. On the other hand, the English doctor Philip, whom she will eventually marry, is a gardener, with 'an obsessive interest in rearranging the landscape ... for no other reason than the pleasure of it and making the plants do exactly what he wanted them to do; and it made great sense that he would be drawn to this activity, for it is act of conquest' (143). Kincaid's novel is saved from didacticism by the complex humanity of Xuela, and by the tone which she herself characterizes as 'vulnerable, hard, and helpless' (4). The hardness provides the surface judgments that divide the world relentlessly into victor and vanquished, that hold at bay the contradictory feelings of loss, desire, and need for comfort and mother love, for ancestral connections.

The outer facts of Xuela's life at first appear to be quite clear and blunt, but upon inspection they flicker into a liminal realm of imagination and interpretation. This is especially true of her interactions with substitute mother figures such as the step-mother she accuses of trying to poison her; Madame LaBatte, who bestows Xuela on her husband to bear him a child; and Philip's wife, whom Xuela accuses herself of poisoning. On the broader canvas of the cultural episteme is the folk figure known in the Caribbean as Mama Dlo:

> We saw a woman in the part of the river where the mouth met the sea ... she was dark brown in skin, her hair was black and shiny and twisted in small coils all around her head ... She was surrounded by fruit, mangoes ... She beckoned to us to come to her. Someone said it was not a woman at all, that we should not go, that we should run away (35-6).

One boy swims and swims toward her and he disappears forever. Most importantly, a group of children, including Xuela, witnesses the event, but she reflects that

> they no longer believe what they saw with their own eyes, or their own reality. This is no longer without an explanation to me. Everything about us is held in doubt and we the defeated define all that is unreal, all that is not human, all that is without love, all that is without mercy. Our experience cannot be interpreted by us; we do not know the truth of it (37).

Xuela is able to find a connection to her ancestors through the landscape of Dominica. She is able to resist the colonizer's imposition of European dualism and 'rationality' through investment in her own body and in the body of the environment surrounding her. Thus, Xuela first dreams a partial vision of her mother while sitting in the landscape she embraces, 'the harsh heat that eventually became a part of me, like my blood' (17). As she lies in bed listening to the environment, she says,

> I could hear the sound of those who crawled on their bellies, the ones who carried poisonous lances, and those who carried a deadly poison in their saliva ... And it ended only after my hands had traveled up and down all over my body in a loving caress (43).

Her intense perception of the world outside her bedroom fuses with her sexual connection to her own body. Throughout Kincaid's novels, the self-hatred involved in a mother's preference for boys is a source of anger. Here it becomes part of the larger system of colonized consciousness: 'to people like us, despising anything that was most like ourselves was almost a law of nature' (52). But Xuela fights back by loving herself and loving everything about herself that culture and patriarchy reject — her menstrual flow, the smell of her underarms, and between her legs. This is at once a rebellion against patriarchy, against western philosophy's elevation of mind over body, and against Europe's conquest of New World peoples and environment through both might and, especially, scientific knowledge, rationalization, naming and renaming in an alien language.

At the heart of Xuela's life story is what happens when she becomes pregnant by Monsieur LaBatte, to his wife's joy. She goes to a woman healer for an abortion, and after suffering a 'volcano of pain', she is a new person. Afterwards, she narrates a kind of visionary/ritual walkabout around the perimeter of Dominica, a mythological journey that joins her with the history and geography of the island, concluding

> And that is how I claimed my birthright, East and West, Above and Below, Water and Land: In a dream. I walked through my inheritance, an island of villages and rivers and mountains and

people who began and ended with murder and theft and not
very much love. I claimed it in a dream (89).

Xuela's abortion is an act of self-assertion against the nets cast
around her by gender and racial hierarchies. She escapes the
LaBattes and goes into a kind of dark night of the soul, de-
gendering herself and working as a manual labourer. As is
typical of the narrative, Xuela at once proclaims in mythological
terms her triumphal decision never to be a mother, while also
showing that she is experiencing a sense of severe loss and
emptiness:

> inside me there was a vault made of a substance so heavy I
> could find nothing to compare it to; and inside the vault was an
> ache of such intensity that each night as I lay alone in my house
> all my exhalations were long, low wails, like a lanced boil, with a
> small line of pus trickling out, not like a dam that had burst
> (99).

She regresses into a narcissistic state: 'My own face was a
comfort to me, my own body was a comfort to me' (100).

Autobiography of My Mother and *Wild Decembers* have some
thematic commonalities: both novels centre on a motherless
young female whose sexuality and pregnancy form a crux, not
just for the story but in symbolic relation to the once colonized
land. Both explore the constraints and possibilities of being
gendered female and being a female body within a particular
landscape marked historically by cultural, national, and global
events. As in many feminist texts, questions of voice and
agency are of central importance. Like Xuela, Breege is
motherless. She and her brother, Joseph, are orphans, and
Joseph sees himself as her guardian in ways that extend to a
kind of sexual ownership over her, and, ultimately, to abusing
her physically. The novel suggests that invoking conquest and
colonialism provides a rationale for ongoing masculine battles
for mastery over the land of Ireland, land that is always
feminized, a gendering that passes seamlessly over to actual
women's bodies, and even to the female dog, Violet Hill, whose
sex and topographical name fuse these different levels of abject
femaleness.

At first glance, the style and tone of O'Brien's novel could not be more different from that of Kincaid which appears flat, realistic, concrete, angry. O'Brien's appears lyrical with a kind of Biblical grandeur and excess, mythic rather than realistic. While Xuela is the first person narrator of *Autobiography*, Breege is only partly the narrator of her own story, and she is represented as relatively innocent, sensitive, and helpless, not someone who is prepared to assert herself against the powerful forces around her. It is also noticeable that Breege speaks in plain language, which is less forceful than Xuela's, but which does not participate in the lyricism of the third-person narrator. It is that lyricism, that exalted and timeless sense of the land that is Ireland in myth, which justifies epic struggles that go on generation after generation. O'Brien uses the excess of language to insert the tragic tale of the main characters into a larger legendary, almost timeless historical cycle of feud, war, and colonialism, in which the fields of Ireland, intrinsically gendered as female, are imbricated with repeated cycles of death and loss. Old Testament references are mingled with Celtic and Greek ones. Through Breege's first-person narration the theme of her voicelessness plays itself out, the individual woman versus the almost cosmic force of Irish masculine nationalism, the actual woman versus Cathleen Ní Houlihan, whom a rival in love sarcastically identifies with Breege, just as Joseph identifies her with the Greek goddess Persephone. Breege's struggle is in one sense to emerge from this engulfment by myth and history as an individual voice, her own self rather than the self con-structed by mythologies. Xuela survives her role as a victim by choosing herself, her body, her culture, her vision, though not without cost. Breege suffers a breakdown and spends some time in the asylum, but she is not insane, and she re-emerges with some strength.

Like most of O'Brien's novels, *Wild Decembers* is about being female in Ireland, specifically in relation to the land. Two interconnected traditions weigh heavily on what this means in twentieth-century Ireland: the Catholic worship of the Virgin Mary, and the nationalist identification of conquered Ireland with a woman who inspires and requires redemption. Eileen Morgan points out that

> nationalist representations of Ireland as a victimised woman popularised an ideal of femininity predicated on woman's passivity, including their dependence on male rescuer figures and repression of all but one simplified emotion: grief for Ireland's subjugation (3).

While Kincaid's novels are highly critical both of the African-derived patriarchal preference for boys and for the European-derived repression of female sexuality, she does not have to struggle with an ideal of feminine passivity. Within Afro-Caribbean tradition, women are not typically seen as shrinking violets or as weak and helpless. The legacy of slavery forced women to do demanding physical labour and to be subject to brutal physical punishment, as it also allowed white women to exercise brutality upon enslaved people. *Wild Decembers* does offer alternatives to the Catholic nationalist ideal, but for Breege, her role as a woman is defined in relation to conventional Catholic morality, including the iconography of the Virgin Mary as the ideal feminine prototype. This Catholic ideal also includes the virtues associated with martyrdom — the opposite of aggression or self-assertion. In the opening description of the contested mountain, a notion of blood sacrifice is invoked by the name of the wild dog rose, '*Sangria Jesu*' (3). Self-sacrifice for purity is the highest feminine virtue. One of the features of this gendered logic is that virginity and purity are absolute. Virginity cannot be lightly tampered with; once it is damaged one becomes the opposite of a virgin, a whore. The character Crock, whose physical deformity mirrors his twisted motivation, is both obsessed with Breege, whom he calls Ivory Mary, and bent on disrupting all love relationships with his venom; he is a reverse Cupid. When he hears from the town gossip, the hairdresser Josephine, that Breege has feelings for Bugler, Crock thinks 'Ivory Mary no more. Mary Magdalene now. "I will lay a trap for her"' (79). Breege's brother shares a similar view of her purity. A more modern secular view is articulated by the remnant of colonial presence in the vicinity,

Lady Harkness, who identifies sexuality with nature and with goodness.

When Joseph falls out with Bugler, the quarrel demonstrates his identification of his sister's body with the land. He asks whether Bugler was a gentleman and she answers, 'More of a gentleman than some'. Joseph responds, 'I expect you pointed out to him the boundaries between his lands and ours' (69). This dialogue conflates the boundaries of sexual propriety that Bugler should observe toward Breege with the property boundaries between the two families, identifying Breege as male property to be marked and inscribed and fought over. Breege's response prompts her brother to hit her. Later, when he finds she harbours feelings for Bugler, he calls her '[n]o better than a streetwalker' (86).

Breege and Bugler consummate their attraction on a holy island in a lake, within an ancient, roofless oratory. While the archeological ruins on the island are Christian and not pagan, like many early Christian sites they are built in places that would have had sacred significance to pre-Christian people. Moreover the island contains the cemetery where Breege's ancestors are buried:

> It was Breege now showing him her world as if it were her house, a place she moved about in as easily as in her own yard or her plantation, walking over the graves, calling out the names, old people and not so old, young people, infants, handwritten mildewed messages under broken glass domes where obviously the cattle had broken in and trampled. Last of all, she read him her own family names and then pointed to a strip of ground next to theirs but bordered off with smooth round stones which she had painted white (171).

Breege's relationship to the island cemetery is an organic one, marked by exile and diaspora, but continuous with the past.

Early on, Bugler, the ambitious returned son of an emigrant to Australia, takes Breege on his intrusive alien tractor up the mountain to a ruined cottage his mother used to talk about. It is a magical moment between the two as, emblematically,

> in the river below, a salmon rose up out of the water, bowed
> like a bright sword thrust up into the air, then down in the
> water again and up again, glinting, playful (52).

The salmon inserts a living presence of fecundity, both cultural
and natural, into a landscape of loss where everything is
disfigured and changed. Bugler's mother 'had kept the memory
of it alive for them and had instilled in him the certainty that
one day he must go home' (52). The nation-memory of the
Irish, both at home and in exile, is a blessing and a curse,
inspiring eight hundred years of resistance to conquest. When
Bugler comes back to reclaim what has been remembered, he
encounters a similarly strong but conflicting claim to memory
on the part of his neighbour and hereditary enemy, Joseph
Brennan.

While Breege's femininity is constrained within the
Catholic/ nationalist/masculinist script, other female figures in
the novel have far more freedom and agency in constructing
their gender and sexuality. Part of Bugler's mother's memory of
this place was an encounter with a woman washing her long
black hair who gave her a 'witchlike look. His mother thought
the woman was going to a dance, but it was to the asylum she
was sent' (52). This invokes the counterdiscourses of fairies and
witches which cover and subvert the social control over women
associated with Catholic morality, purity, and sacrifice. Open
sexuality outside the confines of socially sanctioned monogamy
has been enough to put a woman on the wrong side of the
boundary between sane and insane, normal and possessed,
good and evil. The association here — and eventually in
Breege's own story — between dancing and the asylum, is cau-
tionary. The women who do have agency, who are masters over
their own fates and fortunes, and who embrace a lusty sexuality
are Reena and Rita, essentially witch-like in their power, and
feared by many. Reena and Rita entrap Bugler for financial
purposes. He jokingly asks if this is 'the Black Arts'. Reena
seduces and rapes Bugler, as Rita plays the accordion and says,
'Show him who wears the trousers in this hideaway house' (59).
Their behaviour disregards Catholic respectability and they are

successful. Bugler's fiancée Rosemary is a clearly modern woman, with a progressive attitude toward sexuality, who set her sights on Bugler and won him, and has now come all the way from Australia to marry him. Nonetheless it is Breege who wins his heart in the end, suggesting the allure of the wild Irish land that pulled Bugler back from his life in Australia. It is Breege who buries him in her family grave on the holy island where they made love in the moonlight. Thus Ireland is being impinged on by outside influences, but the seductive relationship between the female land and the male farmer has not yet been transformed.

Breege struggles between myth and real life, between inscription by masculine desire/mythology and individual agency. Not only is she associated with Cathleen Ní Houlihan and with the mountain being fought over by Bugler and her brother, she is also associated with Persephone, the Greek fertility goddess who spends half the year underground in Hades with Pluto, who abducted her and holds her captive during the winter. Upon meeting Rosemary, Breege becomes aphasic: 'It was as if a stone or an implement had been put down her throat, cutting her, cutting the words' (204). Breege takes refuge in the nativity scene at the church, 'lying in the straw alongside the donkey, the zebra, the infant Jesus, and the Holy Family' (206). The reaction of the village women is the opposite of compassionate; they by turns accuse her of being possessed, drunk, drugged; they throw cold water on her and laugh at her. Although these women do not know it consciously, Breege has defiled the Christmas scene with her sexually produced pregnancy, her very real body, in contrast to

> those rivers of blue within blue, virgins and martyrs with infants being born not from lower down, but coming out of their chests in clean and undefiled incarnations (203).

Breege is diagnosed with *Hysteria ad absurdam* (213), the diagnosis linking her aphasia to having a womb. As the nurse tells Bugler, sex is the problem of most of the lunatics. But as suddenly as she lost her ability to speak, Breege regains it within the asylum as she sings 'The Castle of Dromore', whose speaker is a mother with a helpless babe appealing to the Virgin Mary to hold off the banshee. Her singing is a miracle in more than one sense because Breege does not know the song herself; Bugler gave her the words printed out, but that would not enable her to sing it. The saving capacity of voice is inscribed in an Irish myth of the evil stepmother Aoife and the children of Lir, read by the immigrant child Aziz aloud to Breege. When Aoife changes Fionnula and her sisters into four swans, Fionnula says,

> though Aoife, our stepmother, could rob us of our human form she could not take our voices away. We learned many things but most of all we learned to sing and soon our music and songs became known the length and breadth of Bamba (95).

Whatever Aoife may represent in the context of *Wild Decembers*, a coalition of patriarchy and Catholic puritanism has conspired to silence Breege and contain her within the asylum. The song is linked with Bugler, who represents both unmediated love and passion on the one hand, and a powerful representation of patriarchy on the other. Nonetheless, in the song it is the woman alone who asks Mary to save her infant from death, and this plea for the life of her unborn child may be the stimulus that restores Breege's voice.

Wild Decembers shifts point of view from third-person limited to third-person omniscient to third-person dramatic or objective, mostly consonant with the epic or mythic tone of the narrative. However, there are four chapters where Breege speaks in the first person and these are significant, given her aphasic response to losing Bugler and being pregnant. They are also significant in a world where her brother speaks for her and seeks to control her and her sexuality. She introduces the story, alternating between household fact and the mythology, within which she becomes inscribed, in this case the story of Helen of Troy. We get a sense of who Breege is when she proclaims, 'I love my deep-red dahlias and I love our Lord' (8). She ends that early chapter feeling light-hearted and giddy, as if she were waltzing, but, like the woman seen by Bugler's mother, Breege will end not dancing but in the asylum. The third chapter she narrates is much later, after she has slept with Bugler and just before she falls into speechlessness. She exhibits some agency in going to see him, after consulting the herbal healer. It goes badly:

> You learn lessons in a flash. Along with resenting my being there, he feared me as if I carried a plague. To have said anything, a soft word or a begging word, would have been useless (193).

She realizes that he loves her in his rebuff, but the key is her belief that words cannot help her. Finally, in the mental asylum, though she cannot speak, her thoughts provide the narration:

> I asked Bugler to see me just once. I begged. I hate that I begged. My brother said it was a sickness. McCann and himself said that it was a child's crush inside a twenty-two-year-old woman, a daftness. Maybe it was, maybe it is, but how can you stop liking someone, even loving someone, how. I would have got into the tabernacle that day if I could have fitted. It was a loneliness to get closer to Jesus or the Holy Ghost. Or else to disappear, to vanish … I will know him again (210).

In this final chapter of first-person narrative, Breege shows her sanity, capable of a basically balanced but pained analysis of her situation, and her subjection to the power of her brother and the doctor. By contrast her brother descends into genuine madness, still battling colonial bureaucracy and nineteenth-century British legislation, and ends up in prison for murdering Bugler.

Unmarried pregnant girls in Ireland have, in the past, been subjected to harsh punishment and confinement, what could be termed human rights abuses. But in this novel, the pregnancy seems more an instance of the larger identification between femininity and the land of Ireland, something to be controlled, mapped, legislated, and fought over by men. Thus, while the text does highlight Joseph's and Crock's shifting of Breege from the Ivory Mary to the Mary Magdalene side of the virgin/whore dichotomy, ultimately, her unwed pregnancy is a bruise and not a death-blow. While Bugler's return from Australia to reclaim his piece of Ireland follows in the mythography of *The Quiet Man* and earlier images of Ireland, Aziz and his mother suggest the new reality of Ireland as a host for

immigration, a country about to lose its homogeneity and
become cosmopolitan. It is in that Ireland that Breege's unwed
pregnancy is no longer deemed a serious offence against
society, no more than a passing item of gossip for the hairdresser and Lady Harkness.

Wild Decembers ends with a double rainbow over the coffin of
Bugler. The modern Australian woman Rosemary asserts her
place at the funeral and in Cloontha. The rainbow suggests
God's promise in Genesis not to wreak further destruction on
his people, but the lawyer O'Dea, 'fearing there might be an
outburst,' intervenes between the two women. The novel ends
very much with a question: will it be the old wars and the
insatiate fight, or will life and love triumph in the new Ireland
of tractors and immigrants?

Whereas Breege is carrying Bugler's child at the end of her
story, Xuela refuses ever to bear children:

> I refused to belong to a race, I refused to accept a nation …
> The crime of these identities, which I now know more than
> ever, I do not have the courage to bear (Kincaid, *Autobiography*
> 225-6).

Thus Xuela, and presumably Kincaid herself, refuses the
nationalist answer to the tragedy of conquest, slavery, and
colonialism. She is left with the existential choice to embrace
herself. The etymological root of 'nationhood' — to be born —
is negated by Xuela's body, despite her affirmation of her body
and her sexuality. In so doing, she repeats the resistance of
many enslaved Africans who refused to bear children in slavery,
suggesting that from her part of the world, history has not yet
afforded a better place for women to produce children in.
Unlike Ireland, Dominica and other small West Indian islands
are not on the brink of a new economic life. They are consigned to the margins of the global economy, consigned to be
places global actors go to for vacations, as Kincaid notes in *A
Small Place*.

Works Cited

Ashcroft, Bill, et al. *Post-Colonial Studies: The Key Concepts* (London: Routledge, 1998).

Chatterjee, Partha. 'The Nationalist Resolution of the Woman's Question'. *Postcolonial Discourses: An Anthology*, ed. Gregory Castle. (London: Blackwell, 2001), 151-66.

Hirsch, Edward. 'The Imaginary Irish Peasant,' *PMLA* 106.5 (Oct. 1991): 1116-33.

Ingman, Heather. 'Edna O'Brien: Stretching the Nation's Boundaries.' *Irish Studies Review* 10.3 (2002): 253-65.

Kincaid, Jamaica. *Autobiography of My Mother* (London: Plume, 1996).

--- *Lucy* (London: Plume, 1990).

--- *A Small Place* (London: Plume, 1988).

Morgan, Eileen. 'Mapping out a Landscape of Female Suffering: Edna O'Brien's Demythologizing Novels,' *Women's Studies: An Interdisciplinary Journal* 29.4 (August 2000): 449-77.

O'Brien, Edna. *House of Splendid Isolation* (London: Plume, 1994).

--- *Wild Decembers* (London: Weidenfield & Nicholson, 1999).

Radhakrishnan, R. 'Nationalism, Gender, and the Narrative of Identity'. *Postcolonial Discourses: An Anthology*, ed. Gregory Castle (London: Blackwell, 2001), 190-208.

Slemon, Stephen. 'Post-Colonial Critical Theories'. *Postcolonial Discourses: An Anthology*, ed. Gregory Castle (London: Blackwell, 2001), 99-116.

---

[1] A group of historians in South Asia led by Ranajit Guha produced a journal called *Subaltern Studies* to 'redress the imbalance created in academic work by a tendency to focus on elites and elite culture in South Asian historiography'; See Ashcroft, p.216.

7 | Outside History: Relocation and Dislocation in Edna O'Brien's *House of Splendid Isolation*

Michael Harris

Edna O'Brien's is not a name that one often hears in discussions of postmodernism. Nevertheless, her novel *House of Splendid Isolation*, which some reviewers have described as a new departure for O'Brien, contains postmodernist elements.[1] For instance, the novel is suggestive of pastiche in its almost random juxtaposition of diary entries, snippets of poems, a children's fable, Irish mythology, a 1921 IRA volunteer's journal, and personal notes (included without any introduction) interspersed throughout its short, staccato sections of narrative.[2] These italicized insertions make it difficult to fit the story within the framework of a known history, a de-familiarizing strategy often employed in postmodernist fiction. The narrative itself proceeds achronologically through fragmented bits and pieces that the reader must fit together. This fragmented style, reminiscent of the crosscutting techniques in contemporary cinema and television, makes *House of Splendid Isolation* at times confusing. The novel opens with a short section entitled 'The Child', in which an initially un-identifiable voice speaks from a position outside of time, retrospectively prophetic, as if from the grave. The following

section entitled 'The Present' begins by describing the Northern
Irish IRA gunman McGreevy, hiding under a tree as he is
pursued by a police helicopter. Then Garda Rory Purcell is
presented in a domestic scene with his wife, son, and daughter.
The Purcells are watching a newscast about an 'escaped
terrorist' who turns out to be McGreevy. Subsequent sections
follow McGreevy as he makes his way south to the Irish
Republic. This lands him in the vicinity of the isolated home of
Josie O'Meara, an elderly woman who has returned home to die
after contracting pneumonia. In the following 170 pages Purcell
is mentioned again only once, before reappearing in the novel's
final pages with fellow Gardaí in pursuit of McGreevy.

House of Splendid Isolation obviously concerns more than an
extended chase scene in which the 'good guys' bring a terrorist
to justice. In those intervening 170 pages, O'Brien turns that
cliché on its head, rendering what Christine St Peter has called
'the most sympathetic treatment of an IRA character in [Irish]
women's fiction' (185). The real interest of the story, however,
becomes the exploration of two lonely, isolated people –
McGreevy and Josie O'Meara – by tracing where they have
been. What the reader discovers is that they are products of a
fragmented island, and that they are fated, if not cursed, to act
out the parts assigned to them by place. Thus another of the
novel's postmodernist elements is its emphasis on the spatial
rather than the temporal. Fredric Jameson, for instance, has
asserted that we now

> inhabit the synchronic rather than the diachronic ... [and] our
> daily life, our psychic experience, our cultural languages, are
> today dominated by categories of space rather than by
> categories of time, as in the preceding period of high
> modernism proper (16).

Time – for instance, the difference in the two main subjects'
ages – is less important here than the setting and the subjects'
point of origin. Although O'Brien uses the past to help explain
McGreevy's and O'Meara's present, she consistently critiques
history as a crude and static straitjacket imposed on the complex dynamism of life. Although Jameson criticizes

postmodernism for ignoring history, O'Brien in *House of Splendid Isolation* tries to open up the present to new possibility – perhaps even a peaceful resolution to conflict – by calling into question conventional modes of understanding human history and life.

Heather Ingman writes that '[i]f there is a lesson in *House of Splendid Isolation*, it is that history should be laid to rest' (261). The people in this novel seem inhibited and haunted by the ghosts of history. Thus Josie's late husband James hears ghostly chains on the stairs in their house at night. The narrator calls these 'the chains of history, the restless dead and the restless living, with scores to settle' (78). The narrator also refers to history as a 'yoke' (70), a constraint that forces one to act in socially accepted, but personally self-destructive patterns. James, for instance, is killed as a result of allowing the IRA to hide a cache of arms on his property – something he feels obliged to do – even though Josie opposes it. It is as if James and the hired man Paud feel obligated to perform roles in a patriotic play not of their own choosing. Josie believes '[h]istory [is] holding them ransom, when it should all be put to rest in the annals' (57). Even though no one is able to completely and permanently step outside the confines of history, we might distinguish Josie and McGreevy for their awareness of their subjugation to 'the dark threads of history looping back and forth and catching her and people like her in their grip, like snares' (58).

O'Brien's conception of history resembles the meta-narratives of modernism, which Jean-François Lyotard attacks in *The Postmodern Condition*. According to Lyotard, postmodernism was borne out of 'the crisis of narratives' and is characterized by an 'incredulity toward metanarratives', such as history, which simplify and distort the incommensurable 'little narratives' of local cultures to fit universal categories, thereby serving the legitimacy of those in power. This process of legitimation, Lyotard contends, 'necessarily entails a certain level of terror, whether soft or hard' (*Postmodern Condition* xiii-xiv). According to Lyotard, in the face of events like the Second

World War genocide at Auschwitz, 'the real question is whether
or not there is a human history' ('Universal History' 321). This
view of the master narrative of history as a script to which
everyone must adhere, moreover, is related to the postmodern
shift from the diachronic to the synchronic, identified by
Jameson. Homi Bhabha, who welds postmodernist theory to
postcolonial concerns, challenges assumptions of universal
history by moving away from narrative chronology toward a
spatial analysis of literature and/or culture. For example,
Bhabha speaks of

> the return of the postcolonial migrant to alienate the holism of
> history. The postcolonial space is now 'supplementary' to the
> metropolitan centre; it … redraws its frontiers in the menacing,
> agonistic boundary of cultural difference that never quite adds
> up, always less than one nation and double ('Dissemination'
> 168).

To a considerable extent, Bhabha's perspective dovetails with
the awareness O'Brien brings to her novel. He could easily be
talking in that passage about the threat McGreevy's presence
poses for the Gardaí in *House of Splendid Isolation*.

Written in O'Brien's sixties, after an unusually long silence,
House of Splendid Isolation marks a transition for the prolific
writer. Unlike her previous work, which has been perceived as
being preoccupied with the individual Irish female subject
pursuing personal liberation both at home and abroad, *House of
Splendid Isolation* opens O'Brien's trilogy on contemporary
Ireland which more explicitly examines the national culture that
shapes the individual subject. According to Laura Engel, with
House of Splendid Isolation O'Brien would 'become less focused
on retelling versions of her own history and more concerned
with the way that many stories connect to shape versions of a
collective history' (341). O'Brien's shift in focus from the
individual subject to the national culture is also evident in the
narrative's unrelenting critique of history. This critique, which
runs throughout the other volumes of the trilogy, *Down by the
River* and *Wild Decembers*, is most pronounced in *House of Splendid
Isolation*.

O'Brien's critique of history also connects her novel with other more recognizably postmodernist fictional texts, such as J.M. Coetzee's *Waiting for the Barbarians*, Arundhati Roy's *The God of Small Things*, and Thomas Pynchon's *Mason & Dixon*, which examine the negative consequences of a monolithic conception of history in a similar way. O'Brien's text, in keeping with those by Coetzee, Roy, and Pynchon, aligns history with a master narrative that imposes a hierarchy on a diverse world and arbitrarily consigns all 'Others' to the periphery.[3] Interestingly, Coetzee, Roy, and Pynchon, like O'Brien, work at the intersection of the postmodern and postcolonial, for the master narrative in each case is linked to the phenomenon of colonialism and its aftermath as it continues to play out in South Africa, India, America, and, in O'Brien's case, Ireland.[4]

O'Brien's concern with history is shared with her near-contemporary, Irish poet Eavan Boland, for whom history represents 'a site of forgetting' (McCallum 39). In her poem sequence 'Outside History' – one of the sources of the rubric of this essay – Boland deliberately breaks up the linear sequence into fragments, creating a postmodernist pastiche effect, much like O'Brien does with the chronology of *House of Splendid Isolation*. One poem in the sequence, 'The Achill Woman', describes a chance encounter with an old woman, caretaker of a cottage where Boland was visiting while at college ('Outside History' 35-6). Boland also devotes an essay of the same title to this encounter in her book *Object Lessons*. In Boland's backward gaze, the Achill woman becomes an emblem as well as a messenger for all those forgotten by history, for the old caretaker was the first person to speak to the young poet about the famine, which Boland would later make the subject of one of her best known poems, 'That The Science of Cartography is Limited'. Boland's famous distinction between history and the past is useful to our purposes here. When she defines *history* as the 'official version' of events, which is also a 'narrative of concealed power' ('Daughters' 14),[5] the *past* stands for the 'inert, unchangeable, sometimes brutal reality of what happened' which 'in its silence and inconvenient completeness … must remain in the suffering, powerless place it surely was and is' ('Daughters' 13). The Achill woman, with her personal memories of the dislocation and suffering caused by the famine and with her connection to a specific, affected place, to some extent disrupts and calls official history into question. Only in retrospect, however, did Boland come to understand this woman. At the time, the poet turned her back on this figure, returning to her book of English court poets – 'the songs and artifices of the very power systems which made her own memory an archive of loss' (*Object Lessons* 130). The Achill woman appears trapped by history, in that her memory is covered over and erased by the master narrative; understood in this way, Boland's epiphany might serve as a paradigm for O'Brien's focus on the blighted lives and chance meeting between Josie O'Meara and McGreevy, who are similarly trapped by history.

To trace O'Brien's emphasis on the spatial and her critique of history, I would like to focus on three different episodes in which place becomes important in understanding the dynamics of her novel. McGreevy's flight from Northern Ireland to the Irish Republic obviously involves a significant relocation, and McGreevy displays an ironic awareness of that change of locale: 'Oh, the sunny South, where people had time for love and strawberries, forgot their brothers and sisters across the border, let them rot' (68). During his flight south through the countryside he seeks temporary shelter in a barn. This episode occurs early in the novel and is instrumental in setting up our understanding of the IRA gunman as outsider. Once inside the barn, McGreevy discovers he is not alone: there's a cow in calf and he feels obliged to assist in the difficult birth, undercutting the conventional view of the IRA gunman as the harbinger of death. McGreevy ministers to the animal to help bring about life. In this early episode and others later, O'Brien likens McGreevy to Christ:

> The manure bags don't soak up the wet, but at least they are cover. Three plastic bags and a manger of straw. Like Jesus.

> Not that he's praying. Others pray for him, but he does not
> pray; he's seen too much and done too much and had too much
> done to him to kneel down and call on a God (13).

This internal view of McGreevy contrasts with the external
perspective, just pages earlier, of the policeman Rory Purcell
who appears swearing at the female TV commentator and
imploring her to tell him how the British Army, the RUC, and
the Gardaí could allow a known pimpernel to 'go into a field
and vanish' (*HSI* 12). Interestingly, this manger scene becomes
more complicated when the farm's owner appears. Although he
seems to recognize McGreevy, the farmer nevertheless offers
him a meal; when his wife initially refuses to cook it, he
threatens her. In the background of this short early scene,
O'Brien thus demonstrates the widespread repercussions of the
conflict in Northern Ireland, extending even into husband-wife
relations in isolated, rural areas of the Republic.

Like Christ, McGreevy has been betrayed, though he is
unsure who the Judas figure might be. Unlike Christ, however,
McGreevy intends to get even with his betrayer:

> A car tailing them from the time they left the house. Someone
> grassed. Who. He'd know one day and then have it out. Friends
> turning traitor. Why. Why. Money or getting the wind up.
> Deserved to die they did, to die and be dumped like animals,
> those that informed, those that betrayed. Bastards (7).

Despite his outsider status and his occasional ability to perceive
the snares of history he is caught in, McGreevy is also largely a
product of his environment and thus subject to the cycle of
reprisal that characterizes the paramilitary organizations in
Northern Ireland. The Irish stamp on McGreevy is signified by
his tricolour tattoo and by his name: *Mc* meaning 'son of' and
Greevy, a homonym of 'grieve' or 'grief'. Thus McGreevy is the
son of grief emanating from the land and its violent history.[6]

The second episode I want to examine involves another key
place in the story: the big house that Josie O'Meara occupies. In
this section, entitled 'Captivity', because McGreevy comes to
hold Josie captive in her own home, the novel temporarily takes
on the characteristics of the Irish Big House novel, but with a

twist, since typically such works have come from Protestant writers charting the decline of the Ascendancy. McGreevy comes to this particular house because its isolation suits his purposes splendidly. Just as the house is isolated, so is its lone inhabitant. Josie is a widow who looks down upon most of her neighbours, just as she did her late husband. The first time we meet her, she is being visited by a Nurse Morrissey, who provides a view of Josie probably shared by many in the community:

> To think that once this woman wouldn't wipe the floor with her or her kind, this woman with her style and her finery, flashing eyes that matched the deep blue glass of her rosary beads which she dangled in chapel, eyes that brought shame on herself, her departed husband, and another, no longer so; eyes now as insipid and watery as boiled tapioca (25).

After her bout of pneumonia, Josie has come home to die, and is presented as an 'elderly woman in a fourposter bed, clutching the strings of her bedjacket' when McGreevy first encounters her (65-6). O'Brien then provides a flashback into Josie's past, a silent story of loss parallel to the Achill woman's in its erasure by the official narrative, in this case, of family and nation. After her marriage Josie feels fortunate to join 'the best family in the county' (40), and to move into 'the house of the low-lying lake. Any girl would have given her eye teeth to marry into it' (29). She suffers disillusionment, however, when she realizes that her husband regards her as he does the horses he loses his fortune on: 'Her haunches were what he liked best, wide and yet with a daintiness to them. A good mare' (32). Indeed, James's chief interest in Josie is for breeding purposes, and in retaliation for his ill treatment of her, she aborts their child. Josie deals with her loneliness by attempting love affairs, first with her doctor and then the local priest. These botched affairs poison her marriage and bring resentment and rejection from the community.

Despite her abortion and public opprobrium, Josie attains the upper hand in the marriage. As James retreats into alcoholism, Josie gains more control, finally getting him to sign

over the house to her. When McGreevy breaks in, Josie is most
affronted by his invasion of her property: 'Her house seems so
precious to her, even its decay. Her house should not have to
suffer this' (78). McGreevy perceives her proprietary airs, and
mocks her with a phrase in Irish '*O! Bhean an Tighe*', which Josie
translates: 'O! woman of the house!' (81-2). The house thus
becomes contested space, so much so that Josie feels it is 'her
house, and yet not hers' (81). The odd relationship between
McGreevy and Josie which unfolds over the following five-day
period ironically resembles the complex pattern of attraction
and repulsion that Bhabha and Robert Young have identified as
characteristic of the colonizer-colonized relationship.[7] Bhabha
has used Freudian theory to distinguish two levels of colonial
rule: a *manifest*, official, conscious level, and a *latent*, sub-
conscious level of fantasy and desire. Thus the colonizer's
unconscious desire for the colonized Other is expressed
through a pattern of sexual attraction and repulsion. Josie, with
her 'ascendancy' into the Big House and her air of superiority
over her neighbours, conforms to the former colonizer's role,
whereas McGreevy, who considers himself at war to 'get the
British out of Ireland', and who fights for 'Justice for all. Peace.
Personal identity. Racial identity' (83), plays the part of the
colonized. Assuming these dualistic colonizer/colonized roles
endemic to Irish history leads the two to view each other with
hostility and suspicion, and yet with underlying interest.
McGreevy acknowledges to Josie that his role in the IRA resistance against the British was less a matter of choice than
assignment: 'To be an ordinary bloke with wife and kids – I just
can't imagine it' (121). Josie's latent sexual attraction to
McGreevy surfaces later when she cuts her hair in an effort to
regain her youth and fantasizes having 'wains' by him (210).
Initially, however, she simply wants McGreevy out of her
house, although he feels 'that surely it was big enough for two'
(81). They strike up an uneasy co-existence with occasional
erotic overtones, neither trusting the other, but, as their time
together passes, they mutually benefit from their co-occupancy
of the house.

Their occupation of odd parts of the house – McGreevy sets up temporary quarters downstairs near the kitchen, sleeping on a pile of newspapers, whereas she stays in her upstairs bedroom, pulling a chest of drawers across the doorframe – signifies the sudden, strange turn both their lives have taken, as they seem to step outside history. Their life together in this house is not part of any known script; as they learn to co-exist and to share this spacious house, they come to shed the past and to see and accept each other for what they are, and more importantly, what they could be. From the pathetic figure in the fourposter, Josie is transformed into a forceful woman with vivid memories of her youth. In her scattered journal entries, Josie writes,

> in spite of it all there used to be inside me this river, an expectation for something marvelous. When did I lose it? When did it go? I want before I die to be myself again (85).

The language used here recalls O'Brien's desire in *Mother Ireland* to shed her recent past in order to trace a 'childhood route' that might 'restore one to one's original place and state of consciousness, to the miraculous innocence of the moment just before birth' (129). The miraculous moment in this novel, like the simple timeless acts in Virginia Woolf, one of O'Brien's modernist progenitors, occurs when Josie gives McGreevy a gift – her late husband's tackle box, used for fishing.[8] This gift serves to domesticate McGreevy and grants him temporary status as man of the house, for they suddenly become 'two people united by the sentiment contained in a tackle box ... two people bound for a moment in that caesura of winter light, warmed by each other's company, each other's breath' (99). Although we learn less about McGreevy's past than we do Josie's, we do know he has killed people and intends to kill more, and as a result of his IRA involvement has lost a wife and daughter. His past has been as unfulfilled as hers, having left 'something wiped out in his nature, his human nature' (121), but he, too, is altered by this short interval with the elderly woman. Stepping outside history and into this strange house leads him to question how much of his life is his own:

> If he quit and ran now, what would he do, what was there –
> nothing else, nothing else. His life was graphed by others and
> his deeds punished or rewarded by others (177).

Let us now turn to a third episode – in this case, the novel's ending – that again draws much of its meaning from *where* it takes place. Christina Mahony has called *House of Splendid Isolation* a 'highly imagistic novel' and has shown how, for instance, the policeman Rory Purcell's deer-hunting pastime becomes indelibly linked to his character (214). For Purcell, hunting McGreevy affords the same sporting thrill as hunting deer. By contrast, McGreevy is associated with trees. The first time we meet him, he is 'curled up in the hollow of a tree' (7), and in the end he attempts to escape out of the house by climbing down a tree. O'Brien compares McGreevy to 'Mad Sweeney in the poem' (222), but undercuts the Irish legend by having McGreevy slip on the wet bough and fall to his capture. Again, as in the first passage we examined, this scene is replete with references to Christ and the crucifixion, turning the tree into a symbolic cross and giving McGreevy the 'blind impervious aura of the martyr' (227).

House of Splendid Isolation, like much postmodern fiction, tends toward the allegorical. The re-entry of Rory Purcell and his fellow Gardaí into the narrative equals the reinstatement of the stereotypic media image of McGreevy as a 'terrorist', a 'murderer', a 'criminal', the 'maniac', the 'Beast', the 'animal', a 'savage', a 'psychopath', a 'sicko that held the country hostage' (12, 17, 66, 74, 76, 77, 113, 225). A would-be idyll transforms into farce, as history returns with a vengeance. McGreevy's occupation of the Big House, which proves an odd but fitting home for him, is short-lived; his dislocation coincides with the return of history, the re-assertion of the master narrative with its pre-assigned roles for him and his pursuers. In fact, in this final episode, everything goes wrong, and with disastrous consequences, culminating in the house's destruction.[9] History's need to name and define must be appeased. Two Gardaí with binoculars spy on Josie and McGreevy through a window and misinterpret their chasing bees from the house as an 'orgy';

Josie is then mistaken for a 'second gunman' and shot and killed (221); the two young Guards responsible for killing Josie and Brennan, McGreevy's accomplice, are consequently wracked with fear and guilt since both have taken life for the first time. One of the young Guards

> could only guess at the trouble and disjunction which lay ahead, a blighted family life, cold sweats in the night, and the phone calls: 'We know who you are and we'll get you.' And maybe they would (193).

In this final scene, O'Brien portrays the blighted aftermath of history, exacting its due from its assigned actors.

Postmodern works are known for their open endings, gaps, unanswered questions. One lingering question in *House of Splendid Isolation* is why McGreevy returns to the house a second time. After his initial five-day stay, he leaves to join his two compatriots in carrying out the assassination of a retired English judge, visiting the area on holiday. Before this planned execution, however, McGreevy strangely decides to return to the big house, where he is caught by the Guards. O'Brien leaves the question of his motivation open, as McGreevy himself doesn't have the answer, but one might surmise that he misses what the house afforded him. One of the last things he tells Josie is 'Don't think I wouldn't like things like this. Warmth and food and company. I like it here now' (206). The novel closes with the prophetic voice of 'The Child', which we can now identify as Josie's unborn baby. O'Brien has been asked if *House of Splendid Isolation*, written just after the ceasefire in 1994, was a prophetic call for peace in Northern Ireland. She responded: 'Well, there's a possibility of anything. Because we're human, we have to have hope … And that's where it stands now. I mean a year from now, who knows' (qtd in Pearce 6). Stepping outside of history is shown in this novel to be very difficult, reminding us perhaps of Stephen Dedalus's famous for-mulation: 'History is a nightmare from which I'm trying to awake'. Nevertheless, O'Brien allows the possibility of choice. Looked at in a certain way, that is what McGreevy is doing: choosing to walk away from the violence and to rejoin Josie in the house that's big enough for them both. Josie's act of cutting her hair in 'a great lunatic fork of longing' (210) also reflects a conscious choice: to sever her connection with former selves, 'those gnarled and mawkish people she had always tried to run away from' (209), and to relocate that 'childhood route' that might 'restore one to one's original place and state of consciousness'. Even though the house, which may represent the dream of a united Ireland, has been 'battered and pitted' by history (226), there is surely a sign of hope in their attempts to find their way back to those places.

Perhaps O'Brien's own relocation and dislocation outside of Ireland helped her to empathize with all sides involved in the complex Troubles. Such an unaligned position brings an awareness, as the child expresses it on the novel's final page, that 'the same blood and the same tears drop from the enemy as from the self', defined as 'the future knowledge … the knowledge that is to be' (232). This 'knowledge', appropriately held by a Blakean 'Child', that that which holds us together is greater than that which pulls us apart, is connected to that 'miraculous innocence' O'Brien refers to in *Mother Ireland*. The child becomes a personification of contemporary Ireland here, a poetic voice of the aftermath searching for meaning, as it offers a glimmer of hope. The alternative – to resign oneself to one's pre-scripted role in history – is tantamount to, as Pynchon puts it in *Mason & Dixon*, moving 'back into the Net-Work of Points already known … changing all from subjunctive to declarative, reducing Possibilities to Simplicities that serve the ends of Governments' (345). In *House of Splendid Isolation*, O'Brien thus not only diagnoses a seemingly insoluble political problem in contemporary Ireland, but through the chance interaction of Josie and McGreevy also illustrates how a possible solution could come about.

Works Cited

Auge, Andrew. 'Fracture and Wound: Eavan Boland's Poetry of Nationality'. *New Hibernia Review* 8.2 (Summer 2004): 121-41.

Bhabha, Homi. 'DissemiNation: Time, Narrative, and the Margins of the
    Modern Nation'. *The Location of Culture* (New York: Routledge,
    1994), 139-70.
--- 'The Other Question: Stereotype, Discrimination, and the Discourse
    of Colonialism'. *The Location of Culture* (New York: Routledge, 1994),
    68-84.
Boland, Eavan. 'Daughters of the Colony: A Personal Interpretation of
    the Place of Gender Issues in the Postcolonial Interpretation of Irish
    Literature.' *Éire-Ireland* 32.2-3 (Summer-Fall, 1997): 14.
--- *Object Lessons: The Life of the Woman and the Poet in Our Time* (New York:
    W.W. Norton, 1995).
--- 'Outside History: A Sequence'. *Outside History: Selected Poems 1980-1990*
    (New York: W.W. Norton, 1991).
Coetzee, J.M. *Waiting for the Barbarians* (New York: Penguin, 1982).
Docherty, Thomas. *Postmodernism: A Reader* (New York: Columbia
    University Press, 1993).
Engle, Laura. 'Edna O'Brien'. *British Writers, Supplement V*, eds George
    Stade and Sarah Hannah Goldstein (New York: Charles Scribner's
    Sons, 1999).
Grodin, Michael and Martin Kreiswirth, eds. *The Johns Hopkins Guide to
    Literary Theory and Criticism* (Baltimore: Johns Hopkins University
    Press, 1994).
Hanks, Patrick and Flavia Hodges. *A Dictionary of Surnames* (Oxford:
    Oxford University Press, 1988).
Harris, Michael. 'Pynchon's Postcoloniality'. *Thomas Pynchon: Reading from
    the Margins*, ed. Niran Abbas (Cranbury, NJ: Associated University
    Press, 2003), 199-214.
L'Heureux, John. 'The Terrorist and the Lady'. *New York Times Book
    Review* 26 June 1994: 7.
Ingman, Heather. 'Edna O'Brien: Stretching the Nation's Boundaries'.
    Irish Studies Review 10.3 (2002): 253-65.
Jameson, Fredric. *Postmodernism, or the Cultural Logic of Late Capitalism*
    (Durham, NC: Duke University Press, 1991).
Lyotard, Jean-François. *The Postmodern Condition: A Report on Knowledge*.
    Trans. Geoff Bennington and Brian Massumi (Minneapolis:
    University of Minnesota Press, 1984).
--- 'Universal History and Cultural Differences'. *The Lyotard Reader*, ed.
    Andrew Benjamin. Trans. David Macey (Cambridge, MA: Blackwell,
    1989), 314-23.
Mahony, Christina Hunt. *Contemporary Irish Literature: Transforming
    Tradition* (New York: St. Martin's Press, 1998).
McCallum, Shara. 'Eavan Boland's Gift: Sex, History, and Myth. *Antioch
    Review* 62.1 (Winter 2004): 37-47.

O'Brien, Edna. *House of Splendid Isolation* (New York: Plume, 1995).
--- *Mother Ireland* (New York: Plume, 1999).
Pearce, Sandra Manoogian. 'An Interview with Edna O'Brien'. *Canadian Journal of Irish Studies* 22. 2 (December, 1996): 5-8.
Pynchon, Thomas. *Mason & Dixon* (New York: Henry Holt, 1997).
Roy, Arundhati. *The God of Small Things* (New York: Harper Collins, 1998).
St Peter, Christine. *Changing Ireland: Strategies in Contemporary Women's Fiction* (London: Palgrave, 2000).
Woolf, Virginia. *To the Lighthouse* (New York: Harcourt, Brace and Company, 1927).
Young, J.C. Robert. *Colonial Desire: Hybridity in Theory, Culture, and Race* (New York: Routledge, 1995).

---

[1] Mahony calls *House of Splendid Isolation* 'a departure for O'Brien stylistically as well as thematically', p.214. L'Heureux states that the novel 'marks a dramatic departure for Edna O'Brien in both subject matter and in style', p.7.

[2] See 'Postmodernism' in *The Johns Hopkins Guide to Literary Theory and Criticism*: 'Unlike the heroic modernist, who created works out of pure imagination, the postmodern artist works with cultural givens, trying to manipulate them in various ways (parody, pastiche, collage, juxtaposition) for various ends', p.586.

[3] Postmodernist writers are generally suspicious of the 'universal history or metanarrative' associated with colonialism, as Docherty has asserted: Postmodernism is 'the discourse *of* the periphery, a discourse which imperialism had strenuously silenced but which is now made available', resulting in 'not one world, but rather many worlds ... producing contradictory histories'. A full consideration of the convergences and divergences between postmodernism and postcolonialism is beyond the scope of the present essay.

[4] *Waiting for the Barbarians* offers an especially apt connection to our discussion of O'Brien's novel. Coetzee's narrator, the Magistrate of a colonial outpost, remarks, 'I wanted to live outside history. I wanted to live outside the history that Empire imposes on its subjects, even its lost subjects. I never wished it for the barbarians that they should have the history of Empire laid upon them', p.151. Regarding Pynchon as a postcolonial writer, see my 'Pynchon's Postcoloniality'.

[5] I am indebted to Andrew Auge for my awareness of Boland's essay. Pynchon, in *Mason & Dixon* views history in a similar way to Boland and O'Brien; that is, as linked with the master narrative of

nationalism and/or colonialism. As Pynchon's narrator Wicks Cherrycoke asserts, 'History is hir'd or coerc'd, only in Interests that must ever prove base. She is too innocent, to be left within the reach of anyone in Power', p.350.

[6] Said to have originated in O'Brien's own County Clare where the family claimed Irial the ancient king of Ulster as an ancestor, the name McGreevy can more recently be traced to County Antrim in Northern Ireland. One of its many variants is McGillivray, an anglicized form of the Gaelic *Mac Giolla Bhraith*, meaning, appropriately for McGreevy, 'Servant of Judgment or Doom'. See Hanks and Hodges, p.358.

[7] See Bhabha, 'The Other Question', and Young, *passim*.

[8] An example of a timeless moment of unity in Woolf occurs in *To the Lighthouse* when Mrs Ramsay lights the candles at the dinner table and suddenly all those seated around the table put aside petty concerns and momentarily become one in her presence, pp.146-7.

[9] A corresponding episode occurs at the end of Roy's *The God of Small Things* when policemen, referred to as 'history's henchmen', mistakenly apprehend the title character, Velutha, and beat him to death: 'It was human history, masquerading as God's purpose …, an era imprinting itself on those who lived in it', pp.292-3.

8 | 'Caring Nothing for Sacrifice': The Drama of Solitude in Edna O'Brien's *Iphigenia*.

Loredana Salis

Iphigenia, after Euripides' *Iphigenia in Aulis*, is one of Edna O'Brien's most recent theatrical works and her first adaptation of a Greek drama. The play was 'found' by Michael Grandage, the artistic director of Sheffield's Crucible Theatre, who approached O'Brien at a time when the Irish writer had reworked half of it already. A 'devotee of the Greeks', O'Brien had long been drawn to the story of Iphigenia because it is seldom performed, and because 'it's the genesis of all drama. It's at one moment epic, but domestic' (qtd in Lee).

The production opened at the Crucible Theatre in February 2003; it received good audiences, but never toured. There were mixed reviews, some of which queried O'Brien's alterations and use of language (Billington), or found the main characters 'tremendously under-powered' (Pearson). Others praised it as a 'powerful anti-war play [that] makes a point against what is lost in war' (Paulin); but for the vast majority of critics, the play reiterated O'Brien's feminist agenda. Peter Stothard of the *Times* wrote in the course of his review that 'the Irish novelist has made a lifelong theme of weak and violent men who abuse women for specious causes'. Speaking of *Iphigenia* he maintained that the play 'is ... absolutely clear about what is right and [what is] wrong'. Similarly, the journalist Veronica Lee found herself 'struck by how female-centred O'Brien's adaptation is', despite the author's view that 'rather than being female-centred [*Iphigenia*] is a more equal representation of both ... male and female characters' (qtd in Lee). The war of the sexes is certainly a central issue in the play: in the words of another reviewer, O'Brien

> brings into sharp focus where females fit into this world of war-mongering males – as innocent victims, seductive forces in their own right, and formidable avengers (Basset).

The remarks above bear testimony to a well-consolidated tradition of feminist readings of O'Brien's work. It is a tradition, however, that denies *Iphigenia* its full potential, and sadly reminds us that today a wider critical engagement is still needed if we are to give O'Brien's *oeuvre* the attention it truly deserves.[1] In the present context of re-appraisal of the work of Edna O'Brien, it seems appropriate to re-read her *Iphigenia*, a play that has largely been neglected and misinterpreted. Besides the aforementioned reviews, and despite its publication by Methuen in September 2003, little more has been written about the play.

This essay proposes a reading of O'Brien's reworking centred upon the theme of solitude. Its does not deny the relevance of the feminist issues which run throughout her work, but it also draws attention to the writer's concern with isolation and the lack of solidarity affecting modern society. Solitude lies at the heart of O'Brien's attraction to Euripides: both writers in fact share a similar relation to their homeland as well as their people. Viewed in this light, Edna O'Brien's version of *Iphigenia* becomes a journey of self-discovery and a powerful representation of the writer's perception of her work.

O'Brien is not the first to have translated *Iphigenia in Aulis* for the contemporary stage: since 1999, four 'new versions' of Euripides' tragedy, two by Irish writers, have been staged in Ireland. In 1999, Colin Teevan's *IPH...* premiered at the Lyric Theatre in Belfast, and in 2002 Marina Carr's *Ariel* opened at the Abbey Theatre in Dublin. In 2001, the Gate and Peacock theatres in Dublin put on productions of Euripides' play directed by Katie Mitchell and Neil LaBute respectively.[2] What do we make of the upsurge of interest in 'one of Euripides' least performed plays' among Irish writers?[3]

Over the past twenty years there has been an increasing interest in the reworking of the classics in Ireland. The pioneering work of Marianne McDonald has contributed to a postcolonial reading of contemporary versions of Greek tragedy. In her view, that 'Ireland's history shows the imprint of English imperialism' explains why 'the Irish are ... defining themselves in the terms provided by the Greek dramatists' (16). Nicholas Grene has taken a different view and stresses that the translation of the classics in contemporary Irish theatre should not be dismissed as a form of 'auto-exoticism', since 'to concentrate on Irish drama as primarily a manifestation of national self-examination is to neglect its crucial international dimension' (267). By the same token, to concentrate on its international dimension is not to deny or underestimate its local specificity. A combination of both aspects is a key to investigating contemporary uses of the classics, and, in this context, it helps to understand the appeal of Euripides' *Iphigenia in Aulis* in Ireland.

Iphigenia in Aulis, or *Iphigenia at Aulis* (408 BC), as it is sometimes translated, tells the story of how the eponymous heroine dies for the sake of a Greek victory at Troy. Agamemnon and his fleet have come to a halt on the island of Aulis as the winds are not favourable for sailing. The seer Calchas reveals the oracle that a sacrifice should be made to Artemis: 'There must be sacrifice, a maid must bleed / [her] chafing rage demands it' (Aeschylus 49). Having betrayed the goddess in the past, Agamemnon is now expected to sacrifice his daughter, Iphigenia, to placate Artemis and win the war. The girl is brought to Aulis on the pretext of marrying Achilles. As the plot unfolds, Iphigenia's tragic destiny is fulfilled; she resolves to sacrifice her life and abide by the law of the gods. Taken to the sacrificial altar in front of a bloodthirsty crowd of Greek warriors, she is about to face her death at the hands of a priest when Artemis intervenes. Iphigenia disappears and is replaced by a deer, which appears lying on the floor with its throat cut.

The story is traditionally, and not surprisingly, taken as an exemplar of male oppression: Iphigenia is accordingly a stereotypical female victim who dies at the hands of her unscrupulous father. The play has also been read as emblematic of divine necessity since it shows how human beings are inescapably subject to the gods' will. There is also a tradition of political and/or patriotic readings of the Iphigenia story. In *Ireland and the Classical Tradition*, W.B. Stanford reports on a seventeenth-century treatise on the Catholic cause in Ireland entitled *Bleeding Iphigenia*.[4] The treatise does not expand on the analogy with the Euripidean text, except to observe that it exploits the image of the heroine in such a way that 'readers who knew the moving account of Iphigenia's death ... would feel sympathy. All classical antiquity', Stanford continues, 'had condemned her suffering as unjust. Ireland's suffering ... was equally so' (205). More recently, Tom Paulin has drawn upon similar imagery in relation to O'Brien's adaptation, and has observed that she 'comes out of a culture which is soaked in blood and martyrdom and is revising that against itself'. The Irish connection pointed out by Paulin should not be overlooked; in fact it explains the contemporary appeal of *Iphigenia* to Irish playwrights. At the same time, there is a sense in which the engagement with the classics goes beyond Ireland's troubled history to embrace, in O'Brien's words, 'passions and compulsions that everyone can identify with' (qtd in Hunter).

Like O'Brien, contemporary translators of Euripides' play tend to be critical or sceptical of fate-centred readings of it. In Ireland especially, playwrights who have re-worked *Iphigenia in Aulis* have sought the demythologization of its protagonist's sacrificial act. This is reflected in the unanimous dismissal of its ending as 'non Euripidei' (Teevan xiii), or as O'Brien puts it, 'unthinkable' for an artist of Euripides' 'unflinching integrity' ('Notes' vii). Although divine intervention is topical in Euripidean drama, it appears that in the case of *Iphigenia*, a play that was found incomplete after the tragedian's death, the finale was someone else's work. Thus, Teevan, Carr, and O'Brien all similarly alter their source and omit the uncharacteristic ending. What follows the death of the protagonist in their versions is the actualization (Teevan and Carr) or the prophecy (O'Brien) of Clytemnestra's revenge.

The significance and outcome of these alterations strikes me as pivotal to a contemporary understanding of tragedy, and of tragedy in translation. The centrality of Clytemnestra's revenge in the revised texts mentioned above should not be under-estimated. As René Girard has argued, revenge is beside the point of sacrifice. Sacrifice, by its own nature, is intended to appease societal crises and check vengeance (12). The fact that Iphigenia's death leads to retaliation in the plays by Teevan, Carr, and O'Brien brings me to the conclusion that for them, her 'sacrifice' cannot be ascribed to divine necessity; rather, it may be corrupted from its inception. If the death of Iphigenia is not part of the harness of Fate, these plays seem to ask, then, who or what is to be held responsible for it?

In the *Oresteia*, Aeschylus has no doubt that Agamemnon is the sole perpetrator of Iphigenia's death. A man who 'would not admit to error', the Greek king finds himself confronted with choice between victory and family and simply makes the wrong decision: 'Rather than retreat', Aeschylus writes, '[Agamemnon] endured to offer up his daughter's life / to help a war fought for a faithless wife / and pay the ransom for a storm-bound fleet' (24, 48-9). Here, Clytemnestra's act is a matter of just retribution: 'Where', the Chorus asks, 'Where lies Right? … Reproach answers reproach … *the sinner dies*' (95-6). O'Brien rejects Aeschylus' characterization and, as with the aforementioned miraculous ending, she decides to revise the traditional role of King Agamemnon. In doing so she presents him in a new light, and at the same time she exposes the significance of Iphigenia's death.

Girard's model of the scapegoat mechanism can help us read O'Brien's demythologizing of the Iphigenia story, and see how in her view Iphigenia dies a victim at the hands of the com-munity to which she belongs.[5] In the play, the young girl is taken for a scapegoat and selected by the community as sacrificial victim. Eventually she gives herself in sacrifice: 'I will die. Let me save Hellas', she says, 'if that is what the gods want' (O'Brien 40). The selection and eviction of the scapegoat is a symbolic act through which a community in crisis seeks to purge itself. The selected victim is seen unanimously as a stumbling block, the elimination of which will grant peace and stability to the community. The play presents a number of stumbling blocks or barriers of some sort, all of which cause social division. The notion of language as a barrier is dominant in the play: here, O'Brien deploys images of walls by way of which she explores the dynamics of interpersonal relations and suggests, as in the words of Hélène Cixous, that 'there is more than one kind of wall to get past' (qtd in Suleiman ix). The language barrier in *Iphigenia* serves to mark boundaries between the characters and to limit and delimit characters' interaction (Salis). To this extent it is related to another type of barrier or wall, the wall of sexual difference.

The wall of sexual difference is a major obstacle to social interaction, a tough barrier to get past. In the play, male and female characters speak different idioms: women adopt the language of flowers; they express themselves through ritual, storytelling, and dance. Orality and the arts allow them to communicate and to assert their presence in the world. Early in the play, Iphigenia and Five Girls, corresponding to the Women of Chalkis in Euripides, 'are having a pillow fight. *They speak in a made-up inexplicable language*' (O'Brien 11, emphasis added). In another scene, the Sixth Girl, one of O'Brien's additional characters, tries to seduce Agamemnon by offering him boiled eggs:

> **Agamemnon:** This ... husband ... of yours?
> **Sixth Girl:** What about him?
> **Agamemnon:** What about him ... did you give him boiled eggs?
> **Sixth Girl:** Sometimes ... if we had any ... the morning he left I did ...
> **Agamemnon:** And now you're giving me boiled eggs ... is that a ... (*instead of the word he traces her lips*). Little serpent ...

She starts to dance. He joins her in the dance but is not as carefree with the steps as she (O'Brien 16).

Upon her arrival in Aulis, Iphigenia brings flowers to her father and then presents him with 'a huge embroidery for you ... a lamb in a meadow' (O'Brien 23). Verbal language fails the young girl: 'If I had Orpheus's eloquence ... the voice to charm the rocks ... If I could bewitch with words I would bewitch now ... but I only have tears and prayers' (O'Brien 38).

Unlike women, men in the play exert control over written language and consequently they hold ultimate decisional power. Thus, Agamemnon is pictured walking around with a 'book-shaped pine tablet' (O'Brien 7) as if he were, to quote Helen Foley, in the 'process of rewriting the traditional script by revoking and rewriting his original letter' (94). The image reinforces the patriarchal imagery invested in the Achean leader; quite simply the power to make things happen is in Agamemnon's hands, or in his *logos*.

O'Brien deploys another image of the wall which better reflects her intent in adapting Euripides. This we may call the wall of *in*difference or wall of isolation, a tougher barrier found at the heart of what Turner calls *communitas* – the 'unmediated relationship between historical, idiosyncratic, concrete individuals' (45). In *Iphigenia*, O'Brien shows how within the female communitas women betray, mistrust, and lie to each other; they lie even to themselves. Thus, when the Sixth Girl tells Clytemnestra that her daughter will be 'sacrificed in order that [the Greeks] can hoist the sails and make war on Troy', the queen's reaction is dismissive: 'You rave' (O'Brien 27). Likewise, when Clytemnestra warns Iphigenia that 'your father intends to sacrifice you to Artemis the goddess', the young girl's reply is: 'What a tall story' (O'Brien 35). The Sixth Girl tries to seduce Agamemnon (O'Brien 10) while the Nurse competes with the queen for her child's love: 'The night you were born ... my name was the first you said ... not your noble mother' (O'Brien 14).

The male community is also affected by rivalry and inner isolation. O'Brien draws particular attention to the dilemma of

Agamemnon and to the fact that no one seems to care about it. On the eve of Iphigenia's arrival in Aulis, the king prays to the stars that they may 'send her a dream, tell her not to come here' (O'Brien 8). Later, and to no avail, he seeks advice from the Old Man (O'Brien 8), and from the Sixth Girl (O'Brien 16). For O'Brien, it is this indifference and lack of solidarity between members of the Greek community that cause the death of Iphigenia.

As noted, that the sacrifice of Iphigenia is corrupted is made clear by her mother's act of vengeance. O'Brien reinforces this notion by way of significant additions to her source. In an early scene before she goes to Aulis, the young protagonist is wearing a wedding gown when she 'lets out a cry – her menstrual blood has started to flow, running down her legs' (14). The episode is doubly significant as it marks Iphigenia's transition to adulthood (she is about to become a bride) and at the same time reminds us of her tragic fate (she is about to die). Bearing in mind the fact that blood, and especially menstrual blood is a clear index of pollution (Girard 101), the act of 'becoming a woman' indicates that Iphigenia is no longer pure, and consequently that she can no longer be a proper scapegoat. Yet, she is killed at the altar. It is also in these terms that her sacrifice appears to be corrupted or unnecessary from the start.

The selection and eviction of a sacrificial victim occurs when a community is caught up in what Girard calls 'mimetic crisis' or crisis of differentiation, that is when differences are effaced and two members of the community compete for the possession of the same object or for the status that accrues to that possession (293). In Euripides' play there are two major instances of this type of crisis: the first occurs when Menelaus confronts his brother and questions his right to leadership; 'You are not a king' (O'Brien 19). The second takes place later in the play when Achilles makes a similar claim: 'I no longer see him as my master, for I am his' (O'Brien 31). Almost as if to reinforce Euripides' point, O'Brien adds at least three examples of mimetic crisis. On the eve of Iphigenia's departure to Aulis, Electra is clearly envious of her sister because she receives everyone's attention: 'She gets everything', she laments (O'Brien 12). Envy is also manifest in the Nurse's attitude towards Clytemnestra, as it is in the Sixth Girl's attempts to seduce King Agamemnon (O'Brien 14, 16). The scene is set for the ritual of sacrifice: as Iphigenia begins her journey to Aulis unaware of her fate, the Chorus predicts 'that [which] I would rather not speak of ... for the greatness of war is great' (O'Brien 15). 'Caring nothing for sacrifice', is the Sixth Girl's poignant remark at this stage.

No one cares for Iphigenia's sacrifice in the play; and no one really cares for anyone's sacrifice. O'Brien reiterates the idea in her depiction of King Agamemnon. This is another significant departure from tradition (as represented by Aeschylus and anti-patriarchal readings of the play) and from her Euripidean source. In her *Iphigenia*, Agamemnon is deliberately isolated; his efforts to save the young girl are tragically in vain. From the start, this solitary monarch walks around in desperation. In an early scene, where he asks the Old Man: 'What would you do if it were your daughter', the answer is rather inconclusive: 'My tongue dare not speak at all' (O'Brien 8). Agamemnon knows that he cannot stop the raging mob outside. When the Sixth Girl says, 'If you cannot, who can?' his answer to her – 'I play the role expected of me' – is a convincing statement of impotence vis-à-vis the impending tragedy (O'Brien 16). To make things worse, the seer Calchas intervenes to remind Agamemnon of Artemis' rage, and the curse on his progeny, ultimately putting pressure on him to fulfil the oracle. There is no escape for this broken king; for him, 'gone, gone is every hope' (O'Brien 9). A recasting of Agamemnon in these terms may lead to the conclusion that O'Brien builds some sort of apologia for the Achean leader. On the contrary, I would argue that it is precisely because she does *not* 'exact [Agamemnon's] full price' that O'Brien manages to make everyone in some way responsible for Iphigenia's death.

Solitude was also the fate of Euripides. In a comedy of BC 411, Aristophanes has him facing a group of raging women: 'I fear that this day will be my last. The women have been plotting against me. They are going to discuss my liquidation', he tells an elderly relative. At this, his interlocutor asks: 'But why on earth?' Euripides replies, 'They say I slander them in my tragedies'. 'Well, so you do', the old man says, 'Serve you right if they did get you' (Aristophanes 32). Similarly, in an essay written for the Crucible programme, O'Brien tells of how 'the crimes [of Euripides] were legion. He had questioned the prestige of the state, of pious honour and ancient injunctions' ('Notes' v).

In *Iphigenia*, Agamemnon speaks words which resonate with Euripides' unpopularity among his people to suggest, perhaps, the similarity of their fates. Thus, when the king laments: 'Phantom females dripping with blood visit me in my sleep' (O'Brien 33), he brings to mind his wife's revenge but also the 'hearsay that Euripides was ... torn to death by mad dogs or mad women who could not tolerate his depiction of them' (O'Brien 'Notes' v). In the same essay, O'Brien likens Iphigenia's solitude to that of a martyr-mystic: here, as with Agamemnon's words above, one has the feeling that she is talking about Euripides as much as she talking about herself. To Veronica Lee, O'Brien has said that:

> Most real writers are exiled in their minds always – whether from family, parish or country – because writing by its very nature is an extremely isolating and reflective job. Even though you are embroiled in the human stories, the work is done in the crucible of the imagination (Lee).

A similar suggestion is found in the programme notes when O'Brien praises her Greek master for his 'dedication to his calling', despite the fact that he was 'the scourge of his native Athens, his plays regarded as seditions and corrupting. Born in exile ... he died in exile in his mid-seventies ('Notes' v). The passage alludes to the kind of undeserved criticism the Irish writer is clearly familiar with. As she says of Euripides, O'Brien too has 'shocked public opinion, offended the critics and ... [has been] overlooked' ('Notes' v). There is a strong suggestion in both play and essay that O'Brien identifies with Euripides on a number of levels.

O'Brien's reflections upon Euripides' work and life confirm how, in a contemporary context, classical tragedy can provide fertile ground for an exploration of the dynamics of human relations in society. In *Iphigenia*, the death of the young girl is not justified by the demands of religious ritual. Quite simply, the mythic belief that a sacrificial victim will restore peace to the community is no longer valid in O'Brien's version. As Girard has put it, 'Once understood, the [scapegoat] mechanisms ... collapse one after the other' (10). The death of Iphigenia is a consequence of that social malaise which O'Brien identifies in the community's lack of solidarity. Once this revelation comes about, two myths are simultaneously challenged: one is the myth of necessity (both divine and political); the other is the myth concerning O'Brien's work. As with Euripides', hers has been traditionally 'marginalized' or 'overlooked' (O'Brien, 'Notes' v). The claim that her work is primarily female-centred (that is, anti-patriarchal) does little justice to this writer's concern with universal issues and to her constant investigation of the aesthetic medium. It is a claim which clearly fails to reflect the depth and energy of O'Brien's *Iphigenia*.

Works Cited

Aeschylus. *The Oresteian Trilogy.* Trans. Philip Vellacott (Harmondsworth: Penguin, 1959).

Aristophanes. 'Thesmophoriazusai'. *The Frogs and Other Plays.* Trans. and introduction David Barrett (Harmondsworth: Penguin, 1984).

Bassett, Kate. Rev. of Edna O'Brien's *Iphigenia* at Sheffield's Crucible. *Independent* 16 February 2003.
http://members.aol.com/actorsite3/add00/loindex.htm.

Billington, Michael. Rev. of Edna O'Brien's *Iphigenia* at Sheffield's Crucible. *The Guardian* 12 February 2003.
http://members.aol.com/actorsite3/add00/loindex.htm.

Euripides. *Iphigenia at Aulis.* Trans. William Merwin and George E. Dimock, Jr, ed. William Arrowsmith (New York: Oxford University Press, 1978).

Foley, Helen, *Ritual Irony: Poetry and Sacrifice in Euripides* (Ithaca and London: Cornell University Press, 1985).

Girard, René. *Things Hidden since the Foundation of the World.* Trans.
    Stephen Bann (Books II & III) and Michael Metteer (Book I)
    (London: Athlone, 1987).
Grene, Nicholas. *The Politics of Irish Drama: Plays in Context from Boucicault
    to Friel* (Cambridge: Cambridge University Press, 1999).
Hunter, Sophie. 'In Conversation with Edna O'Brien'. Sheffield's
    Theatres Education Resources online.
    http://www.sheffieldtheatres.co.uk/education/productions/
    Iphigenia [accessed 10 October 2005]
Lawson, Mark, Allison Pearson, Rosie Boycott, and Tom Paulin.
    'Iphigenia', highlights of *Newsnight Review*, BBC 2, 17 February 2003.
    http://news.bbc.co.uk/1/programmes/newsnight/review/2771075.
    stm [accessed 14 January 2004]
Lee, Veronica. 'The anger of heaven is nothing to the anger of men.'
    Independent 9 February 2003.
    http://enjoyment.independent.co.uk/theatre/interviews/article1186
    02.ece.
March, Jennifer. 'Euripides the Misogynist?' *Euripides, Women and
    Sexuality*, ed. Anton Powell (London: Routledge, 1990).
McDonald, Marianne. 'Classics as Celtic Firebrand: Greek Tragedy, Irish
    Playwrights and Colonialism'. *Theatre Stuff*, ed. Eamonn Jordan.
    (Dublin: Carysfort Press, 2000).
O'Brien, Edna, *Iphigenia.* Adapted with introduction (London: Methuen,
    2003).
Pelan, Rebecca. 'Edna O'Brien's "Stage-Irish" Persona: an "Act" of
    Resistance'. *Canadian Journal of Irish Studies* 19 (July 1993): 67-78.
Salis, Loredana. 'Edna's Euripides: Ritual and Language in Edna
    O'Brien's *Iphigenia*'. Paper delivered at the International Association
    for the Study of Irish Literatures (IASIL) Annual Conference,
    Galway. July 2004.
Sheffield's Theatres Education Resources online
    http://www.sheffieldtheatres.co.uk/education/productions/
    Iphigenia [accessed 10 October 2005]
Stanford, William Bedell. *Ireland and the Classical Tradition* (Dublin: Allen
    Figgis, 1977).
Stothard, Peter. Rev. of Edna O'Brien's *Iphigenia* at Sheffield's Crucible.
    Times 14 February 2003.
    http://members.aol.com/actorsite3/add00/loindex.htm.
Suleiman, Susan Rubin. 'Writing Past the Wall or the Passion According
    to H.C.' *Coming to Writing and Other Essays*, ed. Deborah Jenson
    (London: Harvard University Press, 1991).
Teevan, Colin. Introduction. *IPH...* (London: Nick Hern Books, 1999).

Turner, Victor. *From Ritual to Theatre: the Human Seriousness of Play* (New York: Performing Arts Journal Publications, 1982).

---

[1] I refer specifically to an article which appeared in *Canadian Journal of Irish Studies* in 1993 in which Rebecca Pelan called for a wider and more serious critical engagement with O'Brien's work. Ten years on, when O'Brien adapts *Iphigenia*, Pelan's observations are all too relevant.

[2] Katie Mitchell's production, based on Don Taylor's translation of Euripides' *Iphigenia in Aulis* (London: Methuen, 1991) ran from 28 March to 21 April 2001. Neil LaBute's trilogy *Bash* including 'Iphigenia in Orem', 'Medea Redux' and 'A Gaggle of Saints' ran from 27 March to 17 April. The playscript was published by Faber and Faber in 2001.

[3] The words are O'Brien's, p.vi. See her essay in the Programme Notes for Sheffield's Theatres production of *Iphigenia* available online at http://www.sheffieldtheatres.co.uk/education/productions/-Iphigenia. The essay was reprinted as an introduction to her *Iphigenia*. Henceforth, quotations from the essay will be referred to as 'Notes'.

[4] Stanford 204, 205. The Preface, by an anonymous friend of French's explains: 'The picture of Iphigenia … going to be sacrificed … smiling, bearing in her countenance a Majesty and contempt for death; so charming was the art of this picture, that few could view it without teares. Courteous Reader, the Author of this Preface hath drawne another *Iphigenia* of the body of a noble, ancient Catholic Nation, cl'd all in red, not to bee now offered up as a victime; but already sacrific'd, not to a profane Deity, but to the living God for holy Religion: look but on this our bleeding Iphigenia, and I dare say you will lament her tragedy'.

[5] I have developed this argument in 'Edna's Euripides: Ritual and Language in Edna O'Brien's *Iphigenia*', unpublished paper delivered at the IASIL Annual Conference, Galway, July 2004.

9 | 'Meaniacs' and Martyrs: Sadomasochistic Desire in O'Brien's *The Country Girls Trilogy*

Shirley Peterson

> All masochists are just sadists waiting to be cured.
> Edna O'Brien

The IRA's recently-declared disarmament in Northern Ireland, although disputed, signals an encouraging development in an otherwise escalating international climate of terrorism. As a symbolic gesture, it also undercuts a particular gendered nationalism that has helped define not only the IRA but also the Irish Republic, a nationalism that has historically curtailed women's liberation and reinforced gender norms 'for the good of the State' (Pelan 49). As Heather Ingman argues, from 1922 the new Irish nation-state sought to establish 'national norms of gender', in support of a 'homogeneous' postcolonial ideal that increasingly relied on strict female virtue and a 'hypermasculine republican model of masculinity' (253, 255). Consequently, as Eileen Morgan argues, the pure but suffering Irish woman is one of the 'foundational myths of the Republic' that enshrined 'the quintessential maiden-victim' along with her counterpart, the 'Irish hero' (451). Thus, destabilizing this entrenched myth

of victim/hero has decided allure, especially if the hero can also
be a victimizer.

The patriarchal and nationalist underpinnings of this polarized gender division have been amply noted. I would simply
add that they are attended by concomitant sadomasochistic
impulses that drive the mid-century Irish sociopolitical agenda.
To that end, I will focus on Edna O'Brien's 1960s trilogy,
revised and collected as *The Country Girls Trilogy* in 1987.[1]
Together, these texts provide a fascinating study of sadomasochistic desire as contained within the demands of compulsory heterosexuality. O'Brien's protagonists, Cait/Kate
Brady (hereafter referred to as Kate) and Baba Brennan, are
first indoctrinated in the principles of heterosexual/sado-
masochistic desire through the patriarchal family. They sub-
sequently reenact these principles in heterosexual relationships,
as well as in their relationship with each other. As Kate seeks
acknowledgment of herself through male approval and Baba
denies her own feelings of dependency by abusing Kate, both
characters seek to attain an elusive female subjectivity that is
ultimately impossible at this point in Ireland, structured as it
was around a patriarchal and nationalist agenda. Amanda
Greenwood argues that

> [t]he quest of O'Brien's protagonists for an Irish identity with
> which it is possible to be comfortable is analogous with the
> search for a heterosexual relationship which avoids 'sell-out' in
> terms of female sexuality (32).

The failure of this quest in O'Brien's first trilogy owes much to
the demands of a culture simultaneously constructed along
heterosexual and sadomasochistic lines. Furthermore, these
demands thwart the potential for a redemptive sisterhood that
Helen Thompson sees as 'women's salvation' in O'Brien's
novels (23).

O'Brien has argued that the Irish have been the 'least
ashamed of and the most atavistic at mapping out a landscape
of suffering' that some might call 'masochism'. She rejects this
term as imprecise and, citing Joyce, asserts that 'one has not
lived unless one has conceived of life as a tragedy' ('It's a Bad

Time' 20). Semantics aside, however, the extent to which sadomasochism determines the individual tragic life as well as the larger social system that contains it is worth consideration. In *Sadomasochism in Everyday Life: The Dynamics of Power and Powerlessness*, Lynn Chancer illuminates this link between individual and social S/M by applying some basic principles of sexual S/M to nonsexual dimensions of human relationships, thus suggesting that one of the linchpins of modern capitalist society is sadomasochism. Drawing from nineteenth-century sexology through to more contemporary feminist analyses,[2] Chancer argues that 'as a phenomenon [S/M] appears to be more and more common — and undoubtedly an object of cultural fascination' (20). However, she warns, the more recent approach of popular psychology, tends to work toward changing individual behaviour without addressing the underlying cultural conditions that inform workplace, race, and gender hierarchies. Placing these hierarchies squarely in the context of modern capitalism, Chancer finds that S/M desires appear to diminish with prosperity and egalitarianism (39). This suggests not only S/M's dependence on inequality, but also the capacity for transformation within the dynamic itself.

Chancer's work has implications for gender studies in that many modern cultures produce a 'symbiotic need' between members of society that finds expression in gender-specific sadomasochistic behaviour: 'A connection clearly exists between the structural tendencies of a male-dominated and patriarchal society ... and a particular social psychology it encourages between men and women' (146). Most commonly, S/M discourse has focused on deviant sexual practice, or what Barbara Ehrenreich calls 'the ultimately commercial form of sex' (123), something Freudian analysis of S/M has certainly reinforced;[3] however, this concentration eclipses the broader social manifestations of S/M. As a basic indicator on either the sexual or social register, S/M depends on a hierarchical and grossly unequal social arrangement that also contains a central paradox:

> Just as the sadist secretly wishes to acknowledge denied feelings
> of dependency, so a masochist is needed through whom such
> feelings can be genuinely acknowledged: paradoxically, furtively,
> the sadist needs the masochist [in order] to be free. At the same
> time, the masochist wants her or his own strivings for freedom
> to be recognized by a sadist who cannot qua sadist ever really
> acknowledge these desires, too frightened to relinquish his or
> her investment in the masochist's lack of freedom (Chancer
> 139).

Within this Gordian knot of social, cultural, and emotional
'constraints', O'Brien's *Trilogy* evolves from *Bildungsroman*/
romance into what Greenwood calls a 'negative romance', a
subversion of the romance genre that appears to conform to it
(23).[4] Furthermore, the text's subversive S/M narrative exposes
the difficulty of resisting 'national norms of gender' within
patriarchy. On one hand, this narrative appears to suggest that
the only option is to replicate the male/sadist female/masochist
polarization, even when both parties are female; on the other
hand, the narrative retains an essentially subversive element that
ultimately challenges the gender/sex dichotomy and the
masculinist/nationalist ideology that supports it. Thus, as a
strategy for interrogating male-dominated society, the S/M
narrative promotes a progressive, if thwarted, agenda.

The maternal figures in the trilogy operate, more or less, as
models of female masochism at the hands of what Sheila
Rowbotham calls the 'Mean Man' (126), or what Kate and
Baba's Dublin landlady terms male 'meaniac[s]' (215). Kate's
and Baba's mothers present two variations on this theme.
Kate's parents, the Bradys, characterize standard male/sadist
and female/masochist roles. This duality marks the novel's
opening in which Kate and Mrs Brady, the iconic suffering
Mother Ireland,[5] anxiously await the return of Mr Brady, the
first in a long line of O'Brien's 'raving rollicking Irish father[s]'
(*MI* 32). Mrs Brady sits idly awaiting her husband's return,
having kept vigil all night to ensure that Kate did not choke on
a piece of candy, a veritable image of 'maternal martyrdom'
(Morgan 460). Kate herself gets up 'six or seven times every

night' (4) to say prayers, well trained in mortification of the flesh through Catholicism and maternal example. Both anticipate the worst upon Mr Brady's return: 'Would he stumble up the stone steps at the back door waving a bottle of whiskey? Would he shout, struggle, kill her, or apologize?' (6). The uncertainty principle within this familiar scenario of domestic abuse — would he brutalize or beg forgiveness? — acts as an instructional tool for the masochist in patriarchal marriage, a lesson Kate internalizes and repeats later on with both Mr Gentleman and Eugene Gaillard, who keep her in perpetual uncertainty. When Mr Brady finally does return to find his wife gone, he turns his anger on Kate, physically abusing her. The discovery that Mrs Brady has, in fact, drowned while trying to flee this oppressive situation only guarantees her martyrdom and passes the mantle of masochism to her daughter.

If Mrs Brady reenacts the classic masochistic role, Baba's mother, Martha Brennan, has been deemed both a 'second exemplar of maternal suffering' (Morgan 460) or her opposite — 'the alcoholic extrovert' (P. O'Brien 484). In fact, Martha is a study in contradictions. She embodies the contrasting features of the Virgin/Whore with her 'pale Madonna face' (as opposed to Mrs Brady's 'heartbreaking face') and magnetic appeal to men. Yet, she is 'what the villagers called fast' (30-1, 36). When we meet her, she seems the antithesis of female masochism. She reclines like Molly Bloom on her bed, secretly satisfying her appetite — a cooked chicken spread out on the bed so 'the aul fella won't get it' (30). The 'aul fella', Mr Brennan, looks haplessly on in a picture which she playfully — but sadistically — shoots with her right hand. She treats Kate kindly but simultaneously abuses their servant girl, Molly, through stinginess, humiliation, and beatings. Kate even notes a resemblance between Martha and her sadistic father in that 'like all drinkers, she was reluctant to spend on anything other than drink' (31).

In the two maternal figures, then, O'Brien 'restages the battle between female types ... the first of whom [Mrs Brady] epitomizes the lyrical, submissive heroine of late-nineteenth-century nationalist literature, while the second [Mrs Brennan] undermines that romantic ideal through endless pursuit of self-gratification, as well as crass language and bawdy behaviour' (Morgan 457-8). The second category also challenges conventional designations of female/masochist and male/sadist:

> For how can sadism be 'essentially' the province of males or masochism that of females when nearly every observer of sado-masochism (including, ironically, Freud himself) has noted that the two dimensions coexist and are opposite sides of the same coin? (Chancer 129)

We can observe the fluidity of these roles in the economically superior Brennans whose marriage is likely to be more stable than the Bradys' because Mr Brennan, a solidly middle-class family man, experiences a lesser degree of emasculation than Mr Brady, an impoverished and dispossessed farmer. In this respect, the degree of sadomasochism is a function of power rather than gender difference. Even within the same person, roles can shift, as implied by Peggy O'Brien, who also sees the suffering Mrs Brady as 'a repressive force dictating every movement within her domain' (479). In contrast, Martha becomes increasingly masochistic and pathetic, buckling to provincial, social, and religious pressures until she finally dies of the cancer that Kate feared would destroy her own mother and that Baba attributes to women who don't have enough children, that is, who do not conform to their gender specific roles (29). Martha's fate marks the limitations for any Irish woman who deviates from the martyr/masochist role by adopting the male designated sadist position. By the novel's conclusion, then, the destruction of both mothers proves that there is more in question than — in S/M parlance — who's on top. Deviant behavior alone does not short-circuit the social constructions that sustain cultural sadomasochism.

Kate's romantic relationships with Mr Gentleman and later with Eugene extend the principle of female masochism to its logical conclusion: the death of the self. Ultimately, Kate's masochism is so central to her identity that it becomes impossible to imagine a less tragic conclusion. This pattern of behaviour, learned within patriarchy, is highly paradoxical:

Deference to the other's power and ability to affect one's life
may become the only means for forging a vicarious, if estranged
relationship to self. To undergo self-subordination may become
habitual, ringing with the ambivalent comfort of the familiar
and potentially rewardable. That women come to assume a
relatively masochistic role in relationships and in love, then,
may indicate just the reverse of masochism's usual signification
… taking pleasure in pain. Instead, a proclivity in women to
assume a masochistic role more regularly than do men … [is] a
rather predictable, logical, and ultimately defensive outcome of
[patriarchy] (Chancer 27-8).

In other words, Kate's interactions with her abusive father and
suffering mother determine her self-abnegation and deference
in all subsequent relationships, driving her romantic desires because they offer the comfort and reward of the familiar. Therefore, Mr Brady, described as 'a gentleman, a decent man who
wouldn't hurt a fly', ironically foreshadows 'Mr Gentleman', a
more familiar father figure than he first seems (27).

The fact that Mr Gentleman is a married man forever beyond reach makes him all the more alluring from a masochistic
standpoint, what Freud describes as 'an extension of sadism
turned round upon the subject's own self' (*Three Essays* 24). Mr
Gentleman's advances are clearly a mere dalliance in his eyes;
however, Kate's enshrinement of her 'new god' fuels her masochistic idolatry: '[His] face carved out of pale marble and eyes
that made me sad for every woman who hadn't known him'
(57). Interestingly, his compliment that she is 'the sweetest
thing that ever happened to [him]' sounds to her like a
'deathless, deathless song' when, by the trilogy's conclusion, it
seems more a prophetic dirge (56-7). The ending of the first
novel in which Kate receives his devastating rejection, constitutes the fulfillment of romantic masochism. And if the story
were to end here, it would not rise above the level of popular
melodramatic romance, only demonstrating, as Anatole Broyard
puts it, 'a gentleman is a failed promise' (12). Kate mourns Mr
Gentleman while 'a real gentleman', the new lodger, treats her
dispassionately, incapable of communicating: 'No English
speak' (175). What has begun as an 'estranged relation to self'

has developed into nearly complete estrangement from every-one, including herself. In her isolation, she occupies a powerless position within a rigged system that turns a blind eye to masculine infidelity but roundly condemns unsanctioned female sexuality. However, this is not the end of the story as *The Lonely Girl* continues Kate's development, offering an example of what Tania Modleski terms the 'revenge fantasy' of the romance novel. In this genre, masochism works as a '"cover" for anxieties, desires and wishes which if openly expressed would challenge the psychological and social order of things' (30). Here, O'Brien conveys feminist optimism that women can reject their designated masochistic role.

If Mr Gentleman is Kate's childish fantasy of the Good Father, then Eugene Gaillard is the dark underside of this desire, evoking several versions of the 'meaniac'. A Bluebeard — like Mr Gentlemen with a mysterious, absent wife — Eugene is sophisticated and world weary, a cryptic Mr Rochester with a streak of 'Old Heathcliff' (334).[6] When Kate first meets him, 'he [doesn't] look very pleased. He had a sad face [and] … an odd expression of contempt as he spoke' (184). Naturally, these features are magnetic qualities to 'Mary of the Sorrows', as Baba wryly describes Kate. Whereas Baba characteristically fantasizes about a sexual fling with Eugene, Kate masochistically swoons: 'I suppose lots of women have *died* for him' (188). And ulti-mately, in a manner of speaking, she does. He is not entirely a brute, however; he does, after all, retain some Prince Charming qualities, making efforts to raise Kate intellectually and socially (Eckley 43). His more benign paternal side emerges in such things as his instructions on how to brush her teeth and his confession that he misses his three-year-old daughter: 'Once you've had a child you want to live with it and watch it grow' (234). These words take on a more sadistic meaning later, though, as his relationship with Kate evolves and we see *her* as the child he at first nurtures but increasingly controls. At the same time, his love for her begins to resemble Mr Brady's in its sadistic assertion of authority over the powerless.

Finally, the dark side of the marital fairytale emerges, turning the Cinderella fantasy into Greenwood's 'negative romance' and exposing 'the compromised nature of female subjectivity' (23-4). When Kate first agrees to go alone to Eugene's home, her decision is met with dark forebodings: clanging church bells calling her to Mass, a frost-covered city, and Joanna's horrified exclamation that Eugene might be a 'meaniac' (215). When Eugene finally arrives late, he is 'lined and gray as if from lack of sleep' and, seemingly more beast than beau, he greets her by breathing on her face. His remark that she looks like 'a child bride' highlights both Kate's innocence and her lack of power. His home (built with profits from his one Hollywood film, a romance) in Wicklow's 'bleak mountain land' contains ominous relics of slaughter: antlers, horns, heads and skins supposedly left by the previous owner (223). They are greeted by Eugene's insolent housekeeper, Anna, 'a rural Irish Mrs Danvers', a reference to Daphne du Maurier's *Rebecca*, whom Greenwood links to Kate's 'fear of sexuality' (27).[7]

Eugene seems to take a kind of sadistic Freudian '*fort/da*' pleasure in both fulfilling and denying Kate's desires.[8] At their initial clandestine 'marriage', he presents her with a ring accompanied by a lewd vow that unsettles her: '"With this expensive ring, I thee bed", he said, and I gave a little shiver and laughed' (314). On their 'wedding night', he plays the devouring husband cum ideal romantic hero, what Ann Barr Snitow calls 'a hungry monster that has gobbled up and digested all sorts of human pleasures' (197): 'I could eat you', Eugene salivates, 'like an ice cream' (315).[9] Even his expressions of love forebode ill:

> 'That ring has to last you a long time', he said.
> 'How long?'
> 'As long as you keep your girlish laughter' (316).

Of course, the 'child bride' inevitably loses her innocent laughter, and the ring, too big for Kate to begin with, becomes just another sign of her inadequacy and the looseness with which Eugene regards his commitment. She takes no physical pleasure in her sexual initiation, only a masochistic resignation that she has 'done what [she] was born to do'. Eugene's comment that she is 'a ruined woman now' jarringly contrasts with his 'half-articulated words of love' and seems to 'come from a great distance' as he detaches himself emotionally and sadistically threatens her with pregnancy (316-17). The following morning, he is fully dominant:

> 'Lucky you don't snore', he said. 'Or I'd send you back'.
> 'Do you love me?' I asked again.
> 'Ask me that in ten years' time, when I know you better',
> he said as he linked me down to breakfast and told Anna that
> we had got married (319).

Eugene's playful *fort/da* threat to 'send her back' becomes reality when he realizes she is no longer 'a simple, uncomplicated girl' (340). His ten-year deferral of her question indicates that much depends on Kate's remaining in a child-like — and masochistic — state of paralysis as a kind of commodity for male consumption.

The gender poles of this S/M dynamic are not fixed, however, as Eugene's marriage to the conveniently absent Laura suggests. In a flirtatious letter, Laura accuses him of having a 'feudal attitude toward women' (341), yet she wields the upper hand in their own S/M game, using their daughter in a sadistic power play to keep Eugene from divorcing her. Ironically, Eugene seems the victim of women, what Kate deems 'a mad martyr nailed to his chair, thinking and sighing and smoking' (351).[10] In this image of immobility, we see the sadist's paralyzing dilemma: 'power is possible only relative to the masochist's lack of it ... [and] extreme need is the common thread that links the sadist's desire for control to the desire to punish'. At the same time, the sadist 'secretly crave[s] *resistance* to, and challenges of, his ... authority from the masochist' (Chancer 49-50). The American Laura — who 'believes that happiness is her right' (221) — may be up to the game, but Kate is not. Flexing what little sadistic muscle she has, Kate decides to 'teach him a lesson' by leaving him, the typical 'disappearing act' of the angry romantic heroine of the revenge fantasy (Modleski 47). But she is no Laura, and her empty threat becomes a self-fulfilling prophecy, as Eugene will not have her back despite her pathetic attempts to encourage him. The second novel ends like the first with Kate abandoned by her lover. But, on a more hopeful — and feminist — note, she claims to be 'finding [her] feet' in London where she attends university (377). Thus, while the first novel ends in Kate's masochistic meltdown, *The Lonely Girl* offers the possibility that Kate might escape the sadomasochistic trap. We can even believe that this has been a character-building experience as she has adopted Eugene's philosophy of love:

> We all leave one another. We die, we change — it's mostly change — we outgrow our best friends; but even if I do leave you, I will have passed on to you something of myself; you will be a different person because of knowing me; it's inescapable (377).

Sounding on one hand like good advice, on the other hand, the conflicting notions of liberation and entrapment in this statement actually convey the contradictions at the heart of sadomasochistic relationships. If both Kate and Baba are 'trapped in traditional and social scripts', as Kristine Byron suggests (458), they are trapped in sadomasochistic scripts as well.

At this point, the story could become one in a number of novels about rejecting female oppression, a 'feminist' ending some readers would likely prefer.[11] And yet, in O'Brien's third novel, *Girls in Their Married Bliss*, and especially in the 'Epilogue', added later, O'Brien seems to be playing a narrative game of *fort/da* herself with the reader by withdrawing this ending and giving a point of view to Baba, Kate's alter ego and arguably the most sadistic person in the book. Readers are so invested in Kate's problems by this point that at first, like good masochists ourselves, we may resist the narrative shift only to be bitch-slapped by Baba into a heightened awareness of the debilitating effects of masochism. If Kate's romantic enthralment constitutes a denouncement of female masochism, then Baba suggests that the 'S' side of the S/M dynamic is at least preferable to the 'M'. At the same time, her appropriation of the 'natural' male sadistic role demonstrates Judith Butler's point that all gender roles are performative rather than expressive of an internal 'essence':

> That gender reality is created through sustained social performances means that the very notions of an essential sex and a true or abiding masculinity or femininity are also constituted as part of the strategy that conceals gender's performative character and the performative possibilities for proliferating gender configurations outside the restricting frames of masculinist domination and compulsory heterosexuality (140-1).

Thus, in *Girls in Their Married Bliss*, we begin to see what Byron calls the deconstruction of all 'prescribed roles for women in patriarchal Irish society' (448). If there is no masochistic female essence, then the possibility exists for female sadism and both Baba's and Kate's 'performances' simply expose the 'phantasmatic' nature of gendered identity (Butler 141). By extension, gender-specific sadomasochism may seem a self-contained and self-defeating enterprise. At the same time, the fluidity of sadomasochism subverts the binary and opens the possibility for other 'gender configurations'.

At this point, the *Trilogy*, along with its 'Epilogue', presents less a celebration of feminist liberation than a lament for its lost optimism.[12] Baba turns a cold eye on Kate's misty romance and, according to the author, the character is one who 'undermine[s] every piece of protocol and religion and hypocrisy' that she can ('Irish Heroines' 13). Baba keenly observes the psychological dependency of both Kate and Eugene; to Baba, they are both mad. She buys into the Cinderella myth only insofar as it is a vehicle for upward mobility, the literal cash she acquires from marrying Frank an ironically mercenary counterpoint to Kate's child, Cash. But O'Brien does not present Baba as an entirely preferable alternative to Kate either, despite Baba's function as a reality check on romanticism run amok. Baba may survive in the end, but she cannot entirely escape the disabling effects of their masculinist culture. The sociopolitical limits of their rebellion force both Kate and Baba to surrender to the

demands of compulsory heterosexuality, precluding any possibility for fulfillment outside patriarchal marriage, which serves
the needs of both masculinist nationalism and sadomasochism.
To fully understand the S/M dynamic in the novel, therefore,
we need to consider not only the heterosexual relationships in
the *Trilogy*, but also Kate and Baba's friendship.

The interdependence of this friendship is somewhat
surprising given Baba's domination of Kate from the beginning,
when Baba appears as Kate's hateful nemesis on her 'Pink-
Witch bicycle', 'coy, pretty, malicious' and 'the person [Kate]
feared most after [her] father' (14). Kate's conflicting repulsion
from and attraction to Baba even resembles the 'uncanny'
lesbian desire Thompson notes in O'Brien's later works (24-5).
In the *Trilogy*, desire is determined partly by economic status, an
inequity with sadomasochistic implications. While Kate comes
from a downwardly mobile background associated with Irish
decline, Baba enjoys the rewards of middle-class Irish life,
which has seductive appeal for Kate:

> I could smell her soap. The soap and the neat bands of sticking
> plaster, and the cute, cute smile; and the face dimpled and soft
> and just the right plumpness — for these things I could have
> killed her (19).

The friendship is fraught with brutality, yet it has an erotic
dimension as well, as this sensuously charged passage suggests.
In fact, Kate and Baba have experimented erotically with each
other as juveniles:

> Baba and I ... shared secrets, and once we took off our
> knickers ... and tickled one another. The greatest secret of all.
> Baba used to say she would tell, and every time she said that, I
> gave her a silk hankie or a new tartan ribbon or something (8).

This homoerotic play initiates Kate's subordination and Baba's
domination, but through the homosexual taboo, any possibility
for Butler's 'proliferating gender configurations' is suppressed.
Thus, the gifts Kate gives Baba both 'demonstrate [lesbian]
desire and keep it hidden' (Thompson 28). Their occluded
desire leaves a lingering sense, however, that the compulsory

heterosexuality to which they both succumb is performative at best, and consequently its masculinist/nationalist underpinnings are potentially destabilized.

Baba's sadism masks her reliance on Kate, a dependency that illustrates how 'the sadist needs the masochist [in order] to be free' by affirming the sadist's need to control while simultaneously fulfilling the need for an 'Other' (Chancer 138-9). Predictably, Baba's dependency becomes more apparent — and more masochistic — as Kate asserts her independence from Baba. When Kate and Eugene legitimately marry — 'a question of having to' — Baba is 'miserable' and, seemingly on the rebound, she marries Frank, a 'thick' but nice builder who is 'bad in bed' (381-4). Despite Baba's gold-digger mentality, her venality is still surprising: 'I liked his money and his slob ways: I didn't mind holding hands at the pictures, but I had no urge to get into bed with him. Quite the opposite' (385). Baba's mother advises her to 'grit [her] teeth and suffer it', and in the end Frank's financial largesse wins her family's approval over Baba's complaint that she is 'the bloody sacrificial lamb' (386). Baba's association of marriage with female sacrifice and martyrdom, strikingly like Kate's own nuptial experience, places her oddly in the role of masochist at this point. When an extramarital affair ends in pregnancy, Baba fully realizes the sadomasochistic game as a blood sport in which women have a disadvantage: 'There isn't a man alive wouldn't kill any woman the minute she draws attention to his defects' (468). Unlike Kate, Baba also recognizes the danger of masochistic submission in this game: 'I suppose he expected a great slob scene from me about how generous and charitable he was. Not me. I know the minute you apologize to people they kill you' (469). Baba refuses to play the contrite 'Magdalene', even showing no remorse when Frank boasts that he has been to a brothel in retaliation for her infidelity (470). But when Frank begins to weep, she accepts the sadomasochistic terms of marriage: 'Never, never was I to do it again or he'd slay me alive' (471). Ironically, Baba is as trapped within the ever-fluctuating S/M dynamic as Kate is, if for different reasons: 'Never one to be held down by punishment,

[Baba] was cornered in the end by niceness, weakness, dependence' (502). Even Frank's indifference seems a barrier to her escape. Later, when a stroke reduces him to 'a fucking vegetable', she resigns herself to the role of reluctant caretaker for a witless 'spaniel' (519). Contrary to what Snitow sees as 'a push for power in female fantasy' through the 'theme of male mutilation' (192), Frank's debilitation actually disempowers Baba further, lashing her to a husband who is completely dependent. Ultimately, either side of the S/M equation presents a trap for all, male or female, sadist or masochist.

If Baba denotes a kind of impotent female sadism, Kate ironically illustrates the destructive potential of masochism. When she reads about a plane crash caused by starlings nesting in the engine, she recognizes herself: 'I feel like the starlings ... I sort of destroy [people], with weakness' (476). Consequently, she reconsiders her enshrined mother as a 'self-appointed martyr ... Smothering her one child in loathsome, sponge-soft, pamper love' (477).[13] As if to ensure she would never do the same, Kate has herself sterilized, an act that has been called a 'self-destructive act of resistance to "femininity"' (Greenwood 29) and 'a radical refusal to conform to her nation's view that the natural vocation of women is motherhood' (Ingman 257). Within the romance genre, Modleski argues, such acts are 'the fulfillment of the fantasy of ultimate revenge through utter self-destruction' (47). While these explanations are valid, within the framework of sadomasochism, however, we might also explain Kate's action as 'an effort to exert control from a powerless position' with the goal reconceived from 'pleasure in pain' to pleasure 'as the goal itself' even at the cost of pain and self-destruction (Chancer 59). In a perverse way, then, Kate's masochism seems oddly satisfying, even assertive.

Following her sterilization, Kate reads about women who, isolated in an underground cave, form a female community that offers a kind of subjectivity through mutual recognition: 'Doctors in touch by telephone from an adjacent cave continue to be astonished at the physical resilience and lively spirits of the women, who were unknown to each other before the vigil began' (507). Critics have generally interpreted this as a hopeful image, as a representation of 'self-knowledge, sexual freedom, and independence' or a symbol of 'women's common ties to each other', an underground female community outside the control, or even the comprehension, of men (Thompson 34; Carpenter 267).[14] As compelling as this reading is, the image remains troubling. While it suggests the powerful nurturing quality of female solidarity in a society organized along both patriarchal and sadomasochistic lines, it also conveys the stasis and confinement of a community powerless to change its situation or even to communicate with an 'Other'. Moreover, it insinuates that by embracing the masochistic/victim role as women's common bond, neither the 'cavewoman', nor her 'caveman' counterpart, achieves a satisfactory end. They remain separated and isolated rather than connected, which is finally the problem with the S/M dynamic in general. Ultimately, sadomasochism is 'irrational, unable to produce its alleged aim — namely, a feeling of contented control for the sadist or of sated subordination on the part of the masochist' (Chancer 189). It is an endgame with no hope of resolution, and at the social level it simply results in a stalemate.

Published in the early days of second-wave feminism, O'Brien's *Trilogy* seems sadly unable to sustain the feminist principle of an insurgent sisterhood as antidote to sadomasochistic masculinist culture. O'Brien's 1966 novel *Casualties of Peace* only makes this failure more explicit in the story of Willa and Patsy, whose friendship threatens to short-circuit their sadomasochistic relationships but has deadly results when Willa is mistakenly murdered by Patsy's husband. Regarding O'Brien's more recent novels, Greenwood has suggested that the 1990s trilogy offers a more optimistic alternative through 'deconstructions of masculinity' (78). She points to Breege of *Wild Decembers* 'holding it together' as indicative of the 'potential for revisions of [the social and symbolic] orders' (92). Greenwood complements Sandra Manoogian Pearce's observation that O'Brien's later works shift from the suffering Kate figure toward the surviving Baba figure (63) and towards

the notion that, increasingly in O'Brien's work, 'women's salvation lies in their relationships with each other' (Thompson
23). *Wild Decembers* offers ambiguous hope, however, that a
sisterhood can prevail. Divided by their love but linked in their
grief for Mick Bugler, victim of another 'meaniac', Breege and
Rosemary form an uneasy alliance as each claims a right to his
legacy. Yet Breege wonders

> if the old wars are brewing again and will they, as women, be
> called on to fight the insatiate fight in the name of honour and
> land and kindred and blood. Will their hearts too turn to
> treason (259).

Of course, O'Brien's consummate 'meaniac', Michen O'Kane
of *In the Forest,* is a critique not only of violent masculinity
through the 'development of "country boy" into
"Kinderschreck"' (Greenwood 104), but also of a community
all too complicit in his dehumanization. Against this
annihilating combination, the sisterhood of Eily and Cassandra
is defenceless.

While *The Country Girls Trilogy* fails to deliver the promise of
a powerful sisterhood, it nevertheless initiates a subversive
element into O'Brien's work that resonates throughout the later
work as well. In the 'Epilogue', written twenty years after the
conclusion of *Girls in Their Married Bliss,* both 'girls' have
reverted to type. Kate has given into her 'Dido desperado
predilections' and probably committed suicide (523). Despite
what O'Brien calls Baba's 'asperity to prevail' ('Irish Heroines'
13), Baba lives a life devoid of love or hope, imprisoned by
cynicism, bitterness, and loneliness. Interestingly, Baba's husband has blamed Kate for his troubled marriage, a suspicion
that may not be unfounded. For the bond between Kate and
Baba, as sadomasochistic and debilitating as it is, carries seeds
of destruction for the masculinist nationalism that sanctions
patriarchal tradition and ensures male domination. By its very
existence, in fact, their bond suggests that sadomasochistic
desires are not necessarily fixed or gender specific, and
consequently they have the potential to deconstruct the entire
social and symbolic system. Alas, O'Brien gives us more hope

than assurance of this upheaval in her first trilogy, in which
Baba's final wish for the deceased Kate — that 'she rises up
nightly like the banshee and does battle with her progenitors' —
announces the author's own feminist agenda (523).

Works Cited

Broyard, Anatole. 'The Rotten Luck of Kate and Baba'. Rev. of *The
    Country Girls Trilogy and Epilogue. New York Times Book Review* 11 May
    1986: 12.
Butler, Judith. *Gender Trouble: Feminism and the Subversion of Identity* (New
    York: Routledge, 1990).
Byron, Kristine. '"In the Name of the Mother ...": The Epilogue of
    Edna O'Brien's *Country Girls Trilogy'. Women's Studies: An
    Interdisciplinary Journal* 31.4 (2002): 447-65.
Cahalan, James M. 'Female and Male Perspectives on Growing Up Irish
    in Edna O'Brien, John McGahern, and Brian Moore'. *Colby Quarterly*
    31.1 (1995): 55-73.
Carpenter, Lynette. 'Tragedies of Remembrance, Comedies of
    Endurance: The Novels of Edna O'Brien'. *Essays on the Contemporary
    British Novel,* eds Hedwig Bock and Albert Wertheim (München:
    Max Hueber, 1986), 263-81.
Chancer, Lynn S. *Sadomasochism in Everyday Life: The Dynamics of Power and
    Powerlessness* (New Brunswick, NJ: Rutgers, 1992).
Du Maurier, Daphne. *Rebecca* (New York: International Collectors
    Library, 1938).
Eckley, Grace. *Edna O'Brien* (Lewisburg, PA: Bucknell University Press,
    1974).
Ehrenreich, Barbara, Elizabeth Hess, and Gloria Jacobs. *Remaking Love:
    The Feminization of Sex* (New York: Doubleday, 1986).
Freud, Sigmund. 'Beyond the Pleasure Principle'. *The Standard Edition of
    the Complete Psychological Works of Sigmund Freud.* Vol. 18. Trans. James
    Strachey (London: Hogarth, 1955).
--- *Three Essays on the Theory of Sexuality* (New York: Basic, 1962).
Greenwood, Amanda. *Edna O'Brien* (Hornden, Tavistock, Devon:
    Northcote House, 2003).
Ingman, Heather. 'Edna O'Brien: Stretching the Nation's Boundaries'.
    Irish Studies Review 10.3 (2002): 253-65.
Pearce, Sandra Manoogian. 'Redemption through Reconciliation: Edna
    O'Brien's Isolated Women'. *Canadian Journal of Irish Studies* 22.2
    (1996): 63-71.
Modleski, Tania. *Loving with a Vengeance: Mass Produced Fantasies for Women*
    (Hamden, CT: Archon, 1982).

Morgan, Eileen. 'Mapping Out a Landscape of Female Suffering: Edna
    O'Brien's Demythologizing Novels'. *Women's Studies: An
    Interdisciplinary Journal* 29.4 (2000): 449-76.
O'Brien, Edna. *Casualties of Peace* (New York: Simon and Schuster, 1966).
--- *The Country Girls Trilogy* (New York: Penguin, 1987).
--- *In The Forest* (Boston: Houghton Mifflin, 2002).
--- 'It's a Bad Time Out There for Emotion'. *New York Times Book Review*
    14 Feb. 1993: 1+.
--- *Mother Ireland* (New York: Harcourt, Brace, Jovanovich, 1976).
--- 'Why Irish Heroines Don't Have to be Good Anymore'. *New York
    Times Book Review* 11 May 1986: 13.
--- *Wild Decembers* (Boston: Houghton Mifflin, 1999).
O'Brien, Peggy. 'The Silly and the Serious: An Assessment of Edna
    O'Brien'. *Massachusetts Review* 28.3 (1987): 474-88.
Pelan, Rebecca. 'Edna O'Brien's "Stage-Irish" Persona: An "Act" of
    Resistance'. *Canadian Journal of Irish Studies* 19.1, (1993): 67-78.
--- 'Edna O'Brien's "World of Nora Barnacle"'. *Canadian Journal of Irish
    Studies* 22.2 (1996): 49-61.
Roth, Philip. *Shop Talk* (Boston: Houghton Mifflin, 2001).
Rowbotham, Sheila. *Hidden from History: Rediscovering Women in History from
    the 17th Century to the Present* (New York: Pantheon, 1974).
Salter, Mary Jo. 'Exiles from Romance'. Rev. of *The Country Girls Trilogy*,
    by Edna O'Brien. *The New Republic* 30 June 1986: 36-9.
Shumaker, Jeanette Roberts. 'Sacrificial Women in Short Stories by Mary
    Lavin and Edna O'Brien'. *Studies in Short Fiction* 32 (1995): 186-8.
Silverman, Kaja. 'Masochism and Subjectivity'. *Framework* 12 (1980): 2-9.
Snitow, Ann Barr. 'Mass Market Romance: Pornography for Women is
    Different'. *Feminist Literary Theory: A Reader*, ed. Mary Eagleton
    (Oxford: Blackwell, 1986).
Thompson, Helen. 'Uncanny and Undomesticated: Lesbian Desire in
    Edna O'Brien's "Sister Imelda" and *The High Road*'. *Women's Studies:
    An Interdisciplinary Journal* 32.1 (2003): 21-44.

---

[1] The sadomasochistic impulse at the heart of the *Trilogy* permeates many
    of Edna O'Brien's works, as critics have noted. See, for instance,
    Eckley, p.11, and Shumaker.
[2] Chancer draws on the work of R. Krafft-Ebing, Sigmund Freud,
    Marquis de Sade, Leopold von Sacher-Masoch, Erich Fromm, Angela
    Carter, Barbara Ehrenreich, and Robin Wood to trace the
    development of critical approaches to S/M, pp.15-42.
[3] See Freud, *Three Essays*. For an analysis of Freud's arguments on S/M,

---

see Chancer, pp.82-8: 'Freud's set of explanations did not encourage the consideration of historical and social factors as causes of sadomasochism *sui generis*', p.88.

[4] On the *Bildungsroman*, see Cahalan. On the subversive romance elements in O'Brien, see Greenwood, pp.21-34. On the gothic romance, see Modleski, pp.59-84.

[5] See Morgan on Mrs Brady's resemblance to the allegorical Shan Van Vocht of Irish mythology, p.459.

[6] O'Brien has admitted her attraction to 'the Heathcliff/Mr Rochester syndrome' in that 'sexual excitement [is] to a great extent linked with pain and separation', in Roth, p.111.

[7] Carpenter also notes the *Rebecca* connection, observing that Mr Gentleman's name is actually Mr du Maurier, p.264.

[8] On the *fort/da* point, see Silverman.

[9] Greenwood notes the gender implications in O'Brien's *Mother Ireland* for 'consuming and being consumed' as related to 'cultural paralysis', p.54.

[10] It seems an overstatement of this point to say, as does Anatole Broyard, that Eugene is 'a devoted lover and teacher' who is 'masochistically patient with Kate', p.12.

[11] See, for instance, Salter. For an overview of the critical reception of O'Brien's work, see Pelan, 'Edna O'Brien's "Stage-Irish" Persona'.

[12] As Byron notes, in 1971 O'Brien 'dramatically altered the conclusion of *Girls in Their Married Bliss*, undercutting the optimism of the first ending', p.448.

[13] See Morgan, p.464.

[14] Thompson links cave imagery in O'Brien's short story 'The Mouth of the Cave' and in her novel *The High Road* to lesbian desires, pp.34-5.

10 | Killing the Bats: O'Brien, Abjection, and the Question of Agency

Patricia Coughlan

The *OED* defines the noun 'abjection' as follows:

> The act of casting down; abasement, humiliation, degradation. *Obs.*

> The condition of casting down ... downcastness, abjectness, low estate.

> The action of casting off or away; rejection.

> That which is cast off or away; refuse, scum, dregs. Usually *fig.* of persons.

and the past participle 'abject' with the sense 1. of 'cast off, cast out, rejected. *Obs.*', and the sense 3. of 'down in spirit or hope; low in regard or estimation, degraded, mean-spirited, despicable'. It illustrates the obsolete noun 'abjectedness', defined as 'downcast condition; abasement; abject state or condition' with a 1660 citation from Robert Boyle's *Seraphic Love*: '[Christ] from the height of Glory ... sunk Himself to the bottom of Abjectedness, to exalt our condition to the contrary extreme'. [1]

My title refers to the following episode in O'Brien's trilogy, which takes place after Kate Brady has been forcibly brought home from Dublin to her father's tumbledown farmhouse. It is well after the death of her mother:

I swept the seven lonely, empty bedrooms because bat droppings dotted the floors.

'There's two bats upstairs', I said to my father, merely making conversation.

'Where?' He jumped out of bed and went upstairs in his long underpants, grabbing the sweeping brush on the way. He routed them out of their brown winter sleep and killed them.

'Bloody nuisances', he said, and my aunt swept them onto a piece of cardboard and burned them downstairs in the stove. She said that we must do something about the rooms. The walls were all damp and mildew had settled on some parts of the wallpaper. But we just closed the doors and hurried down to the kitchen, where it was warm (*CGT* 278).

I think this scene is an allusion to a well-known passage in Chapter 5 of James Joyce's *Portrait of the Artist as a Young Man:*

And yet he felt that, however he might revile and mock her image, his anger was also a form of homage. He had left the classroom in disdain that was not wholly sincere, feeling that perhaps the secret of her race lay behind those dark eyes upon which her long lashes flung a quick shadow. He had told himself bitterly as he walked through the streets that she was a figure of the womanhood of her country, a batlike soul waking to the consciousness of itself in darkness and secrecy and loneliness, tarrying awhile, loveless and sinless, with her mild lover and leaving him to whisper of innocent transgressions in the latticed ear of a priest (183).

In O'Brien's bat scene, Kate's father kills the bats without compunction, getting out of bed to do so: one might say that they are abject*ed*. They have not disturbed Kate, she has not minded them, but *he* feels a compulsion to destroy them, despite (or because of?) the dilapidated and indeed abject state of his whole life. In the real world bats come into a house only if it is uninhabited; in this case they have done so because it is no longer properly maintained within the social order but forsaken, becoming empty. One way to read the allusion is to say that their killing indicates, via the Joyce allusion, that there will be no 'waking to the consciousness of herself' by Kate (often called 'Cait', short for 'Caithleen') as long as she remains at home in her father's house, where her potential awakening is blocked and the otherness of her independent being cannot be accommodated. O'Brien deploys Joyce's image, but also goes beyond it: the notorious blindness of bats is emblem, in his narrator's mind, of women's *embodying* 'the secret of her race', but also of her incapacity to *know* that 'secret' as even the brashly overconfident Stephen Dedalus will come to know it. O'Brien also plays subliminally, as she does throughout the trilogy, with the intermittent suggestion that we can see Kate Brady as a figure for the nation.

I propose that the discussion of the abject affords an extraordinarily fertile medium in which to grow, so to speak, experimentally, some interpretative cultures in relation to O'Brien's life's work.[2] The abject is not a neat category: it can be represented by material objects, or by the process of abject*ing*, as an act or a series of acts, by the encounter with that which has been (perhaps incompletely) abject*ed*, and finally by the experience of abject*ion*, whether as a conscious psychological state or as a phenomenon relegated to the unconscious since infancy. This latter sense invokes Julia Kristeva's theorization of the concept in *Powers of Horror* (1980), which has initiated an extensive body of writing and which I draw on.

From my own first readings of O'Brien, when she was banned and therefore already an object of danger and excitement before one opened the books, I have always been struck by the extraordinarily frequent mentions of bodily scenes and of items eliciting disgust. In those days, of course, the transgressiveness of her work was deemed above all to reside in its alleged obsession with sex, but in fact the number of specifically sexual scenes in, for example, *The Country Girls* or *The Lonely Girl*, is not large, and the content of these scenes is not really calculated to inflame the passions, being the very reverse of romantic; I have no doubt that many of my coevals must have read her with disappointment. These texts, and much of her later work, especially when it uses Irish settings (as for example the remarkable 1982 short-story collection *Returning*), instead of offering titillation, dwell rather on a constellation of scenes, topics, and physical facts which are emotionally distressing.

In this essay I shall not focus primarily on the sex as such (what there is of it). My subject is the building-blocks and small-scale constituents of many fictional scenes, items, and motifs which are either unmentionable in polite society, or what was in the 1960s *felt to be* disgusting (the largest category), or indelicate, or a breach of respectability to describe, or advert to at all, let alone by a young woman writing. Let us list them: mud, dust, grease, urine and faeces (human and animal), the penis and testicles unclothed (*CGT* 164 & 319); a stillborn calf hanging dead from its mother, afterbirths human and animal (*CGT* 322); the difficult delivery of a mare in foal (*DBR* 62); the exact bodily signs of a sexually transmitted infection (*AWM* 148); a village street ankle-deep in cowdung after a fair and a pub floor flowing with porter from an opened tap ('Irish Revel' 62); a can of milk offered to a young girl for drinking but visibly filmed with dust (*CGT* 93); a young woman planning to apply veterinary ointment made for cows' udders to make her breasts grow (*TCG* 99-100); an adult who wets his bed (*CGT* 168); the Holyhead boat pulling away from Dún Laoghaire pier described as 'like a hundred lavatories flushing' (the boat is called the *Hibernia*; *CGT* 374); the live-in workman 'making his water' in a tin and throwing the contents out the window onto the cement outside, which is rendered 'green and slippery' (*CGT* 4, 8); the heroine's mother getting off her bicycle to 'do a pooley', unconcealed, on a country road (*CGT* 477); the same character's half-hearted washing of *one* hand after urinating in a strange house or a hotel, while 'at home she just held her legs apart over the sewerage outside the back door, where they also strained potatoes and calf meal' (*CGT* 477); the convent episode which involves the unwitting barring by one schoolgirl of the nuns' entry to their private toilet, and her friend's deliberate obscenity to get them expelled, which begins (and the beginning is all we hear): 'Father John put his long thing ...' (*CGT* 103-5). As O'Brien readers will know, I could easily multiply these instances by a hundred.

In a word, O'Brien deliberately flouts the laws of respectability both by the sheer extent and by the character of her
fictional attention, not just to the exact description of bodies
(once again, animal and human), but, rather more, to that which
is filthy, disgusting, repulsive. It is as if, in the very texture of
her prose, she implacably refuses prettified, decorous surfaces
in the social world, and insists upon the actuality of filth and
the inextricable constancy of human dwelling with, within,
around, and about it. The 'pooley' episode I've mentioned (in
which a male cyclist comically arrives on the scene just in time
to witness the exposure and the event itself), concludes with the
following summary:

> Ah, childhood, Kate thought; the rain, the grass, the lake of pee
> over the loose stones, the palm of her hand green from a
> sweating penny that the Protestant woman had given her.
> Childhood, when one was at the mercy of everything but did
> not know it (478-9).

Evidently the discourse of nature, and, by extension, visibly
throughout O'Brien's work, the received image of nature in the
West of Ireland (the tourist motifs of wistful, lonely beauty and
aesthetically agreeable wildness, here rudimentarily represented
by 'the rain, the grass'), these are being sharply subverted by the
insistence upon physical grubbiness and disorder, earthy bodi-
liness, and emotional and financial impoverishment.[3] And the
whole is placed in childhood, whose disempowered and
ignorant state is expressly noted. Such ideological subversion is
certainly one motivation for the proliferation of 'pee' and other
waste products, but I shall argue that it is not necessarily their
primary or only interest in these texts. Furthermore, the abject
and abjection, if we may so name such passages, continue to
make their appearance as structuring elements on the level of
narrative imagery in later fictions, not all of them set in Ireland,
though I shall not develop this here.

To explain the uses of abjection theory in understanding
O'Brien's vision, it is necessary to consider the specific character of Kristeva's thinking. The general currency of the terms
'abject' and 'abjected' is often only a rather vague rehearsal of

her fundamental and remarkable argument. One of her main innovations in psychoanalytic theory is her positing that we constitute our subjectivity and enter the symbolic order, a patriarchal domain, by disavowing the lived body, and with it the maternal, as abject. This process of abjection, as she defines it, marks a stage in the pre-Oedipal development of the subject. These exclusions form the basis of Oedipal subjecthood and of Cartesian duality, splitting or polarizing mind from body, meaning from being, and subject from object. It is a sacrificial logic that nevertheless lays the foundation for identity (as conventionally understood).[4] Kristeva used classical psycho-analytic theory as her point of departure in developing her abjection theory: I would argue, however, that while apparently working within this quintessentially patriarchal model, she silently turns it against itself, ultimately offering a deeply ironic and dissenting interpretation of the constitution of the self within gendered structures, an interpretation very different from the principal, patriarchal account of culture in Freud, Lacan, and the founding ideology of Catholic Ireland.

I shall focus on those aspects of the theory which are most relevant to the interpretation of O'Brien. Recent feminist thought has pointedly and rightly rejected the Cartesian and subsequent Freudian impasses which deliver an atomized self-hood, seen as destructively severed from the body, the other, and the world; feminist theorists have proposed far more productive alternative narratives of subjectivity.[5] But O'Brien's pervasive melancholy answers much better to the old, con-stitutively misogynist structures, which had after all formed the social order she so sceptically appraised, in the Ireland of the four middle decades of the last century, and Kristeva's analysis of these structures is a singularly powerful one.

Kristeva argues that within the context of infant develop-ment, the constitution of the child's subjecthood depends upon its alienation from its lived, actual body, and the setting up of an imaginary anatomy. Those caring for an infant establish categories of waste, disgust, and repellence, as well as their opposites of prettiness, pleasure, and attractiveness or beauty, by means of their handling and management of the baby's bodily products and its contact with things in the world. Practically speaking, this is, of course, done in the service of hygiene and of basic socialization and acculturation, but its effects exceed these physical requirements. Kristeva observes how gender is central to these processes: caregivers have generally been female, and so these first experiences of objects which must be relinquished and thrown away – that is, abjected – are mediated by mother-figures. The mother herself is the child's first object. However, having given birth and fed the baby, she has an overwhelming physical presence and felt continuity with it; she therefore occupies a dual, and strongly paradoxical or contradictory, role. She is *both* the agent of culture who teaches the necessity of abjection and enacts it for the child and upon the products of its own body, *and* herself one of those physical objects (bodies) which must be abjected for the infant to establish its own subjectivity. As Kristeva puts it, 'maternal authority is the trustee of th[e] mapping of the self's clean and proper body' (72). But it is also true that *the mother herself* is primary among those things which must be abjected.

'Normal' development, in the classical psychoanalytic narrative, subsequently proceeds by, and depends on, intervention by a third: the father, who will breach the dyad between mother and infant and stand for the symbolic order of the culture outside that dyad. This is especially relevant to O'Brien's fictions, where the father-function tends, destructively, to be strong and weak at the same time: weak in empathy and protective love, strong in regulation, assertions of control, and the making of inappropriate emotional demands. Kristeva asserts that 'the subject will always be marked by the uncertainty of its borders ... and these are all the more determining as the paternal function is weak or even nonexistent ...' (59, 63) In the *ur*-narrative of infancy, the crucial role of the paternal presence is defined as enabling the child (by the father's power of prohibition against incest) to separate itself from the mother. The resulting formation of a superego – site of guilt, inhibition, and law – must, or is supposed to, leave certain things outside.[6] According to the textbook account, the child's original longing for its mother's body must be re-linquished in favour of the desire for a more acceptable other or object. This, however, is always imagined as more complete than its realization in actuality, and which is forever just beyond the person's grasp.[7] This totalized object of desire is represented successively by partial objects of demand, in what Lacan sees as a play of successive substitutions, like those of signification or meaning in the structuralist theory of language.[8] However, the process of psychological development is not a straightforward linear one, and it may – perhaps even must – always fall short of completion: Kristeva's stress on the porous-ness, the inefficiency, of the prescribed events is one of her most inspired insights. So the effecting of abjection in infancy is often incomplete, and the abject(ed) can surface intermittently in adult experience, where it is no longer subject to the laws of infantile amnesia, since pre-Oedipal experience is always un-consciously present to the subject.

Furthermore, the incapacity of an ego – a person's self – to perform abjection, and thus form objects according (as it were) to the prescription, may produce a desire (which we may label 'regressive' and call 'abject' in all senses) to *fuse with* the Other rather than to sustain a painful state of subjectivity and difference from the other: and in this case the Other of desire is wishfully – and, as so often in O'Brien's narratives, disastrously – projected as of one substance with the ego, that is, as maternal. Kristeva defines as 'abjects' people who fail to form active, ego-based external objects of desire, and who persist as 'the fascinated victims of abjection ... if not its submissive and willing ones' (9). Kate Brady and many or most other O'Brien heroines seem singularly well described as such psychologically abject characters, whose very being seems defined by a kind of global abjection, whose ultimate result is a destructive wish for self-abjection: such self-annihilating desires seem to define their very being.[9] They 'refuse to or cannot sublimate the death drive, and hence are compelled to enact and re-enact it' (Coats 298).

The theory of abjection is not confined to the sphere of individual development; it also has strong social-structural implications. The division of objects into dirty and clean is always one laden with cultural significance, and the designation of parts of the physical body as more and less proper or improper inscribes cultural values on social bodies. In the 1930s Georges Bataille discussed the concept of abjection as a *physical* state to which the poor are consigned by those in power. He remarked that where, for example, infants are contaminated by snot and infested by lice, this is the result of neglect and destitution rather than some innate quality, as class prejudice might tacitly imply. He also, however, showed a dialectical insight into the psychosocial function of the assignment of the status of filthiness to some, when he described it as a phenomenon of social apotropaism (meaning a gesture of aversion, setting up a boundary between people and/or classes). I abject you to confirm my own subjectness. Thus privileged groups in society use their power to draw boundaries between themselves and others coded as unclean (Bataille 219; Kristeva 64). Kristeva argues that at the still more general level where cultures construct and maintain their ideological and symbolic systems, such differences are also elaborated to set up boundaries of community and nation.[10] The working of this process is very clear in the zealous policing of Catholic, familist, and nationalist ideology in that Ireland of the 1930s and 1940s which saw Edna O'Brien's formation in childhood and adolescence.[11]

Abjection is something that 'disturbs identity, system, order'. Yet what is abjected we do not cause simply to go away; the abject person or group 'operate[s] at the social rim' (Kristeva 4, 65). Indeed, as Bataille argued dialectically, the presence of the abject is required by ideology, paradoxically to sustain by its very exclusion the constructs of the symbolic order. Yet the fragility of these constructs is keenly felt, and they are haunted by their abjected others. This fundamentally paradoxical character of the abject is inherent in Kristeva's theory. She thematizes the *operation* of abjection as foundational to the sustaining of both self and society, while the *condition* to be abject tends to subvert both. When art theorist Hal Foster asks whether the abject is 'disruptive of subjective and social orders [and] a crisis in them', or 'foundational [and] a confirmation of them', the answer must be 'both' (156).[12]

It is central to my argument that O'Brien's work can be productively understood in both these ways, in its relation to Irish ideologies from the 1960s to the 1990s. On the one hand, it confirms the existence, and plays out the specific operations, of Irish social exclusions and prohibitions: those of personal freedoms including that of religious *dis*belief, women's social and sexual agency, sexuality as pleasure and play, for instance. On the other hand, it simultaneously disrupts and subverts them in the very act of representing them. A study, in Irish media archives, of the way Edna O'Brien was herself received – attacked, critiqued, yet simultaneously displayed as flagrant – in the Ireland of the later 1960s would show how she fulfilled this dual role as a transgressive public figure, herself the object of abjection, placed 'at the social rim' of a culture she was still felt to 'haunt'.

Another important aspect of Kristeva's theory is that, while one must perform necessary acts of abjection to constitute oneself, in infancy (and indeed in a continuing way in adult life, to sustain oneself in being), and those acts of abject*ing* and the process, mood, and condition of abject*ion* are painful, disorientating crises, yet on occasion and in certain contexts, by virtue of their very power to destabilize, they are potentially sublime and/or aesthetically inspiring. Kristeva quotes a remark by Proust (a writer with marked similarities of theme to O'Brien) that 'if the *o*bject of desire is real, it can only rest upon the *a*bject, which is impossible to fulfil' (21, emphasis added). An important aspect of the theory of abjection is precisely the role Kristeva believes it plays in artistic production. Drawing on the essentially paradoxical character of the abject, she sees it as capable of expression and representation in aesthetic work, where the dark, negative energies responsible for abjection can be transmuted by aesthetic form into poetic language, image, or dance, which can articulate affects beyond the codes of the symbolic. She argues that '[t]he artistic experience is rooted in the abject [which] it utters and by the same token purifies' (243). This is another formulation strikingly applicable to the aesthetic effects of O'Brien's dark fictions, so often denied the status of 'real' literature in mainstream, especially Irish, criticism: a neglect more than careless or accidental, but perhaps occasioned by an anxiety to distance their capacity to embarrass by instantiating so many awkward little dirty moments, while simultaneously refusing and almost dreamily marginalizing the big, prescribed themes of nation and more or less oedipal identity. During the 1990s Rosalind Krauss and others further theorized the aesthetic abject within art criticism, though following Bataille somewhat more than Kristeva, as 'a kind of feminine sublime, albeit composed of the infinite unspeakableness of bodily disgust: of blood, of excreta, of mucous membranes'. Commenting in particular on Cindy Sherman's work, Krauss and Yve-Alain Bois observe that within this theorization of art,

> the abject is ultimately cast … as multiple forms of the wound. Because, whether or not the feminine subject is actually at stake in a given work, it is the character of being wounded, victimized, traumatized, marginalized, that is seen as what is at play within this domain (238).[13]

What of the view that Kristeva's theory of abjection is itself misogynist, and not just the patriarchal acculturation process she traces? At this level, too, there is a clear analogy with O'Brien, whose work has also sometimes been rejected by feminists.[14] Considering Kristeva first, if we think of the mother as the first abject, does this perpetuate that classic patriarchal binary according to which the (normatively masculine) subject must wrest his individual being from a threatening, engulfing maternal figure, and the mother's constitutive fate is to be abjected, discarded, and left behind as waste product, in order for that subject to attain his selfhood? Would this merely recapitulate the pathologies of patriarchy? Some feminists, soon after *Powers of Horror* appeared, did specifically challenge Kristeva's vision as perpetuating the

archaic mother in positing the notion of a struggle for
subjectivity against the maternal figure. Some see her as
sustaining the pervasive misogyny of the psychoanalytic fathers
by seeming to accept the designation of femaleness as that
which must itself be abjected in order for subjectivity, and
therefore culture, to develop (Stone). Sub-sequently, however,
Mary Jacobus and others have convincingly rebutted such
views, showing that Kristeva's subordinating of the castration
complex in favour of a prior engagement with the maternal is a
decisive displacement of the phallic.[15] Besides, it is naïve not to
distinguish between *describing* and *endorsing* the widespread
attribution in cultures of 'abject or demoniacal power' to the
feminine, and the 'exclusory prohibition' there-fore applied to
women *in patriarchy* (Kristeva 64). Kristeva does describe, and
indeed goes further to anatomize this attribution, but does not
endorse it or the system which depends upon it. Moreover, as I
have said, a key insight in her vision is the incompleteness of
the abjection process and the repeated re-emergence of the
maternal, the abject, the feminine, of all that is supposed to
have been excluded by the formation of subjectivity. I see
Kristeva, therefore, not as the *advocate* of abjection, but as its
searching and eloquent *analyst*: it is pointless to shoot the
messenger. And likewise in O'Brien's case, she does not *celebrate*
the abjection of the maternal and of Ireland in her work: she
rather chronicles, agonizes, and mourns over it. There is a
parallel in the fiction of Jean Rhys, another eloquent writer of
abjection, in whose work it is beside the point to seek healthy
female role-models and upbeat endings. Rhys's achieve-ment
and her triumphant demonstration of feminine agency, like
O'Brien's, are to be found in the aesthetic brilliance and
emotional penetration *of the writings themselves* as articulations of
abjection.

   I have argued from the outset that we should resist a reductionist approach to the presence of abject items in O'Brien:
I believe they are not accounted for by a notion of realist
transcription (such an argument might run: 'ah sure, in County
Clare in the 1930s they weren't too bothered about keeping

clean'). A literalist reception of her fictions by, say, a reader of the *New Yorker* (where a very large number of the short stories first appeared) might, then, have decoded such motifs simply as evidence of poverty and deprivation. This would obviously be a serious over-simplification amounting to a misinterpretation, and another element of Kristeva's conception is actively helpful in escaping such reductionist readings and indeed in suggesting a further dimension in the interpretation of O'Brien. Kristeva drew significantly on a prior classic of anthropology, Mary Douglas's *Purity and Danger*, written during the same years as O'Brien's trilogy, which analyses the vital cultural role of notions of pollution.[16] Douglas observes that ritual defilement and taboo are not opposites, but an indispensable part of the sacred, considered as a (mental, symbolic) realm. The notion of defilement operates especially in religious contexts, which are – or were – at the core of cultures, and cannot be adequately or appropriately accounted for on the merely practical level, by what she calls 'medical materialism' (that is, the coincidence of certain food taboos or cleansing rituals with modern ideas and practices concerning hygiene or disinfection). Douglas argues that

> we would expect the most materialistic-seeming cults to stage at some central point in the ritual cycle a cult of the paradox of the ultimate unity of life and death. At such a point pollution of death, treated in a positive creative role, can help to close the metaphysical gap (176).

She also describes how '[t]he central act in the ritual of mourning [among a Lake Nyasa people] is actively to welcome filth. They sweep rubbish onto the mourners' (177). That which is tagged as dirty is thus used structurally to elaborate and sustain a culture's own sense of order. Douglas's work marked a milestone in understanding the great significance, on the level of cultural symbolization, of dirt and waste matter. Like Kristeva's own emphasis on unconscious anxieties and half-repressed desires, this adds another suggestive layer to our possible interpretations. It is especially suggestive in its possible reconnection of the maternal, via the ineluctable bodily, with

the larger realm of the sacred, rather than assigning it the
negative, daemonic position demanded by its disavowal. The
role of the maternal is vital in O'Brien, and it by no means
retains a merely or simply abject character, as we shall see.

The complexity of abjection theory in its possible ap-
plications to these fictions exceeds the cruder kind of
explanations from ideology (though it does not, of course,
displace ideological critique in O'Brien). By 'explanations from
ideology', I mean the constellation of ideas to do with her
evident intention to debunk the mystique of Ireland by
representing women's experience from women's viewpoint, her
pointed and satiric resistance to the Irish iconic feminine –
Virgin Mother, Mother Ireland, Cathleen Ní Houlihan – and
accompanying constructions of Irish womanhood, whether in
the ideology of 1930s, 1940s, and 1950s Ireland itself, or in its
external or quasi-external stereotyping by others.[17] Furthermore, the continuing work of constructing specifically feminist
understandings of the writings has now well advanced beyond
its initial stages, and as the present volume shows, is becoming
sufficiently subtle and complex to get beyond the biographical
author's own disavowals of a feminist position.

One other way comes to mind of accounting in part for the
prevalence of dirt, mud, urine, and so on in the texts. This is the
hypothesis of a Joycean influence, which I invoked at the outset
in the specific instance of the bat motif. Both writers show a
special tendency challengingly to name what used to be called
the 'lower' bodily functions: sex, defecation, menstruation, and
so forth. But upon closer analysis, it emerges that O'Brien's
litanies of such items are quite different from Joyce's: there is
far more disgust and far less celebration of appetite, gratification, or pleasure. The *affect* differs markedly. In Joyce's case
his flagrant fetishizing of female bodily effluents and his closely
related coprophilia are both evidently important aspects of his
individual erotic life (shown in his letters to Nora Barnacle, as
well as in the fiction itself). While both writers exhibit a degree
of masochism in terms of erotic mood (O'Brien) or stimulus
(Joyce), gender polarities sharply differentiate both their erotic

expression and their representations of the nature of human attachment in general.

In place of Joyce's maternal-erotic, the erotic construction of the Other in O'Brien's writing is the figure of the chill, superior, older male figure who is represented in language suggesting a sacred or even godlike being: angelic, pale, cool, ascetic, and distant. The structure is that of romance (Jane Eyre and Mr Rochester, and their later avatars Rebecca and Max de Winter, for instance).[18] '[Mr Gentleman's] face had that strange holy-picture quality that made me think of moonlight …' (CGT 261); 'I used to think he was God' (CGT 262); 'always the same remote, enchanting smile'; 'that look of his which was half sexual, half mystic' (both CGT 163); Eugene 'reminded me of a saint's face carved out of grey stone which I saw in the church every Sunday' (CGT 185). A rich and powerful lover in a later story also has a 'graven' face.[19] A scene in 'The Love Object' intriguingly merges the abject – a lover's semen on the woman's body – with food and a displaced masochistic allusion: 'She was thinking of egg white in its various stages of being whipped' (AFH 89). O'Brien recurrently stages the sexual relationship of such an older, wealthier, dominant male character with a young, uncertain, and emotionally abject female one. (These disparities are often further encoded in terms of differences of class or of nationality, where the woman's rural Irishness is an important aspect of her subordinate status). The man's aesthetic disdain, claim to superior rationality and education (CGT 323), his sarcasm, and the woman's over-abundant physicality ('the literary fat girl' [CGT 184], 'your fat bottom' [CGT 242]) and her untidiness and seeming lack of capacity for order, recapitulate the abasement of the needy lover, her emptiness and abjection, before the absolute fullness of the lofty beloved (who denigrates the heroine as 'bred in Stone Age ignorance and religious savagery' [CGT 344-5]). Such clear traces of masochistic affect appear in all the rehearsals of love-affairs: the lofty, super-rational, scornful and controlling – in a word, sadistic – character of all the love objects:[20] the unreachable Godlike figures who supply, well to excess, the deficit of paternal authority in the original family of the typical O'Brien female protagonist. This is an inescapable structure. When, in 'The Love Object', the lover 'happened to say that he had *a slight trace* of masochism' (emphasis added: the elaborate casualness itself signals unease), the woman promptly reverses their roles (the phrase used) in love-making and asserts: 'He was not my father. I became his mother' (*FH* 152). In this story, whose title pointedly and sardonically invokes Freudian discourse, O'Brien is consciously playing with the psychoanalytic binaries. It is as if there were only two options, according to which a woman's male sexual partner must perform as either her father or her son, confirming Freud's melancholy observation that human love is out of phase, and also unsettlingly reinscribing the scene of adult sexuality as a mere replaying of childhood's gendered antinomies.

O'Brien's work recalls not just the Kristevan abject, but its distant part-ancestor, the syndrome of the Christian mystic, abasing her/himself before a God impossibly distant and frequently unresponsive: *Deus quia deus absconditus est.* In these writings the self-humbling devotee (whose gender can vary, a Juan de la Cruz or a Teresa) prostrates herself before the distant and unimaginably perfect God-figure who shows His love by making His servant suffer. Kristeva discusses such 'borderline subjects' who, she says, provide propitious ground for a sublimating discourse, aesthetic, or mystical rather than scientific or rationalist (5, 7, 207). At the start I cited Boyle's image of a self-abasing Christ who 'from the height of Glory ... sunk Himself to the bottom of Abjectedness, to exalt our condition to the contrary extreme' to serve as a reminder of the role of self-prostration in this intense mystical erotic.

Taking up another strand in Kristeva's argument, I turn, finally, to the mother-daughter bond as represented in O'Brien's work. As is evident to all readers, the theme of mother-child relations is central to her vision, and this has an obvious relevance to the potential of abjection as an interpretative approach.[21] I approach the mother-daughter relationship in the texts' narration of it as a willed intersubjective connection which is part of conscious emotional experience, not only as an impersonal tension of unconscious drives involving the infant's impulsion towards, or perhaps expulsion into, subjectivity. It is the most intense form of attachment which the texts focus on, far deeper, more wrenching, and occasionally more ecstatic than specifically sexual woman-to-man connections. Sharply conflicted, it involves opposite imperatives: in one direction to escape, to form, and free the separate self and disavow the maternal other, and in the other to remain attached, to resist at all costs the process of detachment from and relinquishing of the mother, and indeed to long for total (re)union with her. This longing is exceptionally strong in the universe of O'Brien's fictions, and I see it as an instance of that desire for fusion with the other, overriding the aim of individuation and precluding the allegedly appropriate abjection of the maternal, which Kristeva describes. Profound and fierce feeling attends this represented relationship: in text after text it is revisited in only slightly altered forms. In *The Country Girls*, first volume of the trilogy (as it was to become), the mother as a character is physically abjected very early on, dying by drowning (a death many times invoked, sometimes narrowly escaped, by characters in O'Brien's fictions), but never really emotionally relinquished. In later texts, long and short, the mother is permitted to live on into the adulthood of the female protagonist and the business of abjecting her remains to be transacted painfully, sometimes bitterly, with resentment and remorse.

This key and originary instance of self-other attachment is a whole wider topic in itself, with implications for O'Brien's representations of Irishness; I consider it here only from the specific perspective of abjection, though with the potential quality of profound meaning which the Kristeva-Douglas theories seek to explore. To use Freud's terms, this is not object-love but identificatory attachment. Indeed, the attachment represented in several of the texts seems almost literally identification, a fusing with or felt return to the one (mother's) body. 'A Rose in the Heart of New York' (1978) is an especially clear example:

> Her mother's knuckles were her knuckles, her mother's veins were her veins … her mother's body was a recess that she would deepen … she would simply wave from that safe place, she would not budge … They slept side by side, entwined like twigs of trees or the ends of the sugar tongs … (*FH* 380)

Later, the narrator recalls herself 'trembling' when her mother goes 'to her father's bedroom for a tick, to stop him bucking' (*FH* 385); and '[a]t the beginning of sleep and at the precise moment of waking, it was of her mother and for her mother that she existed' (387).[22] Later in the story, however, she is sent away to school and, piqued, replaces the mother 'with a new idol: a nun' (389). This is the hinge of the story, and after that it is a case of increasing distance, ending with the savage resentment and estrangement of the adult daughter whose own marriage has now failed. For her part, after a lifetime of abuse from a drunken husband, the mother disbelieves in love between the sexes:

> there was only one kind of love and that was a mother's love for her child … There passed between them a moment … dense with hate (399).

The daughter returns to the family house only for her mother's funeral, and the story ends like this:

> Their life together and all those exchanges were like so many spilt feelings, and she looked to see some sign or hear some murmur. Instead, a silence filled the room, and there was a vaster silence beyond, as if the house itself had died or had been carefully put down to sleep (404).

In this fine but desolating passage, the very fact of the relationship itself seems abjected – 'spilt' – from a world devoid of any 'sign' of possible renewal. Against the apprehension of 'a vaster silence beyond', the concluding phrase heartbreakingly recalls, but only in metaphor, the quintessential gesture of nurturance and maternal love of an infant 'carefully put down to sleep'.

A discussion of abjection and laughter in O'Brien would also yield dividends, though it is beyond the scope of this essay. Her texts produce vividly comic moments from contexts often involving the loss of control or of balance, which defy or transgress the proprieties. These moments commonly have a Rabelaisian character: this is true, for instance, of the scene where Kate's mother gets off her bicycle to pee in the ditch, at which point a strange man comes unexpectedly on the scene and collides with her, inadvertently thrusting his front wheel between her legs. This strand of humour is associated especially with Baba, Kate's alter ego in the trilogy who combines a malicious, manipulative streak with a spirit of reckless, joyful transgression, and performs as comic mask to Kate's tragic one.

Finally, what of the question of agency, the last word in my title? The relentless marketing of O'Brien as a risqué writer about sex, a kind of incarnate Molly Bloom, is a distraction.[23] So is the (closely related) presentation of her as a figure who with difficulty freed herself from a benighted, brutish, backward, and oppressive Ireland, to inhabit advanced, liberal, modern, and enlightened England. The real struggle in the trilogy, and indeed in the work as a whole, is not between, on the one hand, re-pression, regulation, the alcoholic failed father, prudery, co-ercive virginity, the Irish countryside as a cultural and emotional nowhere, and, on the other, urban modernity, relative anonymity, apparent freedom, and sexual opportunity. It is between the different forms of alienation represented by *each* of these opposites, which are both still under the Law of the Father, and the possibility for a woman of autonomy, the right to attempt self-completion, and the capacity to play out one's life for oneself, to seek love and recognition: in a word, agency. Kate Brady is not less, merely differently, regulated and abject in her Dublin or London lives than in the west of Ireland, and she has escaped one controlling father-figure only to find another.

After she first has sex with Eugene Gaillard, she feels 'no pleasure, only some strange satisfaction that I had done what I was born to do' (*CGT* 316), and on the next page we find her longing for her mother's nurturing love (recalled in the small caring gesture of blowing on the child's soup to cool it). At the story level, Kate Brady never sheds guilt, self-reproach, the sense of sinfulness and moral inadequacy, the judgement of herself as bad mother, and, above all, her emotional abjection. That procession of female characters who people O'Brien's fictions, with Kate at their head, are all more or less examples of what Kristeva calls a '*de*ject': one of those 'borderline personalities' who dwell in abjection (8).[24] But, as I have earlier argued about Jean Rhys, their author can nevertheless on occasion attain the sublime on their behalf, and the reader can recognize and experience this at the higher level of fictional discourse. The very expertise of these characters in crisis experiences, in doing without stable boundaries, can make them vessels for forms of vision which creatively unfix and decentre the symbolic order. Sometimes the characters themselves are given access to that vision and the power to express it, though characteristically in melancholy vein. It is at such moments of vision that O'Brien is at her most Proustian, most a classical definer of loss, of always-and-never relinquishing, never completely abjecting, the desired object (or its predecessor or its anticipated successor), and most aware of the profoundly symbolic character of all our desires. I conclude with some instances:

> I went alone to the nearest restaurant ... thinking how lucky I was to be my own mistress, to be saved the terrible inclination of wanting to possess while being possessed, of being separated from myself while being host to another ('The Return' [1981], *FH* 459).

> I did not care. Only one thing was uppermost in me and it was flight, and in my fancies I had no idea that no matter how distant the flight or how high I soared, those people were entrenched in me ('The Bachelor' [1982], *FH* 69).

> I thought how untoward his gloom was and how his melancholy had cut him off from others. In him I saw a glimpse of my future exiled self ('The Bachelor' 72).

Sitting there, I wanted to be both in our house and to be back in my grandmother's missing my mother. It was as if I could taste my pain better away from her, the excruciating pain that told me how much I loved her I thought how much I needed to be without her so that I could think of her, dwell on her, and fashion her into the perfect person that she clearly was not. ('My Mother's Mother' [1982], *FH* 32)

At that moment I realized that by choosing his world I had said goodbye to my own and to those in it. By such choices we gradually become exiles, until at last we are quite alone ('The Connor Girls' [1981], *FH* 16).

Ultimately, we need to remind ourselves that Edna O'Brien, writer, is more and other than the sum of all her protagonists. We have seen how her fictions dedicatedly, even obsessively, rehearse loss and abjection in all the meanings we have explored: but it is the *heroines* who lack, and struggle for, agency, and who over and over again realize their states of abjection, and the acts of abjecting which have produced those states. The *author* must be distinguished from them, by the very fact that she attains agency in the act of imagining and writing them. She has thus entered fully into the symbolic, that place of symbol-making so heavily coded masculine in the culture which produced her and in the psychoanalytic narrative. In that virtual realm of the aesthetic, which endlessly returns to the originary instances of suffering and loss, she stages abjection, darkly, with desperate humour, unevenly to be sure but with persistent insight and beauty. And in her most effective texts, she thereby transforms and transcends it. As Kristeva puts it:

[D]iscourse will seem tenable only if it ceaselessly confronts that otherness, a burden both repellent and repelled, a deep well of memory that is unapproachable and intimate: the abject (6).

Works Cited

Bataille, Georges. *Oeuvres complètes II: Écrits posthumes 1922-1940* (Paris: Gallimard, 1970).

Benjamin, Jessica. *The Bonds of Love: Psychoanalysis, Feminism, and the Problem of Domination* (New York: Pantheon, 1988).

Benvenuto, Bice and Roger Kennedy. *The Works of Jacques Lacan* (London: Free Association Books, 1986).

Bois, Yve-Alain and Rosalind E.W. Krauss. 'The Destiny of the *Informé*. *Formless: A User's Guide* (New York: Zone Books, 1997).

Carriker, Kitti. 'Edna O'Brien's "The Doll": A Narrative of Abjection'. *Notes on Modern Irish Literature* 1 (1989): 6-13.

Chanter, Tina. 'Viewing Abjection: Film and Social Justice'. http://www.orlando.women.it/cyberarchive/files/chanter.htm [accessed 15 April 2005].

Coats, Karen. 'Abjection and Adolescent Fiction'. *Journal for the Psychoanalysis of Culture and Society* 5.2 (1999): 290-300.

Douglas, Mary. *Purity and Danger: An Analysis of the Concepts of Pollution and Taboo* (London: Routledge and Kegan Paul, 1966).

Foster, Hal. *The Return of the Real: The Avant-Garde at the End of the Century* (New York: October Books, 1996).

Jacobus, Mary. *First Things: The Maternal Imaginary in Literature, Art, and Psychoanalysis* (New York and London: Routledge, 1995).

Joyce, James. *A Portrait of the Artist as a Young Man: Text, Criticism, and Notes*, ed. Chester G. Anderson (New York: Viking, 1968).

Kristeva, Julia. *Powers of Horror: An Essay on Abjection*. Trans. Leon S. Roudiez (New York: Columbia University Press, 1982).

O'Brien, Edna. *August Is a Wicked Month* (London: Penguin, 1987).

--- *The Country Girls Trilogy* (London: Penguin, 1988).

--- *Down by the River* (London: Phoenix, 1996).

--- *A Fanatic Heart: Selected Stories* (Harmondsworth: Penguin, 1984).

Oliver, Kelly, ed. *The Portable Kristeva* (New York: Columbia University Press, 1993).

Rooks-Hughes, Lorna. 'The Family and the Female Body in the Novels of Edna O'Brien and Julia O'Faoláin'. *Canadian Journal of Irish Studies* 22. 2 (1996): 83-97.

Shildrick, Margrit. *Leaky Bodies and Boundaries: Feminism, Postmodernism and (Bio)ethics* (London: Routledge, 1997).

Smith, A. 'Kristeva, Sherman, Butler and the Abject'. www.http://english.cla.umn.edu/alumni/asmith/Sherm4.htm [accessed 30 March 2005].

Stone, Jennifer. 'The Horrors of Power: A Critique of Kristeva'. *The Politics of Theory*, ed. Francis Barker, et al. (Colchester: University of Essex, 1983), 38-48.

---

[1] See p.165 for definition of the noun 'abjection'.

[2] Despite the currency of the notion of abjection in the fields of literary and feminist theory, there has been surprisingly little exploration of this as an interpretative strategy within O'Brien criticism, but see Carriker, which deals with one 1979 story, and Rooks-Hughes.

[3] See also *CGT*, when Kate, asked at a London party where she is from, thinks of a landscape wholly turned towards death, abject: 'Ireland, she said. The west of Ireland. But did not give any echo of the *swamp* fields, the dun *treeless* bogs, the *dead deserted* miles of country with a gray *ruin* on the horizon: the places from which she derived her sense of *doom*' (emphasis added), p.494.

[4] In what follows, apart from Kristeva's own writings I have drawn on discussions of the conceptual field of abjection by Jacobus; Oliver, especially pp.225-7; Chanter; and Coats.

[5] See for instance Shildrick and Benjamin.

[6] If the ego forms *o*bjects of desire, the superego forms *a*bjects: 'To each ego its object, to each superego its abject' (Kristeva 2).

[7] The original longing for the mother, if it has not been relinquished, is allegedly a nostalgic one, turned towards death (Kristeva 112).

[8] See Benvenuto and Kennedy, p.121. In literature, this pattern of repeated deferral is characteristic both of Proust, who influenced O'Brien, and of her own fiction.

[9] Thus when Kate visits the psychiatrist she 'resented telling about her marriage. It not only violated her sense of privacy, it left her empty. Life after all was a secret with the self. The more one gave out the less there remained for the centre – that centre which she coveted for herself and recognized instantly in others' (*CGT* 475). One can only covet what one does not possess: Kate in her desolation has abjected her own subjectivity.

[10] See Coats, pp.2-3. Freud famously argued in *Civilization and its Discontents* (1931) that civilization is founded on such exclusions. In Kristeva's view 'identities, communities, and nations' are 'permanently brittle' constructs because they are 'built on abjection, which haunts their borders' (13; and see Oliver, pp.225-6).

[11] While discussing film, Chanter might almost be describing O'Brien's writing when she writes that '[f]rom beneath the unbroken surface of skilful verbalization the outburst of abjection ... calls for

interpretation'.

[12] Here I also draw on Smith.

[13] This discussion makes an illuminating distinction between abject and *informé*.

[14] Chanter's remark that Kristeva 'does not have uncomplicated liberatory potential' might be applied to O'Brien also.

[15] Jacobus argues that 'abjection shifts the emphasis from an oedipalized matriphobia associated with castration anxiety toward the earliest processes of subject formation', p.99.

[16] It may be significant that Douglas's own world-view, like O'Brien's, was formed within Catholicism. I thank Éamonn Ó Carragáin for this observation.

[17] See passages such as the following, which either associate or identify Kate metonymically with Ireland: 'I could hear the bulrushes sighing when he said my name that way, and I could hear the curlew too, and all the lonesome sounds of Ireland.' (*CGT* 163).

[18] Romance's near relative, Victorian melodrama, figures at story level in the trilogy, where Kate and Baba are attending the performance of a classic example, *East Lynne*, when Kate is called out to be told of her mother's death (*CGT* 39).

[19] There is also 'the priest with the soft eyes and the austere, Christ-like, disciplined hands', and the heroine herself reflects how she desires 'being with a certain kind of man that controlled and bewitched her' (*AWM* 72, 81).

[20] Shirley Peterson's essay in this volume offers a thorough analysis of the sado-masochistic dynamics that characterize all relationships depicted in O'Brien's early fiction.

[21] One, the more extensive and in general the earlier preoccupation, is the mother-daughter relationship, which is closely bound up with O'Brien's representation of Irish identity and being; in this discussion I focus more on this than on the other, mother-son bond.

[22] The vocabulary combines the childish ('tick') and the bestial ('bucking'), a term both for animal high spirits and, in Hiberno-English, for rage, which economically indicates the abusive character of the marriage: the effect of the whole is to disavow and sideline the parents' sexual life in favour of the mother's and daughter's life together. The scene is Oedipal, or would be if the daughter was a son, but the tone of dark emotional intensity contrasts sharply with that which Frank O'Connor devises for his child-narrator in the genially humorous story, 'My Oedipus Complex' (1950).

---

[23] Rebecca Pelan's essay in this volume very effectively charts the construction of this figure by the publishing industry and the media in Britain and the United States.

[24] The resilience of Baba is, of course, an important counter-weight, also at story level, to Kate's emotional abjection and self-abnegation: in this connection O'Brien's alteration of the original ending of *Girls in Their Married Bliss* (1964) for the 1988 publication of the trilogy as one volume is highly significant: Kate's suicide by drowning would seem to tilt the balance decisively towards the abject and turn the whole towards death.

11 | 'Sacramental Sleeves': Fashioning the Female Subject in the Fiction of Edna O'Brien

Sinéad Mooney

> It is the only time that I am thankful for being a woman, that time of evening when I draw the curtains, take off my old clothes, and prepare to go out. …. I shadow my eyelids with black stuff and am astonished by the look of mystery it gives my eyes. I hate being a woman. Vain and shallow and superficial.
> Edna O'Brien, *The Country Girls*

> An unsuccessful appearance is more than a pity; it is a pathological document.
> Elizabeth Bowen, 'Dress'

Edna O'Brien's writing has always been interested in the ways in which female bodies are classified, disciplined, invaded, destroyed, altered, decorated, and pleasured. Her writing since 1960 systematically explores the condition of women as embodied subjects, specifically the ways in which western society disciplines women's bodies within a heterosexual economy, and the extent to which women may accept or contest this. Juxtaposed with this, however, is a continual quasi-Swiftian presentation of the carnality of bodies in terms which, in their insistent dwelling on 'filth', decay, contamination, and waste, appear to ignore or actively transgress the norms of the basic hygiene of socialization and acculturation, and suggest a recurring anxiety over that most basic of boundaries, that between the I and the not-I. In this, her writing as a whole is strikingly suggestive of Julia Kristeva's theorization of abjection, a relationship which is explored in detail by Patricia Coughlan's 'Killing the Bats' in this volume. The present essay, however, is primarily concerned with O'Brien's preoccupation with dress, which, itself ambivalent and undecidable, foregrounds precisely the difficulty of establishing the body's boundaries, that topic of so much moment to O'Brien's heroines, who frequently take the body as synonym for the self.

Mary Salmon, in a 1990 essay on O'Brien, notes that '[c]lothes as a metaphor for identity recur in all the novels and stories' (143). As will be argued below, psychoanalytic readings of clothing suggest that dress both promises to complete the gapped and lacking self by constructing or framing the body, thereby reinforcing its precarious limits, and also, paradoxically, complicates and blurs the body's edges. My specific aim here is to examine the politics of feminine adornment in O'Brien's writing, in which female protagonists often appear alienated from their own flesh, mere decorative apparatuses constructed out of fabric, or, more rarely, manage to achieve a kind of transient rapture through re-presenting their flesh within a covering of signifying fabric. Clothing is thus frequently presented in terms of a quasi-religious rhetoric, as in the dress with 'sacramental sleeves' worn by Willa in *Casualties of Peace* (138).

There may seem something inherently problematic in aiming to read an author whose writing has too often suffered from being seen in the most superficial terms through the lens of a discourse generally deemed superficial, a surface show, or a cover for a nakedness deemed 'authentic'. Feminist suspicion of fashion has a long history, a distrust which had as its chief motivation the ways in which it reinforces the sexual objectification of women, its association with conspicuous consumption, and its positioning of women as economic chattels.

In part, it is the various debates on postmodernism, as well as cognate reconsiderations of pastiche and eclecticism, that have aided a new interest in dress by enabling a climate in which any cultural or aesthetic object may be subject to serious consideration. Also relevant to any consideration of clothes in O'Brien is the sheer tenacity of the essentialist alignment of masculinity with 'high culture' and femininity with the low, popular, or vulgar; dress is not, I would argue, irrelevant to the frequent relegation of O'Brien to the realm of the lightweight. O'Brien's narratives are crowded with exactly-described items of clothing which are, in their 'un-literary' detail, certainly more reminiscent of the popular romance than the literary novel.[1]

Angela Carter, in an exuberantly hostile 1970 essay on the fetishization of women's clothing in D.H. Lawrence's *Women in Love*, certainly considers the detailed depiction of clothing by O'Brien to be a symptom of false consciousness. She derides her along with Jean Rhys as 'women writers who … pretend to be female impersonators', in what she deems their fictional sponsorship of a trivial and inauthentic surface version of femininity (499). The ascription of triviality to dress derives of course from the frequently misogynistic dualistic tradition within Western thought by which clothing, as opposed to the natural body, is associated with earthly vanity, feminine duplicity, and humanity's 'fallen' state. More recent contemporary writing on dress would argue that clothing is the material with which a representation of the body is inscribed onto a particular cultural context, so that dress produces the individual as social being. As Kaja Silverman notes:

> Clothing and other kinds of ornamentation make the human body culturally visible …, draw[s] the body so that it can be culturally seen, and articulates it in meaningful form.

Clothing, for Silverman, is in fact 'a necessary condition of subjectivity', in that 'articulating the body it simultaneously articulates the psyche' (145). In this, contemporary theories of dress bear out writers on the body such as Elizabeth Grosz, who writes of the body as a form of 'hinge' or threshold between a psychic or lived interiority and a more sociological exteriority that produces interiority through the *inscription* of the body's outer surface (33).

That the identities supplied by clothes are provisional and fictional, yet necessary in enabling a transformation of the chaotic body into a semblance of plenitude, is recognized by Edna O'Brien's fiction; her protagonists button themselves into some tenuous form of selfhood.

Ann Hollander's classic *Seeing Through Clothes* (1975) is chiefly concerned, in terms of its specifically literary analysis, with the nineteenth-century realist novel, its rich costume drama, and its linkage of clothing to social context (447). More recent studies, such as Alexandra Warwick and Dani Cavallaro's *Fashioning the Frame: Boundaries, Dress and the Body* (1998), analyse a more ambiguous relationship between dress and the body. Psycho-analysis proposes a number of relations between psychical structures and the perception or representation of the body. Warwick and Cavallaro argue that, in Lacanian terms, dress operates as a kind of 'rim', which, by virtue of being simul-taneously both 'inside' and 'outside' the body, problematizes the notion of the boundary, that all-important ideological and psychological structure designed to individuate and demarcate the self from the non-self, the same from the foreign (xv-xvi). In *Adorned in Dreams*, Elizabeth Wilson amplifies this in terms of thought emanating from Mary Douglas's *Purity and Danger* (1966):

> Clothing marks an unclear boundary ambiguously, and unclear boundaries disturb us; symbolic systems and rituals have been created in many different cultures in order to strengthen and reinforce boundaries. Since these safeguard purity, it is at the margins between one thing and another that pollution may leak out (2-3).

If individual and cultural identities rely on clear boundaries between 'me' and 'not-me', 'without' and 'within', then dress, in challenging the margin or edge of the body, threatens a dangerous or suggestive fluidity.

Dress both frames and contains the body, delimiting the individual and producing the quality of individuality, yet it also, paradoxically, elides the individual into a communal pheno- menon, connecting it to 'the collective Other and fashion[ing individual] fantasies on the model of a public spectacle, thus questioning the myth of a self-contained identity' (Warwick and Cavallaro xvi). This simultaneous articulation and elision of individuality can be viewed as either the contamination of the self by an external Other, or, alternatively, as a dissemination by which the dressed body disperses itself into the external world. Dress, therefore, is typically both a personal and communal phenomenon, both distinguishing and de-individualizing the wearer. Moreover, clothing, as an aspect of culture, is a crucial feature in the production of masculinity and femininity. As Daniel Roche argues in *The Culture of Clothing*, dress 'turns nature into culture, layering cultural meanings upon the body' (143-4).

While gender distinctions drawn by clothes are arbitrary, they are generally fundamental to 'common sense' readings of bodies, so that, in this respect, dress also turns culture into nature, by *naturalizing* an arbitrary cultural order. O'Brien's writing demonstrates a sharp awareness of this arbitrariness, particularly its deployment of drag performances as a means of highlighting the constructed and performed nature of 'femininity', performances which are often juxtaposed with the painful realities of the embodied female subject.[2] Indeed, Maureen O'Connor's 'Edna O'Brien, Irish Dandy' in this volume argues for a drag-informed reading of O'Brien's autho- rial persona, suggesting that the 'Connemara Dietrich' should be regarded in the tradition of Irish dandyism's play with dress and mannerism as social critique. If O'Brien can in fact be viewed as in some sense a 'female impersonator', it is only in the sense that her work is conscious of *femininity* as a specific or exacerbated instance of the performance of identity in general. The conventional, decorative accoutrements of femininity – clothing, cosmetics, perfume – in O'Brien's fiction, rather than

any intrinsic quality, constitute sexual identity; surface determines character.

O'Brien's fiction, I want to argue, in shaping significant
elements of its meaning through clothing, underscores themes
of suffocation, negation, and entrapment, in haunting rehearsals
of the removal of women from family romance and suffocating
rurality to the alienated processes of the modern city. In that
her protagonists in either place remain subject to the constraints of the heterosexual economy and cultural forces acting
in the interests of masculinity, O'Brien performs an analysis of
alienated female bodies as hostages to the scopic regimes they
inhabit, via the whole cultural apparatus of a policed
'femininity'. Her subjects are, variously, Foucauldian 'docile'
bodies, passively subjected to the operations of power, or, in
ways more reminiscent of later Foucault, participants in
'technologies of the self' which allow for active self-fashioning
but within culturally defined limits. Unclothed, they appear not
to exist, risking reversion to the shapeless and abject which
continually threaten the precarious female selves of O'Brien's
fiction; her women seem to achieve a form of muted interiority
only through subjection to discipline and surveillance, or from
the management and scrutiny of their own surfaces. In an *oeuvre*
which takes as its main theme the compromised nature of
female subjectivity, dress, if considered as a 'representative
trifle' is extremely significant, in that it represents the body as a
fundamentally liminal phenomenon, precariously located between the physical and abstract, symbolic and imaginary. Dress
in O'Brien is both decarnalizing, in that it covers up the *improper*
aspects of bodily existence, yet also articulates imaginary
yearnings that defy symbolic orderliness.

There is a certain logic to beginning a survey of dress in
O'Brien with a moment of nakedness. Mary Hooligan, heroine
of *Night*, unwillingly posing as a life model – 'like a polyp
without my robes and my decoys' (72) – for an evening art
class, offers a significant point of entry, suggesting at once
O'Brien's pointed examination of the life class as aesthetic

endorsement of patriarchal power, and her subversion of a
pervasive cultural myth. As Lynda Nead has argued, '[m]ore
than any other subject, the female nude connotes "Art"' (1).
The naked female model, as a cultural commodity, highly
formalized and conventionalized, functions specifically as a sign
of the male artist's authority and stature. She signals also the
various ways in which examining the female body internally and
externally, in medicine and art, represent instances of the
thorough surveillance of femininity, and the regulation of the
female body through the definitions of norms of health and
beauty which is a continual preoccupation in O'Brien's work.
Mary Hooligan, vulnerably parted from her clothing and
displayed 'lotus wise' on a tea-chest, wondering 'what sort of
spectacle I presented, face blazing, muscles fibulating, skin
white and knees a deep purple' and longing for the reassurance
of her mirror (74), typifies O'Brien's heroines as continually
surveying themselves in terms of the gaze or judgement of a
monitoring, panoptical masculinity interiorized as a dominant
value.

However, *Night*'s life-class will not allow the female nude to
remain as the utmost expression of contained form, nature
'clothed' in art, to use Kenneth Clarke's formulation. It is one
of the many instances in O'Brien's fiction which suggest Julia
Kristeva's statement that 'the subject will always be marked by
the uncertainty of its borders' (63). The scene teems with
anxieties about boundaries and subjecthood, thematized
through dress and its absence. Undressed, O'Brien's women are
subject to the scopophilic gaze that threatens to return them to
base matter, alarmingly unstructured, fluid, and undifferen-
tiated, dissolving. Significantly, when undressed, Mary does not
reveal some form of naked 'authenticity' but is rather a 'polyp',
an octopus or cuttle-fish, suggesting both a time-hallowed
symbol of (feminine) changeability, and also an animality or
monstrosity suggesting a reversion to a more primitive form of
life. (The fact that this threatening shapelessness and animality
is linked to her damply threatening rural Irish home place is
also significant.)

Later in the novel, the nakedness of Mary and one of her lovers is represented in terms of a frightening reversion to the pre-Symbolic: they are '[n]o longer like people, but bits of meat, uncooked, flinching, and still infants betimes looking for some little balsam, a crumb, the gob-stopping tit' (86). Harangued by the teacher for concentrating on drawing Mary's 'outer edges' and 'sacrosanct' perimeter, the art students are instructed to 'internalize' her, while Mary is repeatedly ordered to '[g]et that arse open, get those hams out', as the gaze of the 'Michelangelos' becomes increasingly voyeuristic (74). She ceases to be a nude, and becomes merely naked, a body qua body troublingly lacking containment, a nexus of faltering out-lines and broken surfaces, assaulted by sudden memories of 'senna and the brews that Lil used to give us on Saturday night to be cleansed within and without for the Sabbath day' (74).

This involuntary memory of excrement and its purgation, and the odd description of Mary's naked body as 'fibulating', an archaism meaning 'to perform the act of buttoning and un-buttoning' (OED), suggest the incompletion of the abjection process and the threatening re-emergence of all that was meant to have been excluded by the formation of subjectivity. Mary is alarmed at the proximity of the world of matter and the body, with its alarmingly porous contours, which she attempts to seal with clothes, which hence have a form of almost 'sacramental' power in O'Brien. As there is no semiotically innocent and un-mediated body, no unadulterated and self-identical com-munion with an 'authentic' body beneath the 'disguise' of clothing, O'Brien's heroines typically embrace instead the necessary sartorial 'disguise', thereby interrogating the con-ventional surface-depth relationship. Part of the capacity of O'Brien's writing to disturb comes from its presentation of the female body as a surface which can be endlessly modified or transformed to the extent that there appears to be no 'natural' body at all, merely the presentation of the self, its 'robes and decoys', as what Angela Carter calls 'a three-dimensional art object' (106).

Of course, the body, whether naked or dressed, can never be approached as a purely natural entity, operating as it does as a constant in the formation of cultural mythologies. Given its inevitable ideological conscription, its representations are always incarnations of belief systems, bearing witness to social validation of some beliefs and stigmatising others. Dress participates in the processes of cultural mythologization and legitimization, particularly, in O'Brien's writing, in the linked cultural processes of Catholicism and Irish nationalism. In the case of the modern Irish state, the masculine body politic constructs itself as homogenous nation-state by founding itself upon establishing certain norms of gender as 'natural', as Heather Ingman and others have shown in relation to O'Brien's writing and its perennial fascination with the pervasive figures of Cathleen Ní Houlihain, Mother Ireland, and their cognate figure, that of the Virgin Mary. The female body and its policed purity act as conscripted guarantors for the integrity of the Irish (Catholic) nation state and, as such, strongly suggest Mary Douglas's linkage of the body's boundaries to the operation of other social and cultural boundaries, and hence bodily transgression to social deviation. O'Brien's most trenchant instance is in her X-case 'faction' *Down by the River* (1996), in which a Supreme Court judge – 'a character personified by the spill of the gown or the angle of a coiffed wig', ritual clothing showing 'the whole paraphernalia of the law in motion' – describes the breaking scandal of the incestuously-raped teenager as 'some little slut about to pour piss on the nation's breast' (6, 190). Dress, in being instrumental to collective orchestration of cultural experience through its ability to mould the body into obedience to certain culturally-specific definitions of reality, renders the body docile.

In many ways, *The Country Girls* is typical of Edna O'Brien's female *Bildungsromane* in tracing the processes of the socialization and acculturation of the female body and psyche via apparel.[3] The punitive uniforms of the various O'Brien convents are typically Foucauldian, representing a secular version of the all-enveloping nun's habit with its signals of submission to supernatural power, and its positioning of the body as vessel of spirituality: uniformed nuns 'sealed inside their garments, are not women' but are marked as nonsexual (*DR* 37). Uniform, according to Foucault's analysis of surveillance and the nineteenth-century growth of uniforms in *Discipline and Punish*, nullifies the subject and prevents the establishment of an identity; like the criminal or pauper, the right to individuality has been removed and the individual enrolled in the dominant discourse of propriety, morality, and appropriate gender. Similarly, the quasi-military yard drill endured by the schoolgirls in *The Country Girls* suggests the subordination of the female body to the Foucauldian notion of the 'docile' institutionalized body enacting its 'representation' of efficiency and order, subjected to the policing of Catholic doctrine. That this drill is followed by a reading from the life of Teresa of Avila who, working in a laundry, 'let the soap spatter into her eyes as an act of mortification' (*CG* 73), suggests a set of parallels with that other female group subjected to the discipline of the nuns for their physical transgressions, the 'fallen women' for whom 'sin in a field' brings 'the long awful spell in the Magdalen laundry scrubbing it out' (*AWM* 27). However, the failure of the underwear and stockings to entirely cover the skin during drill in *The Country Girls* – the emergence of 'that space where their black stocking tops ended which the legs of their knickers did not cover' (65) – signals the recalcitrance of the body, which can never be entirely subdued.

On the other hand, the hint of sexual voyeurism or fetishism in the description of the fissure between the different bodily coverings which give the female body the gloss of propriety should alert us to the fact that the use of dress as an instrument of social subjugation is not restricted to the religious or educational realm; nor is there any kind of simple opposition between uniform and self-expression. *The Lonely Girl*, for instance, makes it explicit that the 'schoolgirl' can be differently read as sexually titillating, by the introduction of a cosmetics salesman whose car is painted all over with the slogan: 'GIVE HER PINK SATIN, LOVELY PINK SATIN FOR THAT

SCHOOLGIRL BLOOM' (180). Dress can render the body docile through enforced *required* clothing, but also through self-selected dress; non-uniform clothes simply make the body and the self *differently* subject to surveillance, differently docile. (The instance pointed to by dress historians is frequently the abolition of uniforms in women's prisons to promote 'appropriate' femininity and an acceptably heterosexual culture [Ash and Wilson 10]). Instances in O'Brien are multiple, noticeably in the continual alignment in various texts of the town dressmaker, who 'knew when girls were in trouble, even before they knew it themselves' (*CG* 112), with an all-seeing law and religion.

On her first holidays from the convent, Caithleen in *The Country Girls* begins to be disciplined within the heterosexual economy with the suggestively fairy-tale gift of high-heeled shoes and 'golden nylon stockings': 'I looked in the wardrobe mirror at myself and admired my legs a thousand times. ... I was grown up' (*CG* 86). This adult, newly-sexualized status, which, the narrative stresses, is *produced* by clothing, inaugurates Caithleen's career as an object of the male gaze, subjected to the series of panoptical male connoisseurs which begins with the genteel predator Mr Gentleman: 'You got plump', he said, '... It reminded me of young chickens when they were weighed for market' (*CG* 90). The emphasis on woman as commodified object is evident throughout *The Country Girls* trilogy: Eugene Gaillard says Caithleen has 'a face like the girl on the Irish pound note' (*LG* 187), aligning her both with the object of monetary exchange and with the image of Hazel Lavery as Ireland, in a colleen-like head-shawl, which was in circulation on the Irish pound note from 1928 to 1976. Quite clearly, the subtly coercive equation between O'Brien's protagonists and a feminized icon of Ireland involves another specific form of control.

That O'Brien's female characters exist in a close relationship with the 'colleen' archetype with which their author also plays *in propria persona* is obvious throughout: Jack Holland hails Caithleen, with her 'long coils of auburn hair' and 'innocent

look of a very young girl' as an 'Irish colleen' (*CG* 172, 92), and
the assimilation to various purportedly representative types of
Irish femininity is still continuing as late as *The High Road*
(1988). That the sexual continence of the colleen as a 'proper
body' is crucial to the maintenance of the nation's boundaries
becomes explicit in *The Lonely Girl*, when Eugene Gaillard's
relationship with Caithleen is compared by Jack Holland to a
form of invasion: 'The tragic history of our fair land ... alien
power sapped our will to resist' (*LG* 299), Gaillard's putative
penetration of Caithleen is aligned with the *aisling*. However,
O'Brien exposes the colleen as a male-authored sexual fantasy:
Eugene Gaillard in *The Lonely Girl*, having chosen his colleen
for her naïve charms, anglicizes Caithleen to 'Kate', finding her
name 'too "Kiltartan" for his liking' (*CG* 202), while O'Brien
also underscores the implicitly pornographic quality of the
archetype by having Kate and Baba attend a private showing of
a travel film of Ireland: 'All lies, about dark-haired girls roaming
around Connemara in red petticoats. No wonder they had to
show it in private' (*LG* 182).

Clothes, however, become a strategy of at least partial
resistance for her heroines, who resist being the passive bearers
of Irish national meanings. This is frequently achieved by
escaping into an embrace of metropolitan consumerism, thereby allowing for erosion of social and national genealogies, with
their underlying ontologies of race and belonging. When
Eugene Gaillard derides Caithleen/Kate's new 'red lantern'
earrings as cheap and mass-produced, exclaiming 'Hong Kong!'
as he throws them into the fire, he is dismissing the importance
of the artificial, synthetic, and fake in the Edna O'Brien
heroine's rejection of the restrictions of Irish/rural/Catholic
authenticity (*LG* 227). Failing to find shelter in a group or
collective identity, the national or religious collective gives way
to a new aesthetic understanding of collectivity that attempts to
come to terms with the consumer and productive economy of
capitalism, achieved through an act of dissociation from
traditional identities. *Mother Ireland* sketches a similar arc, as the
'irreplaceable integrity' of the country girl is rejected in favour

of the elaborately performative femininity of the Technicolour showgirl, with her 'slit skirts, suntanned thighs, boleros, sequins, saucy looks' (80). One of the roles played by clothes in O'Brien's fiction, thus, is an embrace of this form of 'cinematic' or plastic femininity as a form of resistance to organic paradigms of nationhood and blood-related collective definitions of ethnicity. Her women fall for predetermined, prepackaged images of fashionable femininity as a way of rejecting blood paradigms of identity.

If at times the female body in Edna O'Brien appears to be perpetually collapsing under its sartorial freight, there are, however, also many instances of 'self-fashioning', offering versions of the body/self which are provisional, manipulable, and hauntingly, even gothically, insecure. One of the most notable tropes in early O'Brien is the many items of female clothing which are borrowed, inherited, second-hand, or makeshift: a few examples will suffice to show a general trend. The protagonist of the Joycean 'Irish Revel' excitedly attending the party to which it emerges she has only been bidden as unpaid help, is allowed to wear a 'black lace dress that had come from America years ago and belonged to no one in particular' (*FH* 178); Caithleen in *The Country Girls* borrows her elderly landlady's antiquated and ill-fitting trousseau night-gown for her own abortive tryst, and is reminded of 'a girl playing Lady Macbeth for the Sacred Heart Players' (*CG* 168) and later, in *The Lonely Girl*, goes to bed with her controlling lover in a borrowed night dress identical to the unworn one her dead mother kept in a trunk in case of a hospital visit (*LG* 234); Kate and Baba, who lend or steal clothes back and forth to an extent that suggests a shared, transferable subjectivity, hire tawdry, ill-fitting formal gowns for a dance, and consider selling their bodies for medical research in order to pay the cost: 'They come and collect you when you're dead and the students put you on a table with no clothes on and take you to pieces' (*LG* 189).

Rather than achieving the seductive dazzle of the showgirls idolized by the protagonist of *Mother Ireland*, clothing in

O'Brien, particularly earlier O'Brien, strongly suggests a make-shift, unowned, or insecure feminine identity, or simply acts as a reminder of the fundamental disunity on which all identity rests. The eloquently ill-assorted 'rubber boots and a feather hat' (*LG* 183) in which Caithleen attends a Dublin wine-tasting may seem a comical sartorial recognition of the incongruity of her rural origins and metropolitan aspirations, via the hybridity or intertextuality of dress, which allows her to be misread as bohemian by male onlookers. However, many of O'Brien's depictions of women's clothes are linked to mourning, death, and corpses. These suggest what Judith Halberstam terms the 'Gothic body' which begins with Mary Shelley's *Frankenstein*, a kind of patchwork entity or piecemeal being, stitched together from fragments and scraps of discourse, challenging the post-Enlightenment notion of the well-balanced organic whole.

Dress may appear to signify primarily symbolic orderliness, in covering up the less seemly elements of corporeality, but, lingering as it does at the borders of selfhood as an apparently unifying system, it concurrently hints at dissolution and break-down. In contrast to the Foucauldian sex manual Eugene Gaillard gives Kate in *The Lonely Girl*, its title, *The Body and Mature Behaviour*,[4] stressing singularity and cohesion, dress in O'Brien appears frequently to reactivate pre-Symbolic fantasies and the free-floating drives of the semiotic. Despite the con-trolling sartorial regimes of institutions, husbands, and lovers in O'Brien, dress retains a penchant for the carnivalesque, a dimension of potentially disruptive semiotic forces suggesting unstructured and unrestrained instinctual gratification. This often takes the form of a haunting by the absent body of the dead mother, whose loss marks the initiation into life and culture and who must be replaced with the substitute love objects found throughout O'Brien: the mother's black ring in *The Country Girls* and the 'imitation crocodile handbag and an imitation fur bolero' of 'A Rose in the Heart of New York' (*FH* 403) represent the missing maternal body as a doubly pivotal site. Combining, as Elizabeth Bronfen argues, the primordial mother who collapses the distinction between self and other, healing the fragmented body and source of hope for wholeness, with the castrated mother who is 'midwife of individuation', source of disillusion, loss, and lack (33), the mother both heals and reaffirms the split female subject. As she must be abjected for acculturation to take place, the haunting mother makes her presence felt sartorially, via the reirruption of fluids suggesting abjected matter, as when the white kid gloves, inherited from her dead mother, which Caithleen plans to wear on her trip to Vienna with her lover, are marked with mould (*CG* 172).

Other moments in several of O'Brien's novels and short stories depict a wardrobe opening eerily 'as if there were a ghost in it' (*LG* 358), inviting the contemplation of that quasi-Gothic constant, clothes without people.[5] Various clothes historians have written on the popularity in art of the depiction of empty garments indicating the presence of the absent body, and the investment of these images in pain and dismemberment. One of the effects of the emphasis on dress and self-adornment in O'Brien is the erasure or effacement of the body beneath this 'mask', the odd absence that is the female body without its 'robes and ... decoys' (*Night* 72). Clothing transmits its qualities to other surfaces, flattening out or emptying out that which is inside or within, rendering it merely one more link in the signifying chain. One of the most quietly chilling sartorial effects achieved by O'Brien is when Kate in *Girls in Their Married Bliss*, numb and solitary after the end of her marriage, notes that her clothes are lined up permanently 'pristine ... like clothes waiting for an outing' (488). Thus external appearances are represented as more constitutive of personal identity than the apparently interior aspects of the self, suggesting a kind of 'possession' by appearances: a denial of substantive presence beyond a profoundly unstable continuum of surface effects (Spooner 7).

This interest in empty clothes is not of course unique to O'Brien, but is remarkable in its investiture with the qualities of the uncanny in her work. Clothing is frequently explicitly linked to the Gothic in O'Brien: some of these dresses, or moments of self-decoration, are painfully eloquent on the subject of lack.

The heroine of 'Paradise' looks at her lover's Gothic gift of a dress, 'laid out on the bed, its wide white sleeves hanging down at either side ... uncannily like a corpse' (*LO* 187); the protagonist of 'Baby Blue' in *Mrs Reinhardt and Other Stories*, a collection which depends heavily on Gothic motifs, leaves her crystal earrings on during sex with her vacillating married lover, and is left with 'the semblance of a gash on each side of her neck' (19). Both suggest, again in Gothic terms, the woundedness of the female subject, the pain of compromised feminine consciousness, or the acknowledgement of difference and insufficiency.

However, dress, as suggested above, is inherently paradoxical, and other moments in O'Brien's fiction illustrate the manner in which items of clothing are seen as holding the promise of completion, apparently allowing the desiring, but incomplete, subject to fashion a satisfying identity. Lacan's *Ecrits* is eloquent on the masochism of clothing (in its widest sense including make-up, piercing, and tattooing) through which the subject is continually reminded of his or, more typically, *her* own unfinishedness and fragmentation, in the case of the female subject who is seen as the victim of fashion (11). Lacan's theorization of sexual difference differs little from Freud's: for both, woman is constituted by lack, with the phallus as the signifier of that which she lacks, so that the necessity of attempting to complete the unfinished self is accordingly more urgent. He thus argues that female self-decoration allows women to circumvent their inevitable failure to cure or repair this lack by reconstituting themselves as objects rather than subjects of desire; if they themselves cannot possess the phallus, they can *become* it in relation to men.[6]

Analysis of this transaction is visible throughout O'Brien, in passages such as the one from *The Country Girls* which is the epigraph to this essay; Caithleen, changing her 'old clothes' and performing an elaborate *maquillage* in preparation for a dinner date, simultaneously relishes and feels contempt for the process of 'making herself up' via cosmetics and costume, into a coherent self whose apparent completion is a 'mystery' to her (while her cosmetically-shadowed eyes signal mystery and unattainability to her lover). Clothes and methods of self-decoration participate, for Caithleen and other O'Brien protagonists, in the fantasized drama of subjectivity, with clothes, as an appendix of the body, serving as the Lacanian *objet petit a*, or substitute object, which plugs the fissure that betrays the self as fragmented. Oddly eloquent garments, such as the incongruously adult dress in which the fourteen-year-old Caithleen first has dinner with Mr Gentleman – a low-necked 'ice-blue dress with blossoms on it' with a skirt 'composed of millions of little pieces that flowed when I walked' (*CG* 55) – suggest both clothing's seductive function of containing and completing the body by giving it identifiable shape, and, paradoxically, the painstaking way in which dress fills the gap, pulls together the fragmented identity of the subject as woman. Eugene Gaillard uses a sartorial metaphor when he complains of having to 'educate' Caithleen from scratch: 'It's too difficult, there's not enough time left in the world anymore, and hundreds of girls, ready-made' (*LG* 358). However, for O'Brien's heroines, this is simply not true; identity is, at best, a carefully assembled costume.

The complex intermingling of clothes, desire, and lack is particularly important to the thematics of *August is a Wicked Month* (1965), a novel in which the nihilistic nature of the holidaying protagonist's post-marital foray into the sexual exchange market is conveyed through the purchase and wearing of emblematic garments. Published in the same year as the United States re-launch of *Cosmopolitan*, the novel implicitly examines and debunks many of the magazine's chief preoccupations: personal fulfilment through sex and shopping, the reiteration of stereotypes of heterosexual romance, and the frenzied consumption of clothes and cosmetics. That desire is mediated through capitalist consumption is immediately evident from the passage close to the beginning of the novel in which Ellen stands looking into a shop window at insistently sexualized garments – 'freedom clothes ... fast clothes' – and feels a sexual 'aggravation between the legs' (28, 26). The garments she

impulsively buys for her holiday seductively promise a reno-
vated selfhood, a holistic repair also suggested in the attention
paid to the beautiful navels of the bikini-clad models in the
holiday advertisement.[7] Ellen's seductive 'green silk [trousers]
with a coatee to match' (28) are chosen in deliberate rejection
of the cultural stereotype of the Virgin Mary, who blushes at
the immodesty of clothing that draws attention to the female
legs; and also suggest a sardonic disjunction between the Irish
national colour and the modish, metropolitan Ellen. They are
also objects of desire because they hold the promise of
renovation via completion, as discussed above, the last piece
necessary to close the gap in selfhood. However, the novel
ultimately explodes the *Cosmopolitan* ethos, as summed up by
Ellen McCracken, as the reinforcement of conservative values
under 'the impression of a pseudo-sexual liberation and a
vicarious participation in the life of an imaginary "swinging
single" woman' (159, 162).

O'Brien's commodified examination of romantic love, with
its tropes of insatiability and indefiniteness, suggests Barthes's
argument in *The Lover's Discourse* to the effect that 'love's eternal
self-perpetuation and recurrence [is] akin to the endless circulation of the commodity in post-industrial culture' (136).
Ellen, setting out to attract new lovers, is a classically O'Brien
instance of the split and striving feminine identity, continually
self-monitoring, probing her own sense of lack:

> She could look well talking to herself in a mirror, or again
> talking to herself through the pool of a loving man's eyes, but
> most times she looked mawkish. And curiously unfinished
> (110).

As the ego is constituted by the complex of relations between
itself, others, and the image of the body, and the fundamental
misrecognition that is a condition of the Lacanian mirror stage,
wherein the infant experiences its own body as fragmented and
desires its 'whole' mirror image, the subject's sense of identity is
an alienated one. Ellen, however, wearing her new clothes, does
undergo a solitary moment of happy self-communion suggesting the Lacanian *stade du miroir*.

> In the mirror she danced with the portable radio, she saw
> herself in the new clothes with the milk-white waist showing
> and her toe-nails glistening a wicked carmine in new gold
> sandals (29).

But, if dress can act as a Lacanian mirror, it is in the specific
sense that this guarantee of cohesion and plenitude is based not
on an actual corporeal unity but on a dream of union between
the mirror image and reality; that is, it is a *mis*recognition. In
part due to the transitory nature of the satisfaction yielded by
any idealized image or role, it actually breeds desire not
satiation; Ellen actually avoids the hotel dance for fear of sexual
rejection, 'fores[eeing] herself sitting by the wall, ignored, and
the magic falling away from her like fake frosting or gold dust'
(57). While dress can glue a precarious identity together on the
surface or lend, as it does in *August is a Wicked Month*, a
theatrical aspect to the selection of costumes in which the
individual chooses to present herself to the world, this is a
temporary 'seduction'. Ellen, rejected by a lover in whose gaze
she might have temporarily appeared to overcome her
'unfinished' state, frantically tries on 'hundreds of piled sunhats'
outside his bedroom (74). The dress-object is always a displacement, a substitute; the gap in selfhood, by definition, is un-
pluggable; while it appears to promote the myth of a unified
identity, it also splinters the subject into a succession of
possible masks or costumes.

Mourning the death of her son during her holiday, Ellen is
bought another of those curiously sacramental O'Brien
garments, a

> costly white dress … made of linen, with big sleeves in which
> her hands could nestle. Like the saints that appear in the liturgy
> of the church, white and limbless and very still (130).

The imagery is chilling, suggesting both a form of death and a
revisioning of dress as punitive agent of the Symbolic, via forms
of dress intended to cover up 'improper' aspects of the body,
sanitizing and ordering it. Yet the close of the novel sees an
irruption of the Kristevan abject; Ellen contracts a venereal

disease from her lover. For Kristeva, the forms of corporeality on which the Symbolic lays its heaviest ban can always re-irrupt in the dissolving agency of bodily functions, through which defiling matter wounds the mythically seamless subjectivity. Disease leads to a reassertion of the 'disgraced part', a return of the material, under the sanctifying clothes (*AWM* 149). The circumstance, and the deliberately shocking depiction of the symptoms of the disease – 'the dark mesh of hair had a blight … a nest of sobs now with ugly yellowing tears' (148) – recall Kristevan abjection, in turn closely allied to the notion of the Lacanian rim alluded to earlier, associated with anxieties about the relationship between the inside and outside of the body, and the fissures through which the material processes inducing abjection are passed. The fact that 'in tense situations' Ellen's discharge worsens, 'as if she were crying down there' (165) suggests a form of hysteria, the body intractably acting out a mourning at odds with its sanitizing clothing.

The novel ends with Ellen receiving treatment and thinking gladly 'of how the lotion would stain all her pants and the stains in themselves would be a testimony of mourning, ugly irregular purple shapes' (168). Specifically, this act of bodily mourning, marking the garments which aim to 'seal off' and delineate the body from its discharges, would appear to be for Ellen's dead son, but, more generally, it is an act of mourning for the failure of dress to encapsulate the fantasy of the ideal ego, a failure signalled in the fact of the contamination of the vulnerable body. The integrity of the body as a personal possession is accordingly exploded by the re-incursion of the carnal into the domain of the Symbolic. Lack, however, metaphorized in the novel in terms of the female genitals, which have for so long been a privileged trope for lack, castration, and split, keeps re-asserting itself as a kind of basic condition of being under clothing used as a projection of an ideal ego.

Dress in O'Brien may appear to presage only gloom for her protagonists, eloquent on lack and absence, and suggesting only illusory forms of selfhood. Certainly, by its liminal nature, it emphasizes the uncertainty of the spaces the female body may inhabit, and their associated sense of transit and disorientation, split identities, and bewildered or fretful questing. O'Brien's female subjects, dramatized by dress, are symbolically rootless beings, wandering in what Barthes refers to as 'the site of loss, the seam, the cut' (*Pleasure of the Text* 7). Warwick and Cavallero suggest the potential of dress discourse, albeit in highlighting ontological insecurity, 'for critical and creative relocation and reinscription' (8). The potential for this in O'Brien, barring some fleeting moments of pleasure, is slim indeed. Rather, her thematics of dress sharpen our sense of the subject's stark reality of lack, of inhabiting a condition of perpetual homelessness.

Works Cited

Ash, Juliet and Elizabeth Wilson, eds. *Chic Thrills: A Fashion Reader* (London: Pandora, 1992).

Barthes, Roland. *A Lover's Discourse; Fragments*. Trans. Richard Howard (London: Cape, 1979).

--- *The Pleasure of the Text*. Trans. R Miller (Oxford: Basil Blackwell, 1990).

Bowen, Elizabeth. 'Dress' [1937] *Collected Impressions* (London: Longmans, 1950), 111-15.

Bronfen, Elizabeth. *Over Her Dead Body: Death, Femininity and the Aesthetic* (Manchester: Manchester University Press, 1992).

Brook, Barbara. *Feminist Perspectives on the Body* (London and New York: Longman, 1999).

Butler, Judith. *Gender Trouble: Feminism and the Subversion of Identity* (London and New York: Routledge, 1990).

Carter, Angela. *Shaking a Leg* (London: Chatto and Windus, 1997).

Clarke, Kenneth. *The Nude: The Study of Ideal Art* (London: John Murray, 1956).

Douglas, Mary. *Purity and Danger: An Analysis of Concepts of Pollution and Taboo* (London: Routledge and Kegan Paul, 1966).

Foucault, Michel. *Discipline and Punish: The Birth of the Prison*. Trans. Alan Sheridan (London: Allen Lane, 1977).

Grosz, Elizabeth. *Space, Time and Perversion: Essays on the Politics of Bodies* (New York: Routledge, 1995).

Halberstam, Judith. *Skin Shows: Gothic Horror and the Technology of Monsters* (Durham and London: Duke University Press, 1995).

Hollander, Anne. *Seeing Through Clothes* [1975] (Berkeley: University of California Press, 1993).

Ingman, Heather. 'Edna O'Brien: Stretching the Nation's Boundaries'. *Irish Studies Review* 10.3 (Dec 2002): 253-65.

Kristeva, Julia. *Powers of Horror: An Essay on Abjection*. Trans. Leon S. Roudiez (New York: Columbia University Press, 1982).

Lacan, Jacques. *Ecrits; A Selection*. Trans. Alan Sheridan (London: Tavistock Publications, 1977).

Laing, Kathryn S. 'Addressing Femininity in the Twenties: Virginia Woolf and Rebecca West on Money, Mirrors and Masquerade'. *Virginia Woolf and the Arts: Selected Papers from the Sixth Annual Woolf Conference*, eds. Diane F. Gillespie and Leslie K. Hankins (New York: Pace University Press, 1997), 66-75.

McCracken, Ellen. *Decoding Women's Magazines: From* Mademoiselle *to* Ms (Basingstoke: Macmillan, 1992).

Nead, Lynda. *The Nude: Arts, Obscenity and Sexuality* (London and New York: Routledge, 1992).

O'Brien, Edna. *August is a Wicked Month* (London: Penguin, 1965).

--- *Casualties of Peace* (London: Jonathan Cape, 1966).

--- *The Country Girls Trilogy and Epilogue* (New York: Farrar, Strauss, Giroux, 1987) .

--- *Down by the River* (London: Phoenix, 1997).

--- *A Fanatic Heart: Selected Stories* (London: Weidenfeld & Nicolson, 1985).

--- *The High Road* (London: Weidenfeld & Nicolson, 1988).

--- *The Love Object* (London: Cape, 1968).

--- *Mother Ireland* (Harmondsworth: Penguin, 1978).

--- *Mrs Reinhardt and Other Stories* (London: Weidenfeld & Nicolson, 1978).

--- *Night* (London: Weidenfeld & Nicolson, 1972).

Pointon, Marcia. *Naked Authority: The Body in Western Painting 1830-1908* (Cambridge: Cambridge University Press, 1990).

Roche, Daniel. *The Culture of Clothing*. Trans. Jean Birrell (Cambridge: Cambridge University Press, 1994).

Salmon, Mary. 'Edna O'Brien'. *Contemporary Irish Novelists*, ed. Rüdiger Imhof (Tubingen: Gunter Nach Verlag, 1990), 143-58.

Silverman, Kaja. 'Fragments of a Fashionable Discourse'. *Studies in Entertainment: Studies in Mass Culture*, ed. Tania Modleski (Bloomington: Indiana University Press, 1986).

Spooner, Catherine. *Fashioning Gothic Bodies* (Manchester and New York: Manchester University Press, 2004).

Warwick, Alexandra and Dani Cavallaro. *Fashioning the Frame: Boundaries, Dress and the Body* (Oxford and New York: Berg, 1998).

Wilson, Elizabeth. *Adorned in Dreams: Fashion and Modernity* (London: Virago, 1985).

---

[1] There is none of the obvious ambivalence expressed by writers such as Virginia Woolf and Rebecca West, both of whose work demonstrates an enduring fascination with dress as a mode of exploring a collision between the production of literature, an activity coded masculine, and the decoration of the self, a conventionally 'feminine' activity, as argued by Kathryn Laing, p.67.

[2] Particularly significant examples of this occur in *Down by the River*, when the London bed-and-breakfast owner puts on a drag performance for Mary, the incestuously-raped teenager seeking a London abortion, pp.159-60, and in *August is a Wicked Month*, in which an apparently female stripper is revealed to be a transvestite, just before Ellen becomes infected with a venereal disease, p.67.

[3] While I refer for clarity's sake to the individual novels in the trilogy, all references are to the 1987 Farrar Straus Giroux *The Country Girls Trilogy and Epilogue*.

[4] This is a real text by Moshe Feldenkrais, published in 1949, subtitled *A Study of Anxiety, Sex, Gravitation and Learning*.

[5] See also 'A Rose in the Heart of New York', p.385.

[6] See Warwick and Cavallaro, p.35 and following, for a good discussion of this.

[7] The navel is the marker of what Elizabeth Bronfen calls an 'ambivalent wound' associated with Eve, the opposite type of the Virgin Mary, the feminine stigmatized as associated with sex and death, and as decorative supplement to Adam, p.68.

12 | Famished: Alienation and Appetite in Edna O'Brien's early novels

Mary Burke

> Food is the prototype of all exchanges with the other, be they verbal, financial, or erotic.
>   Maud Ellmann, *The Hunger Artists*

> Down in the Underground there was a gas advertisement. It said, 'Do nothing until you've read Vogue'. Well, in our plight, and with people starving … I thought it was very vital advice.
>   Edna O'Brien, *Girls in Their Married Bliss*

> Bhí naire orm.
> Bhí glas ar mo bhéal
> (Shame was upon me.
> My mouth was under lock).
>   Nuala Ní Dhomhnaill, 'Féar Suaithinseach'

In Edna O'Brien's early fiction, hunger is both physical and metaphysical: in Hiberno-English usage, to be 'famished' may mean to be hungry, thirsty, or, significantly, to be cold, a concept easily stretched to ideas of alienation, exclusion, or a dearth of love. This paper will examine how the anorexic/bulimic imperative of consumerism becomes a controlling force in the lives of O'Brien's heroines, and the conceptual 'anorexia' posited by critics Anna Krugovoy Silver and Edna Longley will be used to interrogate the broader subjugation of Irish women

by church, state, and medical practices also depicted by
O'Brien. Food functions as a problematic facet of a woman's
life in O'Brien's *The Country Girls Trilogy* (1960-64) and in *August
is a Wicked Month* (1965), in which concerns and themes
developed throughout O'Brien's first three novels culminate.
The trilogy follows the coming to maturity, marriages, and subsequent disillusionment and marital strife of the heroines, Cait
(anglicized as 'Kate' in the second and third novels) and Baba,
who are followed from rural Ireland to Dublin and on to
London. The sexual-revolution era *August is a Wicked Month*
centres on separated thirty-something Ellen, whose son is killed
while camping with her estranged husband while she has a
holiday affair on the continent. Images of food in these novels
permeate memory and are entwined with issues of beauty,
gender inequality, sex, class, and religion. O'Brien's women
have an emotional, oftentimes anxious attitude to food, and at
least one reference to eating, drinking, or hunger occurs on
almost every page. The first novel of the trilogy, *The Country
Girls*, charts Cait and Baba's movement from unselfcon-
sciousness in matters of sexuality, food, and consumption and
an unawareness of their lack of true autonomy as females in
mid-century Ireland to a complex and more guilty engagement
with sex, eating, and femininity, while the opening scenes of the
second novel of the trilogy, *Girl with Green Eyes*, consists of a
dash between cafés, bars, restaurants, and parties. The first page
of the final novel of the trilogy, *Girls in their Married Bliss*,
explicitly sets the tone for the weaving together of the themes
of food, drink, alienation, money, and sex:

> Not long ago Kate Brady and I were having a few gloomy gin
> fizzes up London, bemoaning the fact that nothing would ever
> improve, that we'd die the way we were — enough to eat,
> married, dissatisfied … [H]ere in London … over a period of
> eighteen months, we got asked out to about three good dinners
> apiece, which meant six meals for both of us (7).

By *August is a Wicked Month*, the world in which the heroine
moves has reached the logical end-point of the journey from
putative pre-colonial and prepubescent 'innocence' and

'naturalness' to decadence, advanced consumerism, and artificiality begun in the later scenes of *The Country Girls*. As they mature, O'Brien's young heroines are increasingly subject to an anorexic/bulimic imperative to both over-consume processed food and remain desirably slender, and what Anna Krugovoy Silver has referred to as the 'anorexic logic' of patriarchal culture that would keep females compliant and passive. In O'Brien's early novels, as in the Victorian narratives aimed at or concerning young females Silver discusses, 'anorexia becomes a symbolic system in ... text[s] ... not directly "about" anorexia' (71). Edna Longley similarly reads anorexia as the 'ideological *rigor mortis*' of the patriarchal discourses of 'Unionism, Catholicism, Protestantism, Nationalism' to which Irish women are subject, and in a poem by Nuala Ní Dhomhnaill the foreign loan word 'anorexia' is utilized to probe folklore narratives that speak of the physical effects of objectification on young women.[1] Longley's formulation of ideological self-starvation is prompted by what she reads as Paul Muldoon's query in his poem 'Aisling', written near the time of the Northern Irish nationalists' hunger strikes in 1981, as to 'whether Ireland should be symbolized, not by a radiant and abundant goddess, but by the disease anorexia' (3). 'Even on her death-bed', Longley notes in reference to Cathleen Ní Houlihan, the Ireland-as-Woman embodiment *par excellence*, 'Cathleen-Anorexia exerts a residual power over the image and self-images of *all* Irish women' (15-16). Writing of a woman hunger striker in Armagh, the principal detention camp for female terrorists in Northern Ireland, who survived the hunger strike but died within a year of release from prison of anorexia nervosa, Maud Ellmann also reads the Irish woman's hunger as 'a form of speech ... entangled in the rival ideologies of nation, gender, and religion' (3). *Actual* anorexia and bulimia are merely the contradictory demands of consumerism taken to their logical ends, one an extreme capacity to resist desire, the other an absolute capitulation (Bordo 97). Mainstream medical discourse interprets eating disorders as being distinct from the eating habits of 'healthy' women, but O'Brien's early fiction challenges this belief. Although none of the post-adolescent female characters display overtly anorectic or bulimic behaviour, subtly obsessive attitudes to food are more 'normal' amongst them than not. The 'pathological' anorexic is merely the acute end of the spectrum of the manifestation of 'normal femininity' in the West.[2]

The Country Girls commences as a paean to the unadorned country fare of 1950s Ireland, a time when food is seemingly not a source of guilt, stricture, or overindulgence. The novel's celebration of unpasteurized milk, farm eggs, homemade butter, and mustard are all meant to evoke an era before food becomes a problematic aspect of the heroines' lives, a prelapsarian period in which the girls are not yet fully conscious of their secondary status or their coming obligation to monitor food intake. In the Irish context, such foods also subtly invoke an uncontaminated pre-modern and pre-colonial Ireland, pointing to an as yet unimpoverished land in which grains and dairy produce have not yet been overtaken by the more efficient potato crop introduced by the Elizabethan colonizer:

> The raising of cows demanded a considerable amount of grazing land which in 16th- and 17th-century Ireland was made scarce by confiscation, the redistribution of population and the landlords' demands. The ravages of war in the 16th century had also taken their toll of cattle, the slaughtering and driving of which was a common wartime tactic by the Crown forces in Ireland at the time. Some alternative food to livestock produce was therefore needed ... (Ó Sé 85).

Writing in 1960, the year in which the first novel of O'Brien's trilogy was published, C.T. Lucas notes that:

> Only during the dark reign of the potato did [butter] suffer a forced decline but all through that period it continued to be regarded as a symbol of the golden age of plenty and it resumed its ancient status when economic conditions allowed (Lucas 30).

The historical wounds of Cathleen Ní Houlihan are not yet apparent to the young Cait, although some ignored or as yet unacknowledged historical disruption appears to silently hover over the first novel of the trilogy: as suggested by their indoor

plumbing and unused spacious extra bedrooms, Cait's family
live in a 'Big House', though their precarious social standing in
the district and their squatter-like attitude (they leave the
bathrooms largely unused) implies that they are probably not
the descendants of the original occupants. Cait still lives in a
world in which the complexities and wounds of history and
womanhood have yet to be revealed to her. The care taken over
Cait's egg by the family's farmhand, Hickey, and Mama's indulgent school lunches of cake are understood by the child as
tokens of love. The young girl's childhood fantasy of marriage
to Hickey revolves around food ('we would get free eggs, free
milk, and vegetables from Mama' [6]), indicating that in
O'Brien's first novel, innocence in matters of sexuality and food
are enmeshed. Consumerism is not yet advanced in rural
Ireland: shop-bought cakes, tinned fruit, and apple jelly are
considered items for special occasions only. Although Baba's
relatively wealthy family seem to have embraced the new
consumerism of 'gleaming' bicycles and life being 'nicer when
you pay' (21), Cait's Mama spares her 'good' tableware and
furniture for visitors. The greatest indulgence of the school year
is the feast in honour of All Soul's Day, when the girls happily
devour enormous food parcels sent from home. Perhaps
because the schoolgirls are not adequately nourished by the
nuns, food, when plentiful on such feast days, is a communal
and celebratory experience, a far cry from both the bulimic
overindulgence and neurotic attention to calories of the women
depicted in *August is a Wicked Month*. However, by *Girls in Their
Married Bliss*, Kate, depressed by her failed marriage, begins to
doubt the myth of 'thinking that ... when one was young ...the
hedges were full of wild strawberries, when, in fact ... the
strawberries were hearsay' (122). A yearning for the Eden of a
simpler time when food was or is imagined to have been
associated with happiness is continually invoked in moments of
distress by O'Brien's heroines. Trying to recall the happy days
of her failed marriage, Kate muses that it's '[f]unny that she
should only remember meals they had eaten' (*GMB* 88).

O'Brien notes in *Mother Ireland*, her 1976 memoir-as-social-history (whose narrative follows that of her trilogy to a great extent), that when she left her rural home and moved to Dublin as a young woman she found herself suddenly immersed in a delightfully novel consumer culture: 'everything in the city was different ... The city had numerous delights — clothes, cafés where ice cream was served in long-stemmed glasses and three distinct kinds of coffee' (113, 114). The Dublin of O'Brien's memoir and of her first novel is described as a city in which imported shape-hugging fashion and processed foods tempt the young female consumer. There is little or no guilt attached to appetite in the early chapters of *The Country Girls*, set in the economically underdeveloped rural Ireland of Baba and Cait's childhood. O'Brien implies that both obesity and the self-conscious control of food intake only exist in a society of overabundance. However, despite the insistence on the un-complicated attitude to food displayed by the young heroines in the early scenes of *The Country Girls*, by the novel's close the seeds of the more tortured relationship with food they sub-sequently display are already being sewn. The girls' move to Dublin brings a greater awareness of the maddening choice which advanced consumerism brings, and of the nutritional pitfalls of the food industry ('Baba said that all the eggs in the city were rotten' [143]), and such attention to food and its dangers presupposes a consumer society in which women are bombarded by contradictory messages concerning food and the desirability of physical slenderness, a time and place in which affluence has grown to the degree that the 'haves' begin to hanker for a slimness previously only associated with the 'have-nots'.

Given that the first novel of the trilogy discussed is set in its period of publication, Baba and Cait may be said to have arrived in a Dublin in the process of the kind of social, cultural and economic changes that would facilitate such advanced consumerist attitudes to food and thinness. The implemen-tation of economic reforms in the First Programme for Economic Expansion in November 1958 'signalled the end of the post-independence search for a national identity and economy rooted in conceptions of traditional Ireland', and subsequent economic growth 'exceeded anyone's wildest expectations' (Hardiman and Whelan 34). Moreover, the commonly held belief that the decade of the 1950s as a whole was a period of economic stagnation and unimproved living standards in Ireland has been challenged (O'Hagan 34). Political change occurred alongside economic transformation: during the 1960s, the civil rights movement in Northern Ireland, and feminist protests in the Anglophone world 'encouraged the development of an emerging critique of women's rights on the island' (Galligan 111). Similarly, although he acknowledges the transformation wrought by the economic policy implemented by Taoiseach Sean Lemass, Hugh Maguire situates the physical transformation of Dublin in the 1960s within a confluence of international or modernizing influences such as the Kennedy visit, creeping secularization, and the founding of the national television station in 1961. Cait/Kate lodges with an Austrian couple, loves the exotic Mr Gentleman, and later becomes romantically involved with an alien resident of Dublin, and all of these foreigners explicitly admonish the young woman for her healthy appetite: the heroines of O'Brien's first novel are patently exposed to a variety of cultures and imported dis-courses concerning the necessity of female slenderness in the newly-buoyant capital city. Significantly, it is an American guest of Eugene's who enquires of Kate in *Girl with Green Eyes* if she considers sugar to be 'fattening' (189). Such outside influences were, however, simultaneously liberating: the oppressive waif-like ideal of the female form that arose in the wealthier nations of the Anglophone world in the 1960s, and soon impacted on Ireland's urban centres alongside the period make-up and clothes detailed in O'Brien's work, was inextricably and para-doxically bound up with the simultaneous drive for female liberation. Alternative voices cannot be expressed, let alone heard within a monolithic system, which suggests that it was the arrival of such influences in Ireland that created the (admittedly narrow) space within which an educated young woman such as

O'Brien could enunciate both the dissatisfaction of a new
generation with the unquestioned pieties of the post-partition
era, and speak to broader concerns with the female condition
that participated in the arguments of the Anglophone Women's
Movement.[3]

Acknowledging the threat that O'Brien's work posed to the
weakening conservative establishment of the period, Benedict
Kiely speculated that 'the convent girl with her temper riz may
yet do what the strong argument of Seán O'Faoláin failed to do'
(qtd in Morgan 450). Dublin in the 1960s is often depicted as a
provincial city, but ideas concerning liberation from old *mores*
were imported alongside the American and British fashions,
magazines, music, and films that evidently flooded the capital in
that period, as revealed by the most cursory glance at
contemporaneous Irish media.[4] Indeed, it has been suggested
that it was critiques of Ireland's destructive insularity and
Catholic fundamentalism by Irish-American commentators in
the 1950s that inspired subsequent Irish self-examination.[5] The
hysterical reaction of the establishment of the day to O'Brien's
early work — state censors banned her first five novels — was
matched by the positive approval of her work by liberal Ireland.
O'Brien's early work may be too readily read as an indictment
of the Ireland of the period alone, and an insistence on the
absolute link between Catholicism and nationalism and Irish
women's oppression in her early fiction fails to note that she
untethers this subjugation from Irish culture by depicting the
continuation of Baba and Kate's troubles *after* they move to
London in the 1960s, a secular metropolis at the heart of the
new culture of liberation. O'Brien's delineation of the forces to
which Irish women are subject is complex: oppression arises
both from the surveillance of women's bodies engendered by
the attitudes of the post-partition Irish state and from the
newer oppressions concerning slenderness and sexual
promiscuity that emerged as the dark aspect of women's
liberation. (The latter issue is dealt with in the discussion of
August is a Wicked Month.) The sardonic Baba finds the
admonishment of a London Underground station advertise-

ment, 'Do nothing until you've read *Vogue*', a magazine that
proved to be one of the primary vehicles for the promulgation
of the new boyish shape during the 1960s, to be 'vital advice',
what 'with people starving' (*GMB* 110).

'In Anglo-Saxon countries', Margaret Visser notes, 'ice
cream has always represented a kind of apotheosis of milk',
which was considered to be 'innocent, pure, white, and whole-
some … In most of Continental Europe, ice cream delivers an
entirely different message. It has never lost its élite status' (311).
On their first night in the capital city, Baba and Cait have a dish
of ice cream, cream, peaches, and chocolate. Cait has moved
from a place of unpasteurized milk to the location where
nourishing milk is transformed into the nutritionally negligible,
imported luxuries of leisure time, and once the girls have been
inducted into the pleasures of consumerism, there is no
possible return to Eden: 'We got ready quickly and went down
into the neon fairyland of Dublin. I loved it more than I had
ever loved a summer's day in a hayfield' (141). O'Brien's novel
charts the great change in the Irish urban-dweller's diet in the
1960s, a period when, according to ethnologist Patricia Lysaght,
'French, Italian and Chinese foods were introduced and quickly
accepted' (87). Food is one of the means by which men in the
city attempt to purchase sex from impoverished women in
these O'Brien novels (the predatory Harry demands that Cait
snuggle up to him, 'as if I should know the price of a good
dinner' [*CG* 162], while affected sexual availability is traded for
alcohol, for which the young women quickly acquire a taste in
Dublin: '("Look *fast*", Baba said.) We sat near the door and
Baba said that some moron was bound to buy us a drink' [*GGE*
70]). Moreover, the contradictions inherent in advanced
capitalism's conflicting messages become quickly apparent in
the city. It is there that the young women are first made self-
conscious about their appetites and are shocked that the fridge
of rich playboy Harry is unfilled, an emptiness signifying the
fetishization of food that arrives with advanced consumerism:
food is not planned for and stored as of old, but extravagantly
ordered on whim at a moment's notice. The obese wife of the

grocer who employs Cait is the first person in the novel to
display a patently unhealthy relationship to food. She keeps
chocolates by her bed and eats biscuits for elevenses, and the
grocery shop displays posters of '[n]ice girls with healthy teeth'
paradoxically eating chocolate bars (144). Women are cajoled
into indulging in sugar and fat-laden snack food, yet
subliminally warned to maintain the outward indicators of
health and beauty: the implicit anorexic/bulimic imperative of
capitalism cautions women that they must consume (in every
sense) but maintain the appearance of abstinence.

The sixteenth-century British administrator in Ireland,
Edmund Spenser, presciently suggested that 'till Ireland be
famished it cannot be subdued' (244). Strikingly, Victorian
medicine debated the anorexic body through the prism of the
bodies of Irish famine victims, and the latter were generally
represented as female, 'docile', and even culpable in their own
suffering (Kennedy 286).[6] The compliant woman is a thin
woman, just as a hunger silences Cathleen Ní Houlihan's
potential insurrection. In *The Country Girls*, the girls' landlady
gives sausages to the male lodger alone, while the martyred
Mama leaves the smallest portion of trifle for herself. O'Brien's
women struggle with ideals of female slenderness that if adhered to, will lead to physical weakness: '[Baba] was neat
looking, and any man could lift her up in his arms and carry her
off' (*CG* 130). Both a young woman's food intake and her
moral welfare are under constant surveillance in O'Brien's early
fiction: the social system that allows for the informing of Cait's
father of her affair and for a strange taxi-man to help in her
abduction away from her 'sinful' relationship also monitors her
appetite. When Cait accepts a second slice of cake, her landlady
warns that she will get fat, while Kate's soon-to-be-husband
Eugene comments sardonically on her healthy appetite, and,
after their marriage, partially blames the subsequent collapse of
their relationship on Kate's 'slackening midriff' (*CG* 153, *GGE*
37, *GMB* 21). The vulnerability of being seen to eat is akin to
being caught naked ('It was difficult, chewing the food while
she watched me, and I hoped that I didn't make a noise while I

ate' [*CG* 123]). Women, moreover, closely monitor themselves ('I looked in the mirror ... I sucked my cheeks in ... I longed to be thinner' [*GGE* 7]). That women in O'Brien's early fiction are not supposed to indulge in stimulants is indicative of their lesser freedoms: Cait's father in *The Country Girls* does not consider it rude to offer cigarettes to Mr Brennan, who rarely smokes, but not to his wife, Martha Brennan, an habitual smoker. On Kate's train journey home with Dada after her abduction in the second novel of the trilogy, his friends reinforce his denial of Kate's autonomy and adulthood by assuming she will have a soft drink rather than the alcoholic beverages she has developed a taste for in Dublin.

The compliant woman also ensures that she maintains the appearance of conventional beauty. Beauty in O'Brien's work is a hard-won battle over appetite and nature's tendency to atrophy. Beauty is never, as in many texts by male authors, a state of grace into which certain blessed women effortlessly grow. To be 'beautiful' in O'Brien's early novels is a decision that requires constant vigilance to uphold, to the exclusion of more pressing matters: as noted, the only conversation Eugene's reputedly 'intellectual' American woman friend makes with Kate is to enquire whether she considered sugar to be 'fattening'. In *Girl with Green Eyes*, Kate's wish on her pretend wedding day is to 'stay young always' (148), while in the follow-up novel, Baba admits to being exhausted 'keeping my heels mended and my skin fresh for ... Mr Right' (11). On losing her virginity, Kate realizes that the lie of the 'feminine' woman is maintained in order to stimulate the man who will maintain her economically: 'All the perfume, and sighs, and purple brassières, the curling-pins in bed, and gin-and-it, and necklaces, had all been for this' (*GGE* 149). As early as the latter part of *The Country Girls*, the realization has dawned that beauty requires not only time, controlled starvation, and pain, but also money (160). Cait is simultaneously fascinated and appalled by the subterfuge demanded of women:

> I shadow my eyelids with black stuff and am astonished by the
> look of mystery it gives to my eyes. I hate being a woman. Vain
> and shallow and superficial (171).

Unaware of the work put into Cait's 'effortless' look, Mr
Gentleman perceives her as an unaffected representation of
'Oirish' beauty: 'He looked at me for a long time … then he
said my name very gently. ("Caithleen".) I could hear the
bulrushes sighing when he said my name that way and I could
hear … all the lonesome sounds of Ireland' (*CG* 174). Irish
women are defined by the patriarchal embodiment of Ireland-
as-Woman, an entrapment that Longley reads as dis-
empowering to flesh-and-blood women, and Eileen Morgan
posits that O'Brien's *oeuvre* constitutes one of 'the lengthiest and
most intricate negotiations of the received image of Irish
women' (450). The potential for the imaginative immobilization
of Irish women writers in the face of the overwhelming male
tradition of depicting the Irish woman as muse, goddess, or
symbol alone, and to which the young O'Brien herself was
doubtlessly subject when writing the ground-breaking first
novel of the trilogy, is discussed by Irish poet Eavan Boland in
A Kind of Scar. As a young woman struggling with creative self-
expression in 1960s Dublin, Boland was O'Brien's almost exact
contemporary. To Boland's dismay, the 'majority of Irish male
poets depended on women as motifs in their poetry … The
women in their poems were often passive, decorative, raised to
emblematic status', and this 'fusion of the national and the
feminine … simplified both' (12, 7). O'Brien's explicit refusal of
this culturally-mandated female passivity, in daring to explicate
the real lives and sly subversions of nationalist and Catholic
pieties of sexually awakening young Irish women, doubtlessly
shaped the outrage that greeted the publication of *The Country
Girls*, the provocation of which was doubled when the author
was seen to be a rather beautiful young woman who might
herself have been a model for the stereotypically dark-haired
and pale-skinned Cathleen Ní Houlihan. As noted, O'Brien's
implicit refutation of traditional exemplars of female perfection
emanated to a large extent from the outside influences and

voices that flooded Ireland from the 1940s onwards: as Fintan
O'Toole wittily suggests, exposure to the 'sex and drugs and
rock and roll' depicted in the products of foreign media eagerly
devoured in Ireland, 'produced a [youth] culture whose real
presiding goddesses were not Cathleen Ní Houlihan and the
Virgin Mary but A Gal from Kalamazoo and Our Lady Evelyn
of the Follies' (110).

Self-consciousness concerning class intersects the O'Brien
heroine's experience of her own body. When the broke, separated Kate meets her son once a week, the particular details
given concerning food reveal much about her economic
situation and emotional fragility: 'They always went to a café for
tea — the same one each time because she knew the prices —
and he ate chips, and éclairs filled with mock cream' (83).
Habits of consumption determine class in these novels, as does
food vocabulary: 'There are people in the world and you know
they are going to say pudding' (*GMB* 51). Rules concerning
food are created and adhered to by men to perpetuate their
own superior position:[7] Mr Gentleman was 'a big-shot because
he never drank in the local pubs' (*CG* 105), and Eugene is
presumed to be sophisticated because he 'didn't eat potatoes
and he drank water with his dinner' (*GGE* 27). Value-laden
food is the medium through which Cait visualizes Mr Gentleman's higher social status, fantasizing that behind closed doors
he 'eats soufflés and roast venison' (*CG* 16). Moreover, food
choice betrays those who are feigning high birth: 'He affected a
world-weary manner, but it was only put-on, because he ate
loads of bread and jam' (*GGE* 12). In the lower-middle class
world of O'Brien's early novels, food is a social minefield ('I ate
three cakes; he pressed me to eat a fourth but I didn't, in case it
was vulgar' [*GGE* 25]), and the canny Baba understands that
she can aspire to a higher social class by learning the 'correct'
tastes ('Bottles of red wine stood near to warm up … Don't
think we got that information for free' [*GMB* 74]). The mid-
century Ireland of the young Cait and Baba is an un-
sophisticated landscape of ketchup on restaurant tables and
tinned peas served at country hotels, but with the consumer

revolution of the 1960s, even 'good taste' becomes potentially available to anyone able to purchase it: in *Girls in Their Married Bliss*, the décor, alcohol, and food choices of Baba's social-climbing London-Irish building contractor husband are dictated by lifestyle magazines.

O'Brien's fiction 'reflects the intersection of several cultural and historical ideologies which influence its representation of the [Irish] female body', the foremost being 'the ideology of Catholicism' (Rooks-Hughes 83). Religious observance and beauty conventions are equally stern strictures placed upon the Irish Catholic woman. Kate and her mother embody the 'passive images' of 'vulnerable virgin' and 'mourning mother' that Longley notes, linking Cathleen Ní Houlihan with the Virgin Mary (18): Mama in *The Country Girls* takes only powder-puff and rosary beads on her ill-fated boat trip, and her daughter in *Girl with Green Eyes* applies make-up 'in front of the smoky glass of the Holy Picture' (86). Entering a convent is a potential escape route from the hardships of an unhappy marriage, pregnancy, or sex that women 'had to pretend to like' (*GGE* 56), but the price to be paid is that a nun must cease to be 'beautiful' ('[The nun's] eyebrows were black and they met in the middle over the bridge of her red nose. Her face was shiny') and is punished for shirking her reproductive destiny ('Baba said that all nuns get cancer' [*CG* 73, 35]). The Catholic dualism that sets purity and spirit in opposition to sin, appetite, and the physical body, and allows the corpulent body to be perceived as a reflection of 'moral and personal inadequacy ... [and] a symbol for the state of the soul' (Bordo 94), must be taken into account when considering the alienation from their own bodily functions displayed by O'Brien's heroines. The Christian belief of resurrection of the flesh attached moral goodness to slimness (Camporesi 207), and the female body, liable to alien eruptions of menstruation, sexual arousal, and pregnancy, is an enemy of the spirit that must be vanquished: 'The nun read a story about Saint Teresa and how Teresa worked in a laundry and let soap spatter into her eyes as an act of mortification' (*CG* 82). Fat is excessive body and dieting becomes a quasi-spiritual battle, a narrative derived from the Christian ascetic theme of the 'renunciation of the flesh' (Foucault 43). On non-feast days, the schoolgirls are often fed cabbage water for dinner, and are expected to swallow any insects found therein in order to make them spiritually stronger. School, where pious nuns 'starve themselves', and where a ravenous Cait eats vapour-rub to kill hunger, is the site where girls learn tricks of tolerating hunger which will stand them in good stead as dieting women. *Mother Ireland* suggests that the religious strictures against indulgence in the convent boarding school the young O'Brien attended endowed acts of rebellion with an anorectic's sense of the insurrectionary potential of food:

> Sometimes slices of cake, a biscuit or a cherry might be covertly passed to one in the dark, and the pleasure of eating it was not a little mitigated by the realization of the sin that was being committed (98).

It is, therefore, possible to interpret the taboos surrounding food intake in O'Brien's early fiction as vehicles for sly female subversion: it should not be forgotten that within Church history, female self-starvation, though usually interpreted as proof of sanctity and obedience, has occasionally been read as an attempt to force God's hand or even as demonic possession,[8] attitudes which are mirrored in psychiatric discourse that reads adolescent anorexia as a cry for parental attention or defiance of parental control.

In O'Brien's depiction of 1950s and 1960s Ireland and Britain, women are subject to institutionalized patriarchal control through their contact with the medical establishment. In *Girl with Green Eyes*, both Baba and Kate display the alienation from their sexuality and biology that canonical feminist scholarship claims arose in the wake of the pathologization of women's bodily functions.[9] Childbirth and breast-feeding 'terrified' Kate, and menstruation is a 'curse' (151, 184). At the gynaecologist's office, Baba links women's reproductive ability to their secondary position:

> I was thinking of women and all they have to put up with, not just washing napkins or not being able to be high-court judges,

but all this ... poking ... Oh, God ... you hate women, otherwise you'd have made them different (*GMB* 119).

Horror of the 'contamination' of both fatness and pregnancy
coalesce in the critical Baba's comment to a plump Kate: 'You
look like you were going to have a child' (7). Woman is
signified by her body fat since it is her higher proportion of fat
that endows her with her marketable 'womanly curves':

> 'You got plump', [Mr Gentleman] said finally. I hated the sound
> of the word. It reminded me of young chickens when they were
> being weighed for the market (*CG* 98).

Anorexia nervosa, a condition which gradually transforms the
body from fashionable to unattractive slenderness, is a refutation of such marketable 'womanly curves'. The connection
of female sexuality to body fat unites in the use of food imagery
to describe the female body, and constructs female sexuality as
a consumer commodity: purchasable, perishable, vulnerable,
and potentially contaminable. Old age is unacceptable, a facet
of a woman's life that society cannot recognize as legitimate. In
the first novel of the trilogy, the physical decay of Jack's ancient
mother is an abomination:

> The yellow skin stretched like parchment over her old bones
> and her hands and her wrists were thin and brown like boiled
> chicken bones ... I hated to look at her. I was looking at death
> (*CG* 103).

The old woman's body is compared to food, but the food suggested is emblematic of poverty, sickness, and hunger.
Throughout O'Brien's first four novels, there is an ac-
cumulation of food imagery and an ever-increasing association
of the commodification of food with the commodification of
female sexuality that exploded with the sexual and consumer
revolution of the 1960s:

> [M]ost of the sharks ... expected you to pay for the pictures,
> raped you in the back seat, came home, ate your baked beans
> and then wanted some new, experimental kind of sex and no
> worries from you about might you have a baby (*GMB* 11).

It is no coincidence that the women's magazines, which reduced imperfect women to pristine images of slender, air-
brushed forms, were also the source of what Roland Barthes
analyses as a kind of 'look-but-don't-eat' pornography of food
prevalent in post-war women's magazines (78-80). If anorexia
and bulimia are the logical end points of the commodification
of appetite, then the anorectic/bulimic imperative extends to
the over-stimulated sexual appetites of the French Riviera
depicted in *August is a Wicked Month*: 'Two kinds of men, they
fuck everyone or they fuck no one' (99). In *August is a Wicked
Month*, women's bodies are continually presented as food that
stimulates perverse appetites, though the figure-conscious
women themselves avoid eating whenever possible. Rather than
touching her, Mr Gentleman in *The Country Girls* merely looks at
Kate's body, and by *August is a Wicked Month*, the female body is
even more explicitly presented as a delectable consumable to be
devoured or, for the true gourmand, to be merely gazed or
grazed upon: Sidney, the wealthy, world-weary host in
O'Brien's fourth novel, has chosen not to have penetrative sex
for years, and ejaculates outside Ellen's body when they have
sexual relations. Sidney uses his wealth to indulge his appetite
for gourmet food, a stimulant for the jaded palate of one who
can no longer be excited by anything other than what is rare,
exorbitantly priced, or perverse. In O'Brien's fourth novel, girls
have 'chocolate' bellies, and strawberries, menstruation-like,
'leak blood', while the female body, like fruit to a demanding
consumer, is unacceptable when 'slightly blemished' (26, 40).
Food is an over-refined ritual, and foul-smelling, infected
bodies are masked by chemical fragrances. The heroine contracts venereal disease from Sidney, having been seduced by his
talk of the resemblance of lush peaches and artichokes to
female genitalia. Moreover, tanning is equated with cooking,
and elegant, over-priced 'Perrier' is ubiquitous since tap water
induces typhoid and the self-starved women that people the
novel must fill their stomachs with some commodity. The
underlying theme of the transience of the consumer durable (be
it sex or food) in earlier novels is foregrounded in this bleak tale

of decay and death. Sidney seems a corpse as Ellen has sexual
contact with him, while his guests amuse themselves with
pictures of 'a warty breast discharging pus' (76).

In this fallen, sexual-revolution hell, the disquieted Ellen
longs for the impossible and the prelapsarian: 'white peaches
that are imperishable' (141). Throughout her early novels,
O'Brien sets in opposition the 'natural' and artificial in terms of
food and flowers as well as female beauty. We begin to suspect
that all is not well when the recently abducted Kate finds Baba's
mother, Martha, tending 'plastic roses which had been sprayed
with some kind of perfume' (*GGE* 89). It transpires that the
formerly fun-loving Martha has found religion and disapproves
of Kate's plight, leaving Kate without an ally in the village.
Walking the city streets alone, her marriage collapsing, Kate
notes 'plastic chickens motionless on skewers' (*GMB* 89), and,
near to breakdown, she becomes convinced that the soup dis-
pensed by the vending machine is really washing-up water. The
opposition of natural and artificial that occurs throughout the
trilogy is foregrounded in *August is a Wicked Month*. In the
surreal, over-refined resort Ellen stays in, people are 'props' and
lurid flowers have 'no smell' (97, 110). The novel circles upon
feminine artifice and the artificiality of the 'feminine': all of the
wealthy wives and mistresses portrayed own furs, a cultural site
upon which contradictory meanings of 'natural' and 'artificial'
collide.[10] O'Brien exploits the powerful symbolism of the fur-
clad woman, inscribed with violent excess, both material and
sexual, and the emblem *par excellence* of female economic
dependency and the exploitation of animals by the food and
fashion industries. The processed, sewn, deodorized fur is as
authentic in its 'natural' beauty as the artificially enhanced
woman. At the beginning of a striptease scene in O'Brien's
novel, where the hyper-'feminine' stripper turns out to be a
man, a reference is made to a nearby woman wearing 'the
darkest furriest fur Ellen had ever seen' (65). The strip scene is
a culmination of O'Brien's gradual revelation of the 'natural' as
the artificial: the bedecked stripper is finally revealed to be a

smooth boy wearing false breasts, an enactment of Jacques Lacan's definition of femininity as masquerade (694).

According to Barthes,

> milk is cosmetic, it joins, covers, restores. Moreover, its purity, associated with the innocence of the child, is a token of strength, of a strength which is not revulsive, not congestive, but calm, white, lucid, the equal of reality (60).

Significantly, Ellen's young child dies on his way to purchase unpasteurized milk while on a camping trip with her estranged husband. Ellen's son and former husband are temporarily living the fantasy of dwelling in nature and living off the fruits of the land, but it is an immersion in the natural world, mediated by the consumer-driven leisure industry, which makes the experience one far removed from the physical freedom and access to unprocessed food available to the young Cait in *The Country Girls*, despite its superficial resemblance. The early scenes of *The Country Girls* associates childhood innocence and apparent happiness with unpasteurized milk and other unhomogenized farm food, but by *August is a Wicked Month* the heroine has been immersed in a profligate world where Sidney's cook shapes butter and ice into inedible but beautiful sculptures for his cosmopolitan, self-starved guests. This may be read as an invocation of the dichotomy of Southern European/ice cream/decadence/artificiality and Northern European/milk/homeliness/purity first implied in the Dublin scenes of *The Country Girls*. The meandering closing line of *Mother Ireland* intimates that the pre-consumer Ireland of the narrator's 1950s childhood is a prelapsarian womb that cannot be returned to:

> I live out of Ireland because something in me warns me that I might stop if I lived there ... might grow placid when in fact I want yet again and for indefinable reasons to trace that same route, that trenchant childhood route, in the hope of finding some clue that will, or would, or could, make possible the leap that would restore one to one's original place and state of consciousness, to the radical innocence of the moment just before birth (129).

The death of Ellen's child indicates that there is no possible return to what is remembered as a paradisial, life-affirming, and secure childhood world where food is not associated with the guilt of dieting, overindulgence, commodification, and homo-genization. Eden truly was a land flowing with (unpasteurized and full-fat) milk, but it is a place to which there is no possible return.

Works Cited

Barthes, Roland. *Mythologies*. Trans. Annette Lavers (London: Vintage, 1993).

Boland, Eavan. *A Kind of Scar* (Dublin: Attic, 1989).

Bordo, Susan. 'Reading the Slender Body'. *Body/Politics: Women and the Discourses of Science*, eds M. Jacobus, E. Fox Keller, and S. Shuttleworth (London: Routledge, 1990), 83-112.

Bourke, Angela. 'Fairies and Anorexia: Nuala Ní Dhomhnaill's "Amazing Grass"'. *The Proceedings of the Harvard Celtic Colloquium* 13 (1993): 25-38.

Camporesi, Piero. *The Magic Harvest: Food, Folklore and Society*. Trans. Joan Krakover Hall (Cambridge: Polity Press, 1993).

Earls, Maurice. 'The Late Late Show, Controversy and Context'. *Television and Irish Society: 21 Years of Irish Television*, eds Martin McLoone and John MacMahon (Dublin: Radio Telefis Éireann, 1984), 107-22.

Ellmann, Maud. *The Hunger Artists* (Cambridge, MA: Harvard University Press, 1993).

Emberley, Julia V. *Venus and Furs: The Cultural Politics of Fur* (London: Tauris, 1998).

Foucault, Michel. 'Technologies of the Self: A Seminar with Michel Foucault'. *Technologies of the Self*, eds L.H. Martin, H. Gutman, and P.H. Hutton (London: University of Massachusetts Press, 1988).

Galligan, Yvonne. 'The Changing Role of Women'. *Ireland and the Politics of Change*, eds William Crotty and David E. Schmitt (London and New York: Longman, 1998), 107-21.

Garvin, Tom. 'Patriots and Republicans: An Irish Evolution'. *Ireland and the Politics of Change* (London and New York: Longman, 1998), 144-55.

Hardiman, Niamh and Christopher Whelan. 'Changing Values'. *Ireland and the Politics of Change* (London and New York: Longman, 1998), 66-85.

Kelleher, Margaret. *The Feminization of Famine* (Cork: Cork University Press, 1997).

Kennedy, Meghan. Rev. of Anna Krugovoy Silver, *Victorian Literature and the Anorexic Body*. *Victorian Studies* 47.2 (Winter 2005): 285-6.

Kilfeather, Siobhán. 'Irish Feminism'. *The Cambridge Companion to Modern Irish Culture* (Cambridge: Cambridge University Press, 2005), 96-116.

Lacan, Jacques. 'La signification du phallus'. *Ecrits II* (Paris: Seuil, 1966).

Longley, Edna. *From Cathleen to Anorexia: The Breakdown of Irelands* (Dublin: Attic, 1990).

Lucas, C.T. 'Irish Food Before the Potato'. *Gwerin* 3 (1960): 8-43.

Lysaght, Patricia. 'Continuity and Change in Irish Diet'. *Food in Change: Eating Habits from the Middle Ages to the Present Day*, eds Alexander Fenton and Eszter Kisbán (Edinburgh: John Donald in association with the National Museums of Scotland, 1986), 80-9.

Maguire, Hugh. 'Ireland: Torn Between Traditions'. International Conference on the Research of Modern Architecture, 30 August-1 September 2001, Jyväskylä Finland. http://www.alvaraalto.fi/conferences/universal/

Morgan, Eileen. 'Mapping Out a Landscape of Female Suffering: Edna O'Brien's Demythologizing Novels'. *Women's Studies: An Interdisciplinary Journal* 29.4 (2000): 449-76.

O'Brien, Edna. *August is a Wicked Month* (London: Penguin, 1967).

--- *The Country Girls* (London: Weidenfeld & Nicolson, 1989).

--- *Girls in their Married Bliss* (London: Penguin, 1967).

--- *Girl with Green Eyes* (London: Penguin, 1964).

--- *Mother Ireland* (New York: Plume, 1999).

O'Hagan, J.W. *The Economy of Ireland* (London: Macmillan, 1995).

Orbach, Susie. *Hunger Strike* (London: Penguin, 1993).

Ó Sé, Micheál. 'Old Irish Cheeses and Other Milk Products'. *Journal of the Cork Historical and Archaeological Society* 53 (1948): 82-7.

O'Toole, Fintan. *The Ex-Isle of Ireland* (Dublin: New Island, 1996).

Polivy, J. and C.P. Herman. 'Diagnosis and Treatment of Normal Eating'. *Journal of Consulting and Clinical Psychology* (*Special Issue: Eating Disorders*) 55.5 (1987): 635-44.

Rooks-Hughes, Lorna. 'The Family and the Female Body in the Novels of Edna O'Brien and Julia O'Faoláin'. *Canadian Journal of Irish Studies* 22.2 (1996): 83-97.

Roos, Bonnie. 'James Joyce's "The Dead" and Bret Harte's *Gabriel Conroy:* The Nature of the Feast'. *The Yale Journal of Criticism* 15.1 (2002): 99-126.

Showalter, Elaine. *The Female Malady: Women, Madness and English Culture, 1830-1980* (London: Virago, 1985).

Silver, Anna Krugovoy. *Victorian Literature and the Anorexic Body*
    (Cambridge and New York: Cambridge University Press, 2002).
Spenser, Edmund. 'A Brief Note on Ireland'. *The Works of Edmund
    Spenser*. Vol. 9: *The Prose Works*, variorum ed. (Baltimore: Johns
    Hopkins University Press, 1949).
Vandereycken, Walter and Ron van Deth. *From Fasting Saints to Anorexic
    Girls* (New York: New York University Press, 1994).
Visser, Margaret. *Much Depends on Dinner* (Toronto: McClelland and
    Stewart, 1987).

---

[1] Longley, pp.22, 3; Nuala Ní Dhomhnaill's 'Féar Suaithinseach' is an
    account of a young girl who is silenced by the shame of a priest's
    apparent sexual attraction to her. The word 'anorexia' was utilized in
    the subtitle of the poem's initial Irish-language publication, and its
    placement within inverted commas points to it as a foreign loan word
    that readily maps onto what Angela Bourke reads as Ní Dhomhnaill's
    delineation of the effects of objectification as described in Irish
    folklore, the tradition from which the narrative of a mysteriously
    traumatized young woman unable to eat or speak is drawn. See
    Bourke, pp.25-38.

[2] See Orbach; also Polivy and Herman.

[3] 'Many commentators have pointed to increased education of lay
    people, to increased prosperity and therefore increased mental
    independence, to media blanketing from Britain and elsewhere, as
    well as to the events within the Catholic Church commonly termed
    "Vatican II" ... In the 1960s ... an undercurrent of anti-clericalism
    ran through the growing educated stratum of a relatively uneducated
    nation. Hindsight suggests that the resentment of Church power
    dated back much further, perhaps to the Mother and Child incident
    of 1951', Garvin, p.150.

[4] See Kilfeather and Earls.

[5] '[Irish-American priest] Fr John A. O'Brien edited a much-discussed
    collection of essays in 1954 with the alarming title, *The Vanishing Irish*.
    The contributors launched what amounted to a polite but sustained
    and ultimately devastating attack on the intellectual assumptions of
    the Irish establishment. It was suggested in particular that sexual
    repression ... was damaging to family life and ... made Irish people
    unwilling to live and marry in Ireland ... Michael Sheehy, in a book
    entitled *Divided We Stand* (1955), tore apart the official position on
    partition for a newly attentive generation'. Garvin, pp.146, 149.

[6] See also Kelleher and Roos.

[7] Although food has an enormous hold over women, the public

discourse of food is controlled by men in O'Brien's early fiction. Eugene's attempt to 'educate' Kate's palate is a denial of her right to a separate identity. When women serve or cook food in O'Brien's early fiction, it reinforces their inferior position, but when men cook, it is an art and a vocation, as in the case of Sidney's chef in *August is a Wicked Month*.

[8] See Vandereycken and van Deth.

[9] See Showalter.

[10] See Emberley.

Notes on Contributors

Mary Burke received her MA in English from Trinity College Dublin. Her doctoral thesis, submitted to Queen's University Belfast, explored the 'tinker' figure in Irish writing, 1800-2000. She has published on the eighteenth-century European contexts of Synge's *The Tinker's Wedding*, Bohemianism, and the Irish Revival, the depiction of Irish minority culture in Revival-era writing, and Orientalizing theories of Irish Traveller origins. She is currently finishing a book on the Irish Traveller construct in Irish and British literature. She was the Keough Institute at Notre Dame NEH Fellow, 2003-04, and joined the Department of English at the University of Connecticut in 2004 as an Assistant Professor. One of her short stories was included in David Marcus's *The Faber Book of Best New Irish Short Stories 2004-05*.

Bertrand Cardin is a lecturer at the Université de Caen, France. He wrote a book on father/son relationships in the contemporary Irish novel, entitled *Miroirs de la filiation. Parcours dans huit romans irlandais contemporains* (2005) and edited a book on the famine in Irish literature: *Irlande: Ecritures et réécritures de la Famine* (2006). He is also the author of a PhD thesis on John McGahern's short stories and has published articles about contemporary Irish novelists and short-story writers such as Jennifer Johnston, Frank McCourt, and Anne Enright.

Patricia Coughlan is Associate Professor of English at University College Cork. Editor of *Spenser and Ireland* (1989) and co-editor, with Alex Davis, of *Modernism and Ireland: The Poetry of the 1930s* (1995); she has published on a wide range of topics, including English writings about Ireland in the sixteenth and seventeenth centuries, nineteenth-century Gothic, and Beckett. Her recent and current research interests focus on feminist and postcolonialist criticism: she has published essays on Kate O'Brien, Elizabeth Bowen, Peig Sayers, Ronan Bennett, Anne Enright, John Banville, Irish writing in postmodernity, and gender representations by male writers including Seamus Heaney. She led a State-funded inter-disciplinary research project at UCC on women in Irish society, which produced the *Dictionary of Munster Women Writers 1800-2000* (2005, general editor, Tina O'Toole). She is currently writing a monograph on gender, sexuality, and social change in contemporary Irish literature.

Michael Harris, Professor of English at Central College (Pella, Iowa), is the author of *Outsiders and Insiders: Perspectives of Third World Culture in British and Post-Colonial Fiction*, named a *CHOICE* Outstanding Academic Book in 1994. Harris has published on Joseph Conrad, Patrick White, Salman Rushdie, Thomas Pynchon, Peter Abrahams, and Australian Aboriginal poetry. In 1998-1999 he served as a Senior Fulbright Lecturer at the University of Dar es Salaam, Tanzania.

Kathryn Laing teaches in the Department of English at NUI, Galway, having held an IRCHSS Post-Doctoral Fellowship there from 2000 to 2002. She is the editor of *The Sentinel* (2002), an early unfinished novel by Rebecca West, and she has essays forthcoming in two collections on West: 'Rebecca West Today', ed. Bernard Schweizer and 'Rebecca West's Fiction and Non-Fiction', eds Gill Davies, David Malcolm, and John Simons. She has also given research papers and published several articles on other women writers, including Virginia Woolf and Angela Carter.

Sinéad Mooney is a graduate of University College Cork (BA, MA) and the University of Oxford (MSt, DPhil), and has been a lecturer in the Department of English, NUI Galway, since 2002. She is the author of *Samuel Beckett* (2006) and of a number of essays and articles on Beckett. Her other publications include essays on Irish women's writing, including work on Molly Keane, Kate O'Brien, Edna O'Brien, and Elizabeth Bowen. She is currently working on a study of Beckett and translation, as well as various shorter projects, among them an essay on Edna O'Brien and the short story for the *Blackwell Companion to the Irish and British Short Story* (2006).

Ann V. Norton received a PhD in English from Columbia University and has taught nineteenth- and twentieth-century British literature at Saint Anselm College in Manchester, New Hampshire, since 1994. She serves as vice president and newsletter editor of the International Rebecca West Society. Her book *Paradoxical Feminism: The Novels of Rebecca West* was published in 2000, and she has an essay forthcoming in *Rebecca West Today*, a collection of essays from University of Delaware Press, edited by Bernard Schweizer. She has also written on Virginia Woolf, Dorothy L. Sayers, and Mary Lavin.

Maureen O'Connor is an IRCHSS Government of Ireland Post-Doctoral Fellow at the Centre for the Study of Human Settlement and Historical Change, National University of Ireland, Galway, where she is working on a study of nineteenth-century Irish feminism. She is co-editor, with Tadhg Foley, of *India and Ireland: Culture, Colonies, and Empire* (2006) and, with Lisa Colletta, of *Wild Colonial Girl: Essays on Edna O'Brien* (2006).

Rebecca Pelan is Director of Women's Studies at the National University of Ireland, Galway. She lived in Australia for many years, where she lectured in English at the University of Queensland, and returned to Ireland in 2001. She has published extensively on the subject of Irish women's writing, Edna O'Brien's fiction, feminist/literary theory, and women and 'the

Troubles'. She is the author of *Two Irelands: Literary Feminisms North and South* (2005).

Shirley Peterson is an Associate Professor and chair of the English Department at Daemen College in Amherst, New York, where she teaches British and Irish Literature, Gender and Literature, Fiction Writing, and Film. She has published critical articles on novels about the British suffrage movement, women and Modernism, literary uses of the freak, and women and film. She is co-editor with Beth Harrison of *Unmanning Modernism: Gendered Re-Readings* (1997) and is currently working on sadomasochistic desires in literature and film.

Loredana Salis completed her first degree in Foreign Languages and Literatures at the University of Sassari with a thesis on the short stories of Elizabeth Gaskell. She was an Erasmus exchange student at the University of Manchester in 1997, and in 1999 she enrolled for an MA Degree in Irish Literature in English at the University of Ulster, Coleraine. She wrote her dissertation on two versions of Sophocles' *Oedipus Tyrannus* for the modern stage by W.B. Yeats and Ted Hughes, and took interest in the contemporary reworking of classical tragedy in Ireland. She has recently completed her PhD at the University of Ulster with a study of Irish versions of *Antigone*, *Iphigenia*, and *Philoctetes*.

Eve Walsh Stoddard has a PhD in English from UCLA and an AB from Mount Holyoke College. She is chair of the Global Studies department at St Lawrence University in New York State. Her research has been in the intersections between philosophy and literature during the late eighteenth century, feminism, postcolonial and cultural studies, focusing on issues of race and culture in the English-speaking Caribbean. She is working on current and historical representations of the Big House in Ireland in relation to heritage tourism and national identities. Recent publications include a book called *Global Multiculturalism: Comparative Studies in Race, Ethnicity, and Nation* (2001), articles on creolization and hybridity in the Caribbean, and articles on the use of former sugar plantations in the Caribbean as sites that evoke contestations over national memory, identity, and colonial nostalgia.

Michelle Woods is a Postdoctoral Fellow at the Centre for Translation and Textual Studies at Dublin City University. She is currently co-editing an Encyclopaedia of Irish Literature in Translation and her book, *Translating Milan Kundera,* will be published in May 2006.

Index

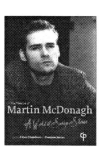

CARYSFORT PRESS

The Press aims to produce high quality publications which, though written and/or edited by academics, will be made accessible to a general readership. The organisation would also like to provide a forum for critical thinking in the Arts in Ireland, again keeping the needs and interests of the general public in view.

The company publishes contemporary Irish writing for and about the theatre.

Editorial and publishing inquiries to:

CARYSFORT PRESS Ltd

58 Woodfield, Scholarstown Road,
Rathfarnham, Dublin 16,
Republic of Ireland

T (353 1) 493 7383 F (353 1) 406 9815
e: info@carysfortpress.com
www.carysfortpress.com

Carysfort Press was formed in the summer of 1998. It receives annual funding from the Arts Council.

The directors believe that drama is playing an ever-increasing role in today's society and that enjoyment of the theatre, both professional and amateur, currently plays a central part in Irish culture.

NEW TITLES

**THE THEATRE OF MARTIN MCDONAGH
'A WORLD OF SAVAGE STORIES'**

EDITED BY LILIAN CHAMBERS AND
EAMONN JORDAN

The book is a vital response to the many challenges set by McDonagh for those involved in the production and reception of his work. Critics and commentators from around the world offer a diverse range of often provocative approaches. What is not surprising is the focus and commitment of the engagement, given the controversial and stimulating nature of the work.

ISBN 1-904505-19-8
€30

**EDNA O'BRIEN
'NEW CRITICAL PERSPECTIVES'**

EDITED BY KATHRYN LAING
SINÉAD MOONEY AND MAUREEN O'CONNOR

The essays collected here illustrate some of the range, complexity, and interest of Edna O'Brien as a fiction writer and dramatist...They will contribute to a broader appreciation of her work and to an evolution of new critical approaches, as well as igniting more interest in the many unexplored areas of her considerable oeuvre.

ISBN 1-904505-20-1
€20

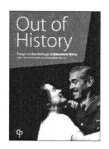

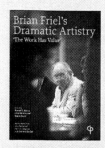

OUT OF HISTORY
'ESSAYS ON THE WRITINGS OF SEBASTIAN BARRY'

EDITED WITH AN INTRODUCTION BY CHRISTINA HUNT MAHONY

The essays address Barry's engagement with the contemporary cultural debate in Ireland and also with issues that inform postcolonial criticial theory. The range and selection of contributors has ensured a high level of critical expression and an insightful assessment of Barry and his works.

ISBN 1-904505-18-X
€20

BRIAN FRIEL'S DRAMATIC ARTISTRY
'THE WORK HAS VALUE'

EDITED BY DONALD E. MORSE, CSILLA BERTHA, AND MÁRIA KURDI

Brian Friel's Dramatic Artistry presents a refreshingly broad range of voices: new work from some of the leading English-speaking authorities on Friel, and fascinating essays from scholars in Germany, Italy, Portugal, and Hungary. This book will deepen our knowledge and enjoyment of Friel's work.

ISBN 1-904505-17-1
€25

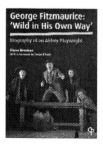

GEORGE FITZMAURICE:
'WILD IN HIS OWN WAY'

BIOGRAPHY OF AN ABBEY PLAYWRIGHT
BY FIONA BRENNAN
WITH A FOREWORD BY FINTAN O'TOOLE

Fiona Brennan's...introduction to his considerable output allows us a much greater appreciation and understanding of Fitzmaurice, the one remaining under-celebrated genius of twentieth-century Irish drama.
Conall Morrison

ISBN 1-904505-16-3
€20

PLAYBOYS OF THE WESTERN WORLD

PRODUCTION HISTORIES
EDITED BY ADRIAN FRAZIER

'Playboys of the Western World is a model of contemporary performance studies.'

'The book is remarkably well-focused: half is a series of production histories of Playboy performances through the twentieth century in the UK, Northern Ireland, the USA, and Ireland. The remainder focuses on one contemporary performance, that of Druid Theatre, as directed by Garry Hynes. The various contemporary social issues that are addressed in relation to Synge's play and this performance of it give the volume an additional interest: it shows how the arts matter.' *Kevin Barry*

ISBN 1-904505-06-6
€20

EAST OF EDEN
NEW ROMANIAN PLAYS
EDITED BY ANDREI MARINESCU

Four of the most promising Romanian playwrights, young and very young, are in this collection, each one with a specific way of seeing the Romanian reality, each one with a style of communicating an articulated artistic vision of the society we are living in.
Ion Caramitru, General Director Romanian National Theatre Bucharest

ISBN 1-904505-15-5
€10

IRISH THEATRE ON TOUR
EDITED BY NICHOLAS GRENE AND CHRIS MORASH

'Touring has been at the strategic heart of Druid's artistic policy since the early eighties. Everyone has the right to see professional theatre in their own communities. Irish theatre on tour is a crucial part of Irish theatre as a whole'. *Garry Hynes*

ISBN 1-904505-13-9
€20

CRITICAL MOMENTS
FINTAN O'TOOLE ON MODERN IRISH THEATRE
EDITED BY JULIA FURAY & REDMOND O'HANLON

This new book on the work of Fintan O'Toole, the internationally acclaimed theatre critic and cultural commentator, offers percussive analyses and assessments of the major plays and playwrights in the canon of modern Irish theatre. Fearless and provocative in his judgements, O'Toole is essential reading for anyone interested in criticism or in the current state of Irish theatre.

ISBN 1-904505-03-1
€20

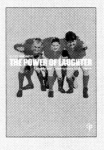

THE POWER OF LAUGHTER
EDITED BY ERIC WEITZ

The collection draws on a wide range of perspectives and voices including critics, playwrights, directors and performers. The result is a series of fascinating and provocative debates about the myriad functions of comedy in contemporary Irish theatre. *Anna McMullan*

As Stan Laurel said, it takes only an onion to cry. Peel it and weep. Comedy is harder. These essays listen to the power of laughter. They hear the tough heart of Irish theatre – hard and wicked and funny. *Frank McGuinness*

ISBN 1-904505-05-8
€20